The Crisis in Economics

W9-CKD-258

Economics today is under more pressure to change than at any time since the 1930s. The charge against it is extremely serious: economics as taught in universities neither explains contemporary economic reality nor provides a framework for the critical debate of economic issues in democratic societies.

In the last few years a world-wide movement to radically reform economics has sprung up. Called the "post-autistic economics movement," it began in France in June 2000 and has already won the support of thousands of economists around the world. The movement is against economics' use of mathematics as an end in itself, against its disregard for many economic realities, against its refusal to take seriously any theory not based on nineteenth-century neoclassical theory, and against its dogmatic teaching style that aims to indoctrinate rather than educate. In lieu of these practices, the movement supports pluralism, critical thinking and engagement with real economic issues and problems.

This book is a lively and idea-packed collection of key texts from the PAE Movement. It is aimed not only at economists and economics students, but also at the general reader. The book's 39 contributors include James K. Galbraith, Geoff Harcourt, Deirdre McCloskey, Bernard Guerrien, Tony Lawson, Anne Mayhew and Geoffrey Hodgson.

This book is a must-read for economists, economics students, and people who want to keep abreast of important changes in intellectual and social trends.

Edward Fullbrook is Visiting Research Fellow at the University of the West of England, UK. *Intersubjectivity in Economics* is another of his books, which is also published by Routledge.

Economics as Social Theory
Series edited by Tony Lawson
University of Cambridge

Social theory is experiencing something of a revival within economics. Critical analyses of the particular nature of the subject matter of social studies and of the types of method, categories and modes of explanation that can legitimately be endorsed for the scientific study of social objects are re-emerging. Economists are again addressing such issues as the relationship between agency and structure, between economy and the rest of society, and between the enquirer and the object of enquiry. There is renewed interest in elaborating basic categories such as causation, competition, culture, discrimination, evolution, money, need, order, organization, power probability, process, rationality, technology, time, truth, uncertainty, value, etc.

The objective for this series is to facilitate this revival further. In contemporary economics the label "theory" has been appropriated by a group that confines itself to largely asocial, ahistorical, mathematical "modeling." *Economics as Social Theory* thus reclaims the "theory" label offering a platform for alternative rigorous, but broader and more critical, conceptions of theorizing.

Other titles in this series include:

Economics and Language
Edited by Willie Henderson

Rationality, Institutions and Economic Methodology
Edited by Uskali Mäki, Bo Gustafsson, and Christian Knudsen

New Directions in Economic Methodology
Edited by Roger Backhouse

Who Pays for the Kids?
Nancy Folbre

Rules and Choice in Economics
Viktor Vanberg

Beyond Rhetoric and Realism in Economics
Thomas A. Boylan and Paschal F. O'Gorman

The Crisis in Economics

The post-autistic economics movement:
the first 600 days

Edited by Edward Fullbrook

Routledge
Taylor & Francis Group

LONDON AND NEW YORK

First published 2003 by Routledge
11 New Fetter Lane, London EC4P 4EE

Simultaneously published in the USA and Canada
by Routledge
29 West 35th Street, New York, NY 10001

Routledge is an imprint of the Taylor & Francis Group

© 2003 Editorial matter and selection, Edward Fullbrook;
individual chapters, the authors

Typeset in Perpetua by Wearset Ltd, Boldon, Tyne and Wear
Printed and bound in Great Britain by The Cromwell Press, Trowbridge,
Wiltshire

All rights reserved. No part of this book may be reprinted or reproduced
or utilised in any form or by any electronic, mechanical, or other means,
now known or hereafter invented, including photocopying and recording,
or in any information storage or retrieval system, without permission in
writing from the publishers.

British Library Cataloguing in Publication Data
A catalogue record for this book is available from the British Library

Library of Congress Cataloging in Publication Data
The crisis in economics / [edited by] Edward Fullbrook.
     p. cm. – (Economics as social theory)
   Includes bibliographical references and index.
    1. Economics–Study and teaching (Higher)–France.
    2. Economics–Study and teaching (Higher) I. Fullbrook, Edward.
   II. Series.

   HB74.9.F8 C75 2003
   330'.071'1–dc21

                                                          2002036909

ISBN 0-415-30897-6 (hbk)
ISBN 0-415-30898-4 (pbk)

Contents

Contents ix

Introduction

A brief history of the post-autistic economics movement

Edward Fullbrook (University of the West of England, UK)

Autisme-économie

In France in June 2000 a group of economics students published a petition on the web protesting *against*:

- the lack of realism in economics teaching;
- economics' "uncontrolled use" and treatment of mathematics as "an end in itself," with the result that economics has become an "autistic science," lost in "imaginary worlds";
- the repressive domination of neoclassical theory and approaches derivative from it in the university economics curriculum; and
- the dogmatic teaching style in economics, which leaves no place for critical and reflective thought.

The French students' petition argued *in favor of*:

- engagement with empirical and concrete economic realities;
- prioritizing science over scientism;
- a pluralism of approaches adapted to the complexity of economic objects and to the uncertainty surrounding most of the big economic questions; and
- their professors initiating reforms to rescue economics from its autistic and socially irresponsible state.

The students' petition carried great weight because its authors and initial signatories were associated with France's "Grandes Écoles," whose enormous academic prestige and selectivity surpasses that of other higher education institutions in France. No one dared say that these students, the *crème de la crème*, opposed the formalist approach to economics because the mathematics was too difficult for them. Thus from the outset defenders of the status quo were deprived of their favorite argumentative gambit.

Meanwhile some economics teachers in France responded with a petition of their own, supporting the students' demands, adding to their analysis, and lamenting the cult of scientism into which economics in the main had descended. The professors' petition also called for the opening of a public debate on the state of economics and economics teaching.

That debate began on 21 June, when the French newspaper, *Le Monde*, reported on the students' movement (soon to call itself *Autisme-économie*) and interviewed several prominent economists who voiced sympathy for the students' cause. Other newspapers and magazines followed suit. As the French media, including radio and television, expanded the public debate, student and teacher fears of persecution if they took a public stand diminished and the number of signatories to the petitions increased. This fueled further media interest. Jack Lang, the French Minister of Education, announced that he regarded the complaints with great seriousness and was setting up a commission to investigate. He put the venerable Jean-Paul Fitoussi, President of l'Observatoire Français des Conjonctures Économiques (OFCE), in charge and instructed him to report within a year.

The movement in France now entered a new stage, as it sought to capitalize on its official recognition and expand the public debate. Meanwhile, news of the recent events was beginning to reach the rest of the world.

The *post-autistic economics newsletter / review*

The first issue of the *post-autistic economics newsletter* appeared in September 2000. It arose out of a conversation the previous month at the World Congress of Social Economics at Cambridge in the UK. Benjamin Balak, then a graduate student at the University of North Carolina at Chapel Hill, told me that some distinguished American universities were eliminating, even as an elective, the history of economic thought from the curriculum, the idea being that the total absence of competing ideas would facilitate students' indoctrination into neoclassicalism. I was incredulous. It seemed too much to believe that the closing down of the horizons of economic enquiry could have gone so far. But a quick check with other conferees not only confirmed Balak's account, but also turned up economists faced with redundancy in consequence of this new narrowing of vision.

Attempts to interest people at the conference in organizing a spirited response, however, came to nothing. The general view was that such a project, no matter how important, stood no chance of success. Sure, economists who either do not subscribe to the neoclassical model or who reject the anti-scientific fundamentalism that surrounds it constitute a sizable and growing minority, but no means existed for mobilizing them as a community. Dissenters survived only as isolated, worried and often persecuted individuals or as members of numerous competing heterodox groups, each zealously guarding their mailing lists against the others. And no one at the Cambridge conference seemed to have heard of the events earlier in the summer in France. My mention of them to a few people appeared to leave them wondering if they were talking to a fantasist.

If it had not been for Geoff Harcourt, that probably would have been the end of my involvement. But in his after-dinner speech at the conference banquet, the old warrior, still fighting and still hilarious, raised spirits with laughter that rattled the timbers of the medieval dining hall. The next day, still buoyed by his performance and returning home on the train to the west of England, I pondered the possibilities for constructive rebellion. Somehow the success and hope of the French students had to be communicated to economists of conscience throughout the world.

The students had a website, *Autisme-économie*, packed with documents, newspaper articles and information. With this to draw on, compiling a journalistic account of their exploits and public reactions proved both easy and fun. But what to do with it? Even if my effort had been accepted in some form by a quality newspaper, it would still largely miss the target audience. Sending it, then just a Word file named "post-autistic economics," out as an electronic newsletter occurred to me as a possibility. Sending it anonymously, giving it an element of mystery, could conceivably spark enough interest for a second issue that would include translations of the French students' and teachers' petitions. It was really these that I thought people should read.

A week passed before I set up an anonymous account with Hotmail, formatted the document as a newsletter, put in pleas for subscribers and for readers to forward the newsletter to potentially interested colleagues, and then emailed it to 99 people. Ninety seconds later the newsletter had its first subscriber, Frank Ackerman, and forty seconds after that its second, Paul Ormerod, and so on until at the end of the first week there were 209. The following email message also arrived from Olivier Vaury, one of the founders of *Autisme-économie*: "I just now got back to Paris. Who are you? What country are you in? What is your organization? What do you want?." This and other messages suggested that the mystery element was working.

However, after the first week uptake fell off: there were 128 new subscribers in the second week, 57 in the third, and 67 in the fourth. The second issue, on 3 October, failed to regain the initial momentum, and likewise the third at the end of November. Furthermore, generating copy was becoming problematic and the project was taking up too much time. Then there was the hate mail, some of it quite nasty and not the ideal way to start the day, and, worst of all, the viruses that were being targeted at the newsletter. So after the third issue I decided the next would be the last. But when my partner, Kate Fullbrook, heard this she implored me to persevere for a few more issues just to see what developed. "The neoclassicalists," she reasoned, "wouldn't be spending their time sending you viruses and hate mail if they didn't see the newsletter as a serious threat."

About this time Joseph Halevi gallantly stepped forward to help out with advice, encouragement and hard copy. So too did James Galbraith. And the French students were proving marvelous to work with, especially Gilles Raveaud. These associations were a real turning point, as they raised the possibility of developing the newsletter into a review with very fast publication of articles received. And although February 2001 saw only 59 new subscribers, this pushed the total past the 1,000 mark. In mid-March, issue number 5 came out featuring six contributors, and in the months that followed circulation grew very rapidly. Today (19 August 2002), the *post-autistic economics review* has 5,500 subscribers.

Fitoussi's report

Meanwhile in France the movement grew in stature and influence. In the beginning the neoclassical mainstream had chosen to ignore the demands and analysis of French economics students and academics, but by autumn 2000 it became clear that in France the call for reform was not about to go away. In October *Le Monde* carried in one issue three pages of articles on the movement, including an ambiguous interview with Amartya Sen. It was about this time that the traditionalists changed tactics and launched a counterattack. This included a long article by Robert Solow in *Le Monde*, another by Olivier Blanchard, the Chair at MIT, and the publication of a counter-petition – a plea for the status quo.

These mainstream initiatives, however, backfired. Solow's article came across as imperialistic and condescending, while the petition, which was mainly an MIT affair, left observers shocked by its cynical misrepresentation of the students' demands. Most of all, however, people on all sides seemed surprised at how feeble were the arguments offered for blocking the reforms proposed by the French students.

Meanwhile the *Autisme-économie* students, led by Gilles Raveaud, Olivier Vaury, Ioana Marinescu and Emmanuelle Benicourt, organized public debates on the issues they had raised in their petition. Through the winter and spring these well-attended events took place at universities all over France, the debate at Nanterre on 10 April attracting more than 400 people.

Articles continued to appear in the French press regarding the issues raised by the movement. In February 2001, *L'Économie Politique* devoted an entire issue to the debate. In articles and interviews in the French national press, various French economists of note, including Bernard Paulré, Olivier Favereau, Yann Moulier-Boutang, Jean Gadrey and André Orléan, came out on the side of the students. Over 200 French academic economists signed the petition of support.

In November 2000, www.paecon.net was launched to give international direction to what had become known as the "post-autistic economics movement" and which by now was receiving media attention around the world. At the beginning of December, Gilles Raveaud and Ioana Marinescu appeared in a round table, "The Future of Economics," at an international conference in Leeds, UK. This event forged important links between the movement in France and emergent initiatives elsewhere. At about the same time, James Galbraith flew to Paris to meet with student and academic leaders of the new movement. In January 2001, Galbraith replied to Solow in the fourth issue of the *post-autistic economics newsletter*.

The French students re-designed and re-launched their website (http://mouv.eco.free.fr) in both French and English. Meanwhile, other PAE-related websites were springing up in various countries. These included one created in the UK by Oxford University students, which came about following an appearance by Raveaud and Marinescu at the Cambridge Workshop on Realism and Economics.

Throughout the academic year 2000–2001, Fitoussi's commission was intensely lobbied. This included a special spring visit to Paris by members of the Executive Committee of the International Economics Association. Big guns and bold maneuvers were called for, because it was perceived by both sides that success by the French reformers would, in all likelihood, have effects far beyond the French borders. Concessions won there would, in time, be demanded in other countries, not just by other students, but also by the thousands of academic economists whose fidelity to the neoclassical mainstream is more survivalist than intellectual.

In June 2001 "the Cambridge 27," 27 embattled economics PhD students at Cambridge University, published their petition "Opening Up Economics." By "opening up economics" they mean becoming mindful of the limitations of the "competing approaches to understanding economic phenomena," of "learning their domain of applicability," and of using "the best methods for the question at hand" rather than "restricting research done in economics to that based on one approach only." Their petition soon had 500 signatures. In September 2001 a cognate petition appeared that resulted from a meeting of 75 students, researchers and professors from 22 nations who gathered in Kansas City for a week of discussion on the state of economics.

People expecting Fitoussi's report to be a whitewash were surprised when it was released in September. It proposed enough reforms to win the support of *Autisme-économie*. And enough for Jack Lang to speak of fundamental reforms, which he has promised to carry through.

Fitoussi's 2001 report, *L'Enseignement supérieur des sciences économiques en question*, calls for two fundamental changes in the teaching of economics (Fitoussi, 2001). First, it calls for the integration of debate on contemporary economic issues into both the structure and content of university economics courses. It means real debate, not neoclassical opinion presented on its own or with only token alternatives. Such an open environment would preclude the standard practice of keeping the ideological content of neoclassicism hidden from students. This change alone would radically transform economics teaching, with inevitable and incalculable effects to economics itself. Second, Fitoussi's report demands that multidisciplinarity be placed at the heart of the teaching of economics. Economics students will be required to study cognate disciplines, such as sociology, history, law, psychology, etc., so as to become familiar with their contrasting views of and methods of treating socio-economic phenomena.

By now over 100 articles have appeared in the French press about the crisis in economics and the efforts to reform it. As this book goes to press, the PAE debate is now also receiving increasing media attention in other countries. Here are a few extracts from international press coverage of the movement:

> The bonfire of revolution has become so bad that the French education minister, Mr. Lang, has ordered a commission to investigate.
>
> *The Melbourne Age* (Australia)

> A movement has begun calling for post-autistic economics . . . If there is a daily prayer for the global economy, it should be "deliver us from the abstraction."
>
> *The Independent* (UK)

> . . . the post-autistic economics movement . . . has spread like wildfire among students in France and Spain, with growing numbers of correspondents in other countries as well.
>
> *Science and Society* (USA)

> The battle lines are being drawn, and www.paecon.net is the site for much of the action.
>
> *The Australian*

> The PAE movement is drawing praise from anti-globalization activists and thinkers. Writing in *The Independent*, Andrew Simms of the United Kingdom-based New Economics Foundation hails the PAE movement as part of an effort to make "the mandarins of the global economy experience a reality check" and protect the environment. The movement's Web site and its e-journal, the *post-autistic economics newsletter* (published every one or two months), showcase PAE's specific critiques of mainstream economics as well as the movement's growing influence.
>
> *Foreign Policy* (USA)

> . . . the "post-autistic economics" (PAE) movement, an academic backlash against traditional economics that is rapidly gaining adherents among disaf-

fected practitioners of the dismal science in developing and advanced economies.

Foreign Policy Magazine (USA)

This [PAE] protest is three-fold: economics as it is taught is completely detached from the "world out there" . . . economic teaching . . . makes an excessive use of maths . . . and economic teaching is monolithic. It does not present the variety of past and present theories.

Arena (Sweden)

. . . in France, a "post-autistic economics" movement erupted in protest against the excesses of formal economics discourses . . . The movement quickly spread to Spain and across much of continental Europe, and is making inroads in the UK.

The Guardian (UK)

Paris has become the birthplace of a revolt against the pre-eminence of theory over practice, of economic abstraction over reality, and statistics over real life. Called "post-autistic economics" . . . the movement has had a worldwide impact, with Cambridge students drawing up their own petition.

New Statesman (UK)

. . . the PAE movement comes at a time of reaction to globalisation and the power of the corporation . . . [and to economists'] continuing loss of students and their increasingly fragile position within the business school.

Arena Magazine (Australia)

The second issue already had readers in 36 countries, today the *post-autistic economics review* has 5,000 (non-paying) subscribers in one hundred countries.

De Morgen (Brussels)

In September 2000 the first internet edition of the *post-autistic economics newsletter* appeared, which spread news of the movement to students, assistant professors and professors throughout the world. Further editions of the newsletter, alongside the post-autistic economics network website (www.paecon.net), have founded a strong platform for discussion.

Süddeutsche Zeitung (Munich)

Tomorrow

Economics has not experienced such pressure to change since the 1930s. Then the complaint was its inability to explain the Great Depression and to effect a recovery. It responded by inventing macroeconomics. Today, the indictment is both more general and more serious: *economics as taught in universities neither explains contemporary reality nor provides a framework for the critical debate of issues in democratic societies.*

One of the founders of *Autisme-économie*, Emmanuelle Benicourt, has described the movement's aspirations as follows:

> We hope it will trigger concrete transformations of the way economics is taught . . . We believe that understanding real-world economic phenomena is enormously important to the future well-being of humankind, but that the current narrow, antiquated and naive approaches to economics and economics teaching make this understanding impossible. We therefore hold it to be extremely important, both ethically and economically, that reforms like the ones we have proposed are, in the years to come, carried through, not just in France, but throughout the world.

The PAE Movement is about bringing economics students and economists of goodwill together to realize these changes, especially by promoting critical public discussion and honest debate. This broadly international collection of 9 documents and 43 short, provocative essays, drawn from the *post-autistic economics review,* is intended to promote these ends.

Finally, it seems worthwhile to ask why the reform movement begun by the French students has, unlike others, so quickly caught the imagination and involvement of so many economists around the world. Three reasons seem to stand out. First, the movement is founded on the sort of optimism that youth is most capable of originating. The French students had the innocent audacity to ask not for a mere amelioration of a deplorable state, but for a total overhaul of economics and economics teaching – in short, for a new beginning. The usual wary vocabulary of the economics of dissent, which presumes that the neoclassical hegemony will continue, is completely absent from the students' documents. Second is their notion of pluralism. Whereas traditionally the representatives of different economic heterodoxies have effected a kind of pluralism by meeting in the name of mutual tolerance and by conspiring through alliance for political advantage, the pluralism of the PAE Movement – and this will become clear as you read this book – is epistemologically grounded. It regards the various "schools" of economics, including neoclassicalism, as offering different windows on economic reality, each bringing into view different subsets of economic phenomena. It rejects the idea that any school could possess final or total solutions, but accepts all as possible means for understanding real-life economic problems. Third, among the decent people of the world there is a growing revulsion against the global financial regime whose policies, distilled from neoclassical dogma and forced on the world's poor, result annually in an invisible slaughter, millions condemned for orthodoxy's sake to needless death and suffering through the withdrawal of life-supporting services in the false name of "good economics."

Reference

Fitoussi, Jean-Paul (2001) *L'Enseignement supérieur des sciences "économiques en question": rapport au ministre de l'Éducation nationale.* Paris: Fayard.

Part I

Documents

The French students' petition

open letter from economic students to professors and others responsible for the teaching of this discipline

We, economics students of the universities of France, declare ourselves to be generally dissatisfied with the teaching that we receive.

This is so for the following reasons:

1. We wish to escape from imaginary worlds!

Most of us have chosen to study economics so as to acquire a deep understanding of the economic phenomena with which the citizens of today are confronted. But the teaching that is offered, that is to say for the most part neoclassical theory or approaches derived from it, does not generally answer this expectation. Indeed, even when the theory legitimately detaches itself from contingencies in the first instance, it rarely carries out the necessary return to the facts. The empirical side (historical facts, functioning of institutions, study of the behaviors and strategies of the agents . . .) is almost non-existent. Furthermore, this gap in the teaching, this disregard for concrete realities, poses an enormous problem for those who would like to render themselves useful to economic and social actors.

2. We oppose the uncontrolled use of mathematics!

The instrumental use of mathematics appears necessary. But resort to mathematical formalization when it is not an instrument but rather an end in itself, leads to a true schizophrenia in relation to the real world. Formalization makes it easy to construct exercises and to manipulate models whose significance is limited to finding "the good result" (that is, the logical result following from the initial hypotheses) in order to be able to write "a good paper." This custom, under the pretence of being scientific, facilitates assessment and selection, but never responds to the question that we are posing regarding contemporary economic debates.

3. We are for a pluralism of approaches in economics!

Too often the lectures leave no place for reflection. Out of all the approaches to economic questions that exist, generally only one is presented to us. This approach is supposed to explain everything by means of a purely axiomatic process, as if this were THE economic truth. We do not accept this dogmatism. We want a pluralism of approaches, adapted to the complexity of the objects and to the uncertainty surrounding most of the big questions in economics (unemployment, inequalities, the place of financial markets, the advantages and disadvantages of free-trade, globalization, economic development, etc.).

4. Call to teachers: wake up before it is too late!

We appreciate that our professors are themselves subject to some constraints. Nevertheless, we appeal to all those who understand our claims and who wish for change. If serious reform does not take place rapidly, the risk is great that economics students, whose numbers are already decreasing, will abandon the field in mass, not because they have lost interest, but because they have been cut off from the realities and debates of the contemporary world.

We no longer want to have this Autistic science imposed on us.

We do not ask for the impossible, but only that good sense may prevail.

We hope, therefore, to be heard very soon.

The French professors' petition

translation of the professors' petition circulated in France

Petition for a Debate on the Teaching of Economics

This petition raises the following problems:

1. **the exclusion of theory that is not neoclassical from the curriculum;**

2. **the mismatch between economics teaching and economic reality;**

3. **the use of mathematics as an end in itself rather than as a tool;**

4. **teaching methods that exclude or prohibit critical thinking;**

5. **the need for a plurality of approaches adapted to the complexity of objects analyzed.**

In real sciences, explanation is focused on actual phenomena. The validity and relevancy of a theory can only be assessed through a confrontation with "facts." This is why we, along with many students, deplore the development of a pedagogy in economics privileging the presentation of theories and the building and manipulation of models without considering their empirical relevance. This pedagogy highlights the formal properties of model construction, while largely ignoring the relations of models, if any, to economic realities. This is scientism. Under a scientific approach, on the other hand, the first interest is to demonstrate the informative power and efficiency of an abstraction vis-à-vis sets of empirical phenomena. This should be the primary task of the economist. It is not a mathematical issue.

The path for "getting back to the facts," however, is not obvious. Every science rests on "facts" that are built up and conceptualized. Different paradigms therefore appear, each of them constituting different families of representation and modalities of interpretation or constructions of reality.

Acknowledging the existence and role of paradigms should not be used as an argument for setting up different citadels, unquestionable from the outside. Paradigms should be confronted and discussed. But this can not be done on the base of a "natural" or immediate representation. One cannot avoid using the tools provided by statistics and econometrics. But performing a critical assessment of a model should not be approached on an exclusively quantitative base. No matter how rigorous from a formalistic point of view or tight its statistical fit, any "economic law" or theorem needs always to be assessed for its relevancy and validity regarding the context and type of situation to which it is applied. One also needs to take into account the institutions, history, environmental and geopolitical ealities, strategies of actors and groups, the sociological dimensions including gender relations, as well as more epistemological matters. However, these dimensions of economics are cruelly missing in the training of our students.

The situation could be improved by introducing specialized courses. But it is not so much the addition of new courses that is important, but rather the linking of different areas of knowledge in the same training program. Students are calling for this linkage, and we consider them right to do so. The fragmentation of our discipline should be fought against. For example, macroeconomics should emphasize the importance of institutional and ecological constraints, of structures, and of the role of history.

This leads us to the issue of pluralism. Pluralism is not just a matter of ideology, that is of different prejudices or visions to which one is committed to expressing. Instead the existence of different theories is also explained by the nature of the assumed hypotheses, by the questions asked, by the choice of a temporal spectrum, by the boundaries of problems studied, and, not least, by the institutional and historical context.

Pluralism must be part of the basic culture of the economist. People in their research should be free to develop the type and direction of thinking to which their convictions and field of interest lead them. In a rapidly evolving and ever-more complex world, it is impossible to avoid and dangerous to discourage alternative representations.

This leads us to question neoclassical theory. The preponderant space it occupies is, of course, inconsistent with pluralism. But there is an even more important issue here. Neoclassicalism's fiction of a "rational" representative agent, its reliance on the notion of equilibrium, and its insistence that prices constitute the main (if not unique) determinant of market behavior are at odds with our own beliefs. Our conception of economics is based on principles of behavior of another kind. These include especially the existence and importance of intersubjectivity between agents, the bounded rationality of agents, the heterogeneity of agents, and the importance of economic behaviors based on non-market factors. Power structures, including organizations, and cultural and social fields should not be a priori excluded.

The fact that in most cases the teaching offered is limited to the neoclassical thesis is questionable also on ethical grounds. Students are led to hold the false belief not only is neoclassical theory the only scientific stream, but also that scientificity is simply a matter of axiomatics and/or formalized modeling.

With the students, we denounce the naive and abusive conflation that is often made between scientificity and the use of mathematics. The debate on the scientific status of economics cannot be limited to the question of using mathematics or not. Furthermore, framing the debate in those terms is actually about deluding people and about avoiding real questions and issues of great importance. These include questioning the object and nature of modeling itself and considering how economics can be redirected toward exploring reality and away from its current focus on resolving "imaginary" problems.

Two fundamental features of university education should be the diversity of the student's degree course and the training of the student in critical thinking. But under the neoclassical regime neither is possible, and often the latter is actively discouraged. Insistence upon mathematical formalism means that most economic phenomena are out of bounds both for research and for the economics curriculum. The indefensibleness of these restrictions means that evidence of critical thinking by students is perceived as a dangerous threat. In free societies, this is an unacceptable state of affairs.

We, economic teachers of **France**, give our full support to the claims made by the students. We are particularly concerned with initiatives that may be taken at the local level in order to provide the beginning of answers to their expectations. We also hope these issues will be heard by all economics students in universities everywhere. To facilitate this we are ready to enter a dialog with students and to be associated with the holding of conferences that will allow the opening of a public debate for all.

post-autistic economics newsletter, Issue No. 1

sanity, humanity and science

post-autistic economics newsletter

No. 1, September 2000

To subscribe, send a blank email to pae_news@btinternet.com

FRANCE

The French economics mainstream is in a state of shock and apprehension following dramatic and unexpected events late in June.

On the 21st the influential Paris daily, *Le Monde*, featured a long article under the headline "Economics Students Denounce the Lack of Pluralism in the Teaching Offered." Economics students at the École Normale Supérieure, France's premier institution of higher learning, were circulating with great success a petition protesting against an excessive mathematical formalization.

The petition notes "a real schizophrenia" created by making modeling "an end in itself" and thereby cutting economics off from reality and forcing it into a state of "**autism**." The students, said a sympathetic *Le Monde*, call for an end to the hegemony of neoclassical theory and approaches derived from it, in favor of a pluralism that will include other approaches, especially those which permit the consideration of "concrete realities." *Le Monde* found French economists of renown, including Michel Vernières, Jean-Paul Fitoussi and Daniel Cohen, willing to speak out in support of the students. Fitoussi, current head of the jury of the economics' agrégation, said that "the students are right to denounce the way economics is generally taught" and that the over-use of mathematics "leads to a disembodiment of economic discourse." Daniel Cohen, economics professor at the École Normale Supérieure, spoke of "the pathological role" played by mathematics in economics. Meanwhile, the Minister of Education, Jack Lang, assured *Le Monde* that he would study closely the appeal from the students.

French radio and television also reported the students' complaints and confirmed their legitimacy. On the 21st, BFM said that it was now recognized that "the teaching of economics no longer had any relation with the real world" and that "this discipline is going through an undeniable crisis." Also on the 21st, *L'Humanité* quoted extensively from the students' open letter, while noting that in recent years several renowned economists had expressed similar views.

On the 23rd, *Les Echos* reported that a government report on university economics teaching had reached conclusions similar to those of the students. In their lengthy article, *Les Echos* noted that it is increasingly recognized that economics' "malaise is general and of long standing" and that "under the guise of being scientific" it has cultivated an anti-scientific environment "which leaves no room for reflection and debate."

On the 26th, the weekly, *Marianne,* carried an article about the student petition against "dogmatism" in the teaching of economics and for its replacement by "a pluralism of explanations." *Marianne* said that the petition, which was now on the Web, had 500 signatures, as well as growing support from economics teachers and interest from the highest levels of the French government.

On June 30th, *Le Nouvel Economiste*, referring to the students' petition and "mobilization," declared that economics had succumbed to a "pathological taste for a priori ideologies and mathematical formalisation disconnected from reality." Economics, it continued, should give up its false emulation of physics and "should instead look to the human sciences."

In July, French media interest continued to fuel the mobilization. On the 3rd, *La Tribune* featured a long article titled "Why a Reform of the Teaching of Economics." It began by saying that all concerned parties agree that economics is in crisis and that "a debate should be opened on this subject" and that the students' initiative aimed to bring this about. Economics, said *La Tribune*, had become lost in "*mondes imaginaires*" and "*l'économie* de Robinson Crusoé" and intellectually enfeebled by "the dogmatism that reigns in the teaching of the discipline." *Alternatives Economiques* carried an article titled "The Revolt of the Students," which noted that French Nobel Prize winner Maurice Allais had, despite his mathematical approach, come to conclusions similar to those of the students.

L'Express, France's equivalent to *Time*, carried an article, "*L'économie, science autiste?*," which aired the students' analysis and complaints. It also reported that the students' petition now had more than 600 signatures, and that their teachers were now starting a petition of their own in support.

On the 22nd of July, *Politis* reported on the students' cause and on the "autism" into which economics had fallen in consequence of its "obsession to produce a social physics." *Politis* noted that student support for the petition was widespread, including students not only from the most prestigious universities, but also from the less celebrated, both in Paris and in the provinces. "Pluralism should be part of the cultural base of economists." Instead, "neoclassical theory dominates because it rests on a simple set of axioms, easily mathematized." The coming academic year, concluded *Politis*, "promises to be agitated."

We have learned that the economics students' petition now has 800 signatures and the economists' petition 147. The latter includes some of the most illustrious names in French economics, e.g. Robert Boyer, André Orléan, Michel Aglietta, Jean-Paul Fitoussi and Daniel Cohen. It concludes by calling for "a national conference that will open a public debate for all."

UNITED STATES

At last month's 10th World Congress of Social Economics at the University of Cambridge, American participants reported that in the USA the purge of non-neoclassical and non-mathematically oriented economists from university faculties continues.

Conferees spoke of the increasing "Stalinization" of the profession. Unlike in France, where the fight-back has begun, in the States there are not yet signs of the formation of the critical mass needed to turn economics away from nineteenth-century dogmas. It is agreed, however, that the number of academic economists in America who are out of sympathy with the orthodoxy comprise a sizable minority. But they are fragmented, often intimidated and lack the means of joining together to exert their collective weight and moral authority. Meanwhile, it was agreed, the American economics' clock runs backwards.

American economists at the World Congress traded horror stories about the new wave of neo-classical "Stalinization." History of economic thought courses are now being targeted as sources of ideas whereby students might question or place in orthodoxy perspective. The goal is to create "history-free environments" in which students can be indoctrinated "more efficiently" into the neo-classical/mainstream belief system. For example, it was reported that from this fall the University of North Carolina is discontinuing all history of thought courses.

American participants also bemoaned plunging standards of literacy among economics graduate students and colleagues as a consequence of the mathematics fetish. The illiteracy problem is said to be particularly acute among new economics PhDs, many of whom are incapable of reading with comprehension a page of complex prose, such as one from *The General Theory*.

UNITED KINGDOM

The ideas expressed by the French students will have a familiar ring to readers of Tony Lawson's *Economics and Reality* (1997). But in Lawson's UK it is reported that economics students, although restless, are not yet rebellious. Meanwhile it is rumored that a French translation of *Economics and Reality* is imminent.

BELGIUM

Interest in the reform campaign launched in France spread quickly to Belgium. On June 24th under the heading "Economie autiste," the daily, *Le Soir*, both reported on the events in France and offered its own analysis of neoclassical economics as a quaint political ideology masquerading as science.

A week later *Le Soir* featured a lengthy article on the crisis in economics. It draws on a recent report by Michel Vernières, commissioned by the French government to investigate the teaching of economics. Vernières emphasizes that economic theories are devices for conceptualizing reality. "Pedagogically, it is therefore essential to articulate conceptual reflection and empirical investigation. . . . [and] to underline the plurality of approaches and the overall coherence of these approaches."

Bernard Paulré, referring especially to neoclassical theory, said that mathematics is often used to hide "the emptiness of the propositions and the absence of any concern for operational relevance." He said that in addition to a priori axioms, it is necessary for economics "to take account of institutions, of history, of the strategies of actors and of groups, of sociological dimensions, etc. . ."

This newsletter aims to link people wishing to bring sanity, humanity and science back to economics. To this end, YOU may help significantly by forwarding this issue to 10 sympathetic colleagues and/or students.

YOU may also help by emailing relevant news items, thoughts and suggestions to: pae_news@btinternet.com

To subscribe to the ***post-autistic economics newsletter***, send a blank email to: pae_news@hotmail.com

post-autistic economics newsletter, Issue No. 3

sanity, humanity and science

post-autistic economics newsletter

Issue no. 3, 27 November 2000

subscribers in 48 countries

to subscribe, email "subscribe" to pae_news@btinternet.com

Amartya Sen Enters the Debate (Edward Fullbrook)

On October 31st the neoclassical mainstream launched a counter-offensive against the French post-autistic economics movement. The amount of planning and co-ordination that obviously had gone into the surprise attack in *Le Monde* ended doubts as to the perceived seriousness of the threat posed by the French reform movement. The Paris daily's three-page spread appeared under the headline: **The counter-appeal that we publish fuels the debate on the excess of modélisation**. The special section on the debate, which has occupied France since last summer, included eight articles. One was a highly ambiguous interview with Amartya Sen.

These new *Le Monde* articles are significant for what they reveal about how the neoclassicalists view their position in strategic terms. Previously one did not know what tactics they would use if forced to come out for a fight. Now we do. For their defense they have adopted the strategy of misrepresenting their adversaries' position. This cynicism stunned members of the French student opposition. (See their response below.) From its inception, the post-autistic challenge to traditionalist practice has been very clear about its two principal points of contention:

    1. the issue of pluralism versus single-minded dogmatism and the imperative need for the former in economics; and

2. the need to liberate economics from its autistic obsession with formal models that have no obvious empirical reference.

Furthermore, to avoid unnecessary misunderstanding, the reform movement has emphasized – and the French students especially – that it does **not** oppose the instrumental use of mathematics in economics any more than it does in the natural sciences, but rather its use as an end in itself. It is mathematics for science versus mathematics for scientism that is the dividing line. The traditionalists, however, have seized upon the possibility here for misunderstanding as their main line of defense. Several of the *Le Monde* articles exploit this possibility as a means of deflecting discussion into a pseudo-debate. Counting on the relative ignorance of their readers, the articles work to convey the false impression that the reform movement wants and only wants to banish **all** mathematics from economics.

One *Le Monde* article goes so far as to use Keynes' $I = S$ and $C = cY$ as examples of the sort of mathematical practice being challenged. Another article, unsigned, leads with the question: "What are the mathematical tools used by economists?" Answer: statistics and "models without numerals." The implication given is that the reformers want to banish statistics and all models, e.g. $I = S$. A third article, signed by fifteen neoclassicalists, repeats this misrepresentation and then equates criticism of the neoclassical mainstream with attacks on "the scientific approach in economics." This reliance on tactics of obfuscation and false representation suggests that the traditionalists themselves regard their position as intellectually indefensible.

The interview with Amartya Sen is disappointing because the interviewer's questions lead Sen away from the real debate and into the pseudo-debate. There is no indication, nor reason to expect, that Sen has read the open letters of either the students or the teachers. Nor does he appear to have the issues that they have raised in focus.

Consequently the interview becomes centered on the non-question of mathematics or not mathematics. Characteristically, Sen takes a diplomatic line. After expounding magnanimously and learnedly on the French origins of the mathematical tradition, he notes that both it and non-mathematical approaches have their place. This is scarcely controversial. Nor is it satisfying. At the end of the interview we are left wondering what are Sen's opinions about the issues that have galvanized the French economics world, and increasingly that of the rest of the world, since June.

Does Amartya Sen believe that economics and economics teaching should be focused less on axiomatics and empirically empty models and more on economic realities? Does he wish to see the influence of scientism in economics reduced? Does he support pluralism, and, if so, in what context? Does he believe that students and economists should be encouraged or discouraged from asking difficult questions? Is he ethically at ease with drives to banish economists and economics that are out of sync with neoclassical doctrines? These are the questions that were not asked of Sen, but whose answers it would be good to hear.

The Students' Response (trans. J. Walter Plinge)

Des cours d'économie pertinents: chiche

So the economic teachers have acknowledged that something is not quite right in the universities (*Le Monde*, Tuesday, 31 Oct). We are delighted at this belated awareness. But, even so, we are perplexed at the direction that these events are taking.

Have we centered our critiques on mathematics? No. Have we questioned econometrics, an empirical practice that must be distinguished from formal models? No. On the contrary, as our open letter states clearly, we are disturbed by the continuous construction of imaginary worlds; that is, the intellectual constructs (the famous models) whose relevance remains to be demonstrated. We also have questioned the manifest lack of pluralism. So also does the petition of the teachers who support us and who contest the near total domination of "neoclassical" theory, whose limits, as well as capabilities, should be clearly presented. One can see, then, that the place of mathematics is secondary in our demands.

But it is true that the excesses of mathematics combined, in the absence of pluralism, with imaginary worlds is disastrous. Is it, then, a simple matter of pedagogy as our critics say? No, surely not, since as we all know, teaching is not just a matter of teaching methods.

What we ask for is simple: to have the empirical and theoretical tools which will permit us to understand the world in which we live. Do economics classes discuss business, the state, or even the market? No. Do they teach us the operation of the French economy; of Europe; of Japan? No. Do the classes offered enable understanding of the recent Asian crises, of the fluctuations of the Euro, or of the reforms in progress for the United Nations Center on Transnational Corporations. No. Etc.

All this can be achieved, suggest the economists who oppose our call for reform, by using a single and unique "scientific" method. That is to say, one which proceeds exclusively by the construction of hypotheses, the development of resulting equations, and then empirical tests which normally lead to refutation of some theories and confirmation of others. But the truth is that this ideal economics is well hidden, since none of us have yet had the good fortune to encounter it. Textbooks and courses are content to repeat the litanies of models without questioning them on an empirical basis.

But beyond that, we are skeptical about the relevance of this approach that wants for itself exclusivity. Should the discipline's role really be reduced to one of providing statistics, or should it not equally play a role in the formulations of hypotheses? Can one abstain from all empirical observation? Is the input of other disciplines (law, psychology, sociology, management) really unnecessary for the understanding of the principal problems of economics? As Amartya Sen, Nobel Prize winner for economics in 1998, said, "It is also necessary to recognize that the over-use of mathematics can be a sad means that deadlocks those subjects which are of ongoing importance, even if one cannot translate them into equations." We are astonished, therefore, to see some economists appealing to the scientific character of their discipline, given its meager results on "important subjects" (unemployment, globalization, fluctuations in the price of oil, etc.).

We desire, then, an end to the pseudo-polemic about mathematics. Explained clearly and in terms of convincing theories, mathematics is obviously welcome in the teaching of economics. We are astonished to have to clarify this point. But what must be taught above all, and which, moreover, some teachers are attempting to do, is the origin of models, their importance and their consequences in terms of the political economy. In short, we have had enough of "economics for children" classes, where the fundamental limits the theories presented, be they empirical or logical, and are only rarely mentioned. Furthermore, each course should be accompanied by a practical work schedule that allows the manipulation of proposed models. That is, in fact, the only means of understanding their logical operation and evaluating their relevance.

A reform of the pedagogy is no doubt one way to renew the appeal of economic sciences. But that is not sufficient. As with all the human sciences, economics should identify its intellectual origins, its political plans and the ideologies of its scientists. Nor should it close itself off to other human sciences, under the pretext of science.

Therefore one must stop taking the students for imbeciles who don't want to do math any more. The debate is now in the hands of the economists: Sirs, Madams, would you like to convince us of the relevance of your theories, of the appropriateness of your science? We ask only that . . . We are waiting.

Movement des étudiants pour la réforme de l'enseignement de l'économie
45, rue d'Ulm, 75005 Paris

Analysis of the Events in France (Joseph Halevi)

France is historically a country where radicalism is deep seated, at the same time it is also a place where power structures around the technocratic élites are extremely well entrenched. The present movement about reforming economic curricula is a central part of the upswing stage of a new radical sentiment and orientation. Its roots are in the awareness generated by the struggles for the defense of the public sector in 1995 and 1996, in the activities against homelessness and social exclusion which have regularly criss-crossed the country in the last five years. A very important role has been played by the monthly *Le Monde Diplomatique*, which has articulated an alternative and very well-informed perspective on economic and social issues at the world level. *Alternatives Economiques* has also contributed to keep open the door of non-conformist thought. Both journals are widely read by high-school (Lycée) teachers and university students.

Yet the main factor which made the awareness possible is that in France the social sciences are not yet monopolized and colonized by economics and they command intellectual respect. Students know that history, politics, and philosophy are not only important but that they ought to impact upon economics as well. Hence the view that economics is in the end Political Economy cannot be erased from people's minds. In this respect Italy is today far more normalized along American lines than France. If we look back to three decades ago, we see that France's economics was rather pluralistic. There was still a large space for literary–descriptive and historical economics of both left-wing and right-wing orientation (Raymond Barre, for instance). There existed, among others, a number of Circuitistes schools, an original French development of Keynes' ideas, as well as a number of Régulation schools, some of which linked up with the US-based social structure of accumulation approach. These contributions are still appreciated among the teachers in the Lycées. But, except for a few places, they rarely feature in the university curricula.

It is with François Mitterrand as President and with Lionel Jospin as Education Minister, whom the radicals of the 1960s and 1970s broadly supported, that technocracy took over totally. This meant giving enormous national importance to those Graduate Schools, programs and research centers that formed economists as *ingénieurs*. The neoclassicists, who ended up seeing their own institutions as little MIT cells on French soil, benefited most in terms of funding and of the power over the nationally-based procedures of academic recruitment. Orthodoxy monopolized the social reproduction mechanism. "Economics is not a discourse about society, it is about testing hypotheses," thundered Edmond Malinvaud in his opening address at the conference Is Economics Becoming a Hard Science? held in Paris at the end of 1992. That was and still is the mindset that the students are confronting.

Their mass movement has frightened the establishment, who responded by relying on the faith in scientism which characterizes and unifies French élites, including part of the radical public. Thus, the clash is being portrayed as revolving around the issue of mathematics rather than around the social and historical significance of what is being taught. Jean-Paul Fitoussi, appointed by the Minister of Education to head the committee for the reform of the economic curricula, is himself a high-ranking cadre of the technocratic vision. Only two years ago he published, with MIT's Olivier Blanchard, a book on unemployment in France where they use a most traditional production function with a natural rate of unemployment as a floor (*Croissance et chômage rapport Conseil*

d'analyse économique; Olivier Blanchard et Jean-Paul Fitoussi, Paris: La Documentation Française, 1998). Furthermore, the same co-author Blanchard wrote in the *Libération* issue of October 16 a rather unsophisticated defense of orthodoxy, claiming even that it helped cope with the Asian crisis! The technocratic élite is attempting to ride the tiger and, in the process, to remain well entrenched. It is up to the students' alertness to invalidate the dictum *plus ça change plus c'est la même chose*.
(Joseph Halevi has taught at the Universities of Grenoble and Nice.)

"Top 40 Economists on the Net" (www.paecon.net)

**pages returned on Google
for name plus "economics"**

1.	Karl Marx	56,000
2.	Adam Smith	32,000
3.	John Maynard Keynes	26,400
4.	David Ricardo	23,400
5.	Aristotle	20,600
6.	John Kenneth Galbraith	11,100
7.	Vilfredo Pareto	9,980
8.	Frederick Engels	9,950
9.	Milton Friedman	9,930
10.	Thomas Malthus	7,880
11.	Paul Krugman	7,270
12.	Thomas Aquinas	7,100
13.	Ludwig von Mises	6,970
14.	E. F. Schumacher	6,760
15.	Joseph Schumpeter	6,050

For the rest of this list and also the "Top 40 Living Economists on the Net," go to http:/www.paecon.net/ These lists are updated bimonthly.

In Brief

United Kingdom, Leeds: On Friday December 1st, Gilles Raveaud, Olivier Vaury, Ioana Marinescu and Pierre-Antoine, four of the student leaders of the post-autistic economics movement in France, will appear with Tony Lawson in a round table on "The Future of Economics." The occasion is The Fifth Postgraduate Economics Conference at Leeds University Business School. Details and booking information are at http:/www.leeds.ac.uk/cipp/pgc.htm

Argentina, Buenos Aires: A meeting has been held at the Institute of Economic Research of the University of Buenos Aires to discuss this newsletter and to consider establishing a pae movement in Argentina.

Australia: Beginning in November a post-autistic economics movement has emerged in Australia. Its website, which features Australian petitions for signing, is http:/www.powerup.com.au/~richleon/

Canada: pae petitions for Canadian economic students and economists are posted at http:/www.geocities.com/nathan_nunn/paestudent.htm and http:/www.geocities.com/nathan_nunn/paeteacher.htm

China: F——- X————, an economist of the Chinese Academy of Social Sciences, is this newsletter's first subscriber in China.

France: Autisme-économie has put up a new website with a new petition at http:/www.autisme-economie.org They also have organized a month of debates at universities throughout France. The first was held last week at the University of Lille, and attracted more than 100 students and teachers. These local debates are part of the build-up to the big national meeting of students and teachers for reform to be held in Paris. The date for that meeting has not yet been set, but it is now expected that it will be in January. Details for foreign journalists wishing to attend will be posted on the announcements page of www.paecon.net as soon as they are available. Meanwhile, student leaders expect soon to have their first meeting with Jean-Paul Fitoussi, the head of the government commission now investigating the state of economics in French universities.

Spain, Madrid: The Asociacion de Estudiantes de Economicas has launched in Spain a post-autistic economics movement based on the one in France. They have translated into Spanish the pae student and teacher petitions, and since mid-November have been actively circulating them. They have been pleasantly surprised by the level of support from professors. The A.e.e. has also put up a website at http:/www.aee.es.org/Post%20autistic%20economics%20index.htm It features the pae petitions in Spanish, a short introduction to the post-autistic economics movement, back issues of this newsletter, and various documents pertaining to economics and the teaching of economics in Spain. The Madrid-based movement is hopeful that in the first instance it will be able to introduce "new subjects" into the economics curriculum, such as heterodox economics and the history of economic thought. But its longer-run goal is to introduce pluralism into the introductory and intermediate micro and macro courses, such as is achieved in Hugh Stretton's superb *Economics: A New Introduction* (London & Sterling, Virginia: Pluto Press, 1999).

USA, Boston: On October 9 *The Boston Globe* noted the appearance of this newsletter as a sign of interesting things to come.

USA, Ivy League: There is a pae student petition for "Ivy League Students" at
http:/www.geocities.com/ivy_league_student_petition

USA, San Diego: On October 13, the *San Diego Union Tribune* featured an
editorial essay, "The faux Nobel Prize?," by Michael A. Bernstein, economist and
historian at the University of California San Diego. The essay describes how
economics has "sought to cloak itself, by use of the Nobel name, in the trappings
of an objectivity it did not and could not possess." Bernstein concludes by citing
the revolution now taking place in France as a real cause for hope for a general
reform of economics.

The Web: November 21, Google lists 286 web pages for "post-autistic
economics."

EDITOR: Edward Fullbrook
CORRESPONDENTS: Argentina: Iserino; Australia: Joseph Halevi, Richard Sanders; Brazil: Wagner
Leal Arienti; France: Gilles Raveaud, Olivier Vaury, J. Walter Plinge; Germany: Helge Peukert; Japan:
Susumu Takenaga; Spain: Jorge Fabra; United Kingdom: Nitasha Kaul; United States: Benjamin Balak,
Daniel Lien, Paul Surlis; At large: Paddy Quick

You are encouraged to post this newsletter to mailing lists and web forums.

To subscribe to the *post-autistic economics newsletter*, send an email with the
message "subscribe" to: pae_news@btinternet.com

To unsubscribe send an email with the message "unsubscribe" to
pae_news@btinternet.com

For requesting website petitions, for reporting news, for offering comments and
ideas, and for general inquiries, email pae_news@btinternet.com

Back issues of this newsletter can be found on over twenty websites, including
www.paecon.net (The Post-Autistic Economics Network)

Why not click on your forward button and send this issue to someone.

Two curricula: Chicago vs PAE

From the post-autistic economics newsletter, issue no. 4; 29 January 2000

Introduction (Edward Fullbrook)

Robert Solow's suggestion in *Le Monde* that there is not really so much difference between what the French students are asking for and what North American economics departments offer appears wildly erroneous and misleading when the core curriculum proposed by the French PAE students is juxtaposed to the core economics curriculum of the University of Chicago, the acknowledged gold standard of American economics curricula.

Below you will find first Chicago's core curriculum (as downloaded from the web) and then the core curriculum put forward by the students in France. In fact the difference between the two curricula is even greater than appears. They have been constructed on the basis of radically different epistemological and pedagogical principles. Whereas the traditional approach lets the theory-generated tool kit determine what aspects of economic reality are admitted for consideration, the post-autistic approach, in line with the natural sciences, reverses the order of determination. Gilles Raveaud, one of the authors of the French PAE core, sums up the new approach as follows: "Our view is: courses can no longer focus on TOOLS (maximizing under constraint, finding local and general extrema), but on PROBLEMS (incomes, poverty, unemployment, monetary policy, international trade, European Union, developing countries, immigration, new economy, ecology, etc.). **The tools would then be used only to the limit of their relevance for analyzing such problems, and not for their own sake.**"

University of Chicago Core Curriculum

Program of Study

The Bachelor of Arts program in economics is intended to equip students with the basic tools required to understand the operation of a modern economy: the origin and role of prices and markets, the allocation of goods and services, and the factors that enter into the determination of income, employment, and the price level.

Program Requirements

The Bachelor of Arts concentration in economics ... must include the **core curriculum**, which consists of price theory (Economics 200, 201) and macroeconomics (Economics 202 and 203). One course in economic history (Economics 221, 222, 223, 225, 229, or 254) and two courses in econometrics are also required; the latter requirement is normally met by Statistics 220 and Economics 210. ... Students concentrating in economics must also take three mathematics courses beyond the general education requirement.

Thus Chicago's core curriculum is divided into ten parts, of which three are pure mathematics, two are econometrics and statistics, four are analytical "tools," and one is economic history. These are listed as follows:

1. **Pure mathematics**

2. **Pure mathematics**

3. **Pure mathematics**

4. **The Elements of Economic Analysis I.** This course develops the economic theory of consumer choice. This theory characterizes optimal choices for consumers given their incomes, their preferences, and the relative prices of different goods. The course develops tools for analyzing how these optimal choices change when relative prices and consumer incomes change. Finally, the course presents several measures of consumer welfare. Students learn how to evaluate the impact of taxes and subsidies using these measures. If time permits, the course examines the determination of market prices and quantities, given primitive assumptions concerning the supply of goods.

5. **The Elements of Economic Analysis II.** This course is a continuation of Econ 200. The first part discusses markets with one or a few suppliers. The second part focuses on demand and supply for factors of production and the distribution of income in the economy. The course also includes some elementary general equilibrium theory and welfare economics.

6. **The Elements of Economic Analysis III.** As an introduction to macroeconomic theory and policy, this course covers the determination of aggregate demand (consumption, investment, and the demand for money), aggregate supply, and the interaction between aggregate demand and supply. The course also discusses activist and monetarist views of fiscal and monetary policy.

7. **The Elements of Economic Analysis IV.** This is a course in money and banking, monetary theories, the determinants of the supply and demand for money, the operation of the banking system, monetary policies, financial markets, and portfolio choice.

8.   Econometrics A. Econometrics A covers the single and multiple linear regression model, the associated distribution theory, and testing procedures; corrections for heteroskedasticity, autocorrelation, and simultaneous equations; and other extensions as time permits. Students also apply the techniques to a variety of data sets using PCs. Students are encouraged to meet this requirement by the end of the third year.

9.   Statistical Methods and Their Applications. This course is an introduction to statistical techniques and methods of data analysis, including the use of computers. Examples are drawn from the biological, physical, and social sciences. Students are required to apply the techniques discussed to data drawn from actual research. Topics include data description, graphical techniques, exploratory data analyses, random variation and sampling, one- and two-sample problems, the analysis of variance, linear regression, and analysis of discrete data. One or more sections of Stat 220 use examples drawn from economics and business and a selection of texts and topics that are more appropriate for concentrators in economics.

10. Economic history.

French PAE Students' Proposed Core Curriculum
(trans. Joseph Halevi)

Proposals for a common core in the curriculum of economics

Three groupings without a predetermined hierarchy

First Group: Descriptive economics: history of economic and social phenomena, actors and institutions

    1. History of economic and social phenomena (including the history of economic and social policies).

    2. Actors, organizations, institutions.
- The State (public administrations, public law, public finance).
- Firms (accounting methods for private firms, commercial law, financial analysis . . .).
- The financial and the banking system (the banks and the Central Bank, money and finance).
- Trade unions (collective bargaining, labor law).
- Associations (diversity, the social economy).
- International economic institutions (international economic relations, the international monetary and financial system, public law, international law . . .).

    3. Descriptive economics (active population, structure of the productive system, household budgets), national accounting systems, economic geography (studying the areas of economic integration, problems of development . . .).

Second Group: Theories and issues

1. History of economic theories (The Classics, Marx and Marxism, Marginalism, Keynes and Keynesianism, the Austrians, the Neoclassicalists, the Institutionalists).
2. Political and moral philosophy (thinking about the concepts of justice, equality, distribution, efficiency . . .). An important part of this course will have to be assigned to the examination of case studies (such as "can health care be left to the free interplay of market forces?," "up to what point should borders be opened?," "should genes be treated as commodities?")

Third Group: Applied economics and quantitative methods

The quantitative and formal techniques available to the economists (statistics econometrics, matrix algebra . . .) are justified only as long as they can be applied to concrete situations. It is necessary therefore to study those quantitative techniques (operation research, forecasting models, simulation models) in relation to questions of current relevance corresponding to political and social issues. This kind of work can be undertaken only in small groups. Here is a non-exhaustive list of the possible themes.

*   taxation (should the petrol tax be lowered? should the income tax system be reformed?)
*   Administered prices and the pricing of public utilities' services (Électricité de France, the national railways (SNCF), prices, the prices of pharmaceuticals)
*   pollution (the market for the rights to pollute, ecotax)
*   the regulation of financial flows (Tobin Tax, prudential regulation)
*   the social minima (the unemployment trap, disincentives)
*   economic forecasting (contribution and limits of modeling)
*   competition (regulation of monopolies, anti-trust policies)
*   insurance (information asymmetries, social insurances such as social security)
*   auctions.

In the same vein we include in this group the topic *economic and social policies*. This inclusion will allow the study of the IS-LM and Mundell Fleming models, etc. as tools addressing specific questions (such as the coordination of budgetary policies in the Euro zone, exchange rate policies, etc.).

Options (such as law, sociology, psychology, history, microeconomics, game theory) can also be pursued during the course of studies in order to facilitate interdisciplinary openness.

Advice from student organizers in France and Spain

From the *post-autistic economics newsletter*, issue no. 4; 29 January 2000

Olivier Vaury, France

When you want to launch a movement like ours, you immediately become aware of three obstacles:

1. the students may not be at all interested: they merely want to pass their degrees, no matter what they learn;
2. the teachers may be satisfied with the current situation; and,
3. last but not least, the journalists may not be at all interested.

I would like to focus on the third obstacle, and to emphasize the fact that it is not that big. And this is the reason why: nowadays, people who want to change something in the society they live in are not very numerous. This makes it easy to be heard: less competition! Moreover, journalists are happy to get some "ready-made" material: do not hesitate to provide them with your articles, and other relevant documents, so that they can simply "copy and paste." Moreover, some of them are really interested in the reform of the economics faculties, and may not be convinced by mainstream's purported "scientificity." You can go and meet them with petitions, with representatives of the teachers, and show them articles by well-known economists (Leontief, Galbraith, Simon, etc.). If you come from a major university, they will be impressed and inclined to take your protest into account.

Gilles Raveaud, France

Our experience is that the very most important point is to focus on TEACHING. Since there are obviously teaching problems (i.e. lots of maths without much relevance), the majority of teachers will agree with you on that point, even if they may disagree on other points. This is even more true now with what is going on in France, because many teachers fear the students' reaction. You just have to prove to them that their misgivings are justified, and not let them continue "teaching as usual" as if nothing is happening. It is also a good argument for the press: journalists have absolutely no idea of what is going on in universities. They are amazed when you tell them how you spend your days.

So focusing on teaching problems is indeed an excellent starting point: most of the people will listen to you, understand what you say, and probably agree with you. Larger consequences (theoretical, or even political in a broad sense) will come afterwards. But it is very important to keep away from such aspects in the beginning, as students are always suspected (in France at least) of being politically biased. And never forget that many social movements have involved students in the past, so when as students you say that you are not pleased with what is going on, lots of people will indeed pay attention. We know that from experience. It is really easier than you would think.

Jorge Fabra, Spain *(Economics Student Association, Madrid)*

The French student mobilization has spread to Spain. Here too it has led to public debate concerning the **future** of economics, but whereas in France the debate has tended to become focused on the excessive use of mathematics, in Spain we are focusing it on the absence of pluralism in the study of economics. However, we see both problems as interrelated. Both escapism into formalism and the exclusion of all analysis that is not broadly neoclassical lead to the same terrifying outcome: economists unable to deal with, maybe even unaware of, the real economic problems of today and tomorrow. Inequalities throughout the world are growing extremely fast; economies are ruining environments and the biosphere; the nature of economic transactions is changing, etc. etc. The study of economics should prepare students to analyze the problems of **their** time.

Opening up economics,
The Cambridge 27

(Released 14 June 2001)

27 PhD students at Cambridge University support the following open letter:

Opening up economics:
a proposal by Cambridge students

As students at Cambridge University, we wish to encourage a debate on contemporary economics. We set out below what we take to be characteristic of today's economics, what we feel needs to be debated and why. As defined by its teaching and research practices, we believe that economics is monopolized by a single approach to the explanation and analysis of economic phenomena. At the heart of this approach lies a commitment to formal modes of reasoning that must be employed for research to be considered valid. The evidence for this is not hard to come by. The contents of the discipline's major journals, of its faculties and its courses all point in this direction.

In our opinion, the general applicability of this formal approach to understanding economic phenomenon is disputable. This is the debate that needs to take place. When are these formal methods the best route to generating good explanations? What makes these methods useful and, consequently, what are their limitations? What other methods could be used in economics? This debate needs to take place within economics and between economists, rather than on the fringe of the subject or outside of it all together. In particular, we propose the following:

1.   That the foundations of the mainstream approach be openly debated. This requires that the bad criticisms be rejected just as firmly as the bad defences. Students, teachers and researchers need to know and acknowledge the strengths and weaknesses of the mainstream approach to economics.

2.   That competing approaches to understanding economic phenomena be subjected to the same degree of critical debate. Where these approaches provide significant insights into economic life, they should be taught and their research encouraged within economics. At the moment this is not happening. Competing approaches have little role in economics as it stands simply because they do not conform to the mainstream's view of what constitutes economics. It should be clear that such a situation is self-enforcing. This debate is important because in our view the *status quo* is harmful in at least four respects. First, it is harmful to students who are taught the "tools" of mainstream economics without learning their domain of applicability. The source and evolution of these ideas is ignored, as is the existence and status of competing theories. Second, it disadvantages a society that ought to be benefiting from what economists can tell us about the world. Economics is a social science with enormous potential for making a difference through its impact on policy debates. In its present form its effectiveness in this arena is limited by the uncritical application of mainstream methods. Third, progress towards a deeper understanding of many important aspects of economic life is being held back. By restricting research done in economics to that based on one approach only, the development of competing research programs is seriously hampered or prevented altogether. Fourth and finally, in the current situation an economist who does not do economics in the prescribed way finds it very difficult to get recognition for his or her research.

The dominance of the mainstream approach creates a social convention in the profession that only economic knowledge production that fits the mainstream approach can be good research, and therefore other modes of economic knowledge are all too easily dismissed as simply being poor, or as not being economics. Many economists therefore face a choice between using what they consider inappropriate methods to answer economic questions, or adopting what they consider the best methods for the question at hand knowing that their work is unlikely to receive a hearing from economists.

Let us conclude by emphasizing what we are certainly not proposing: we are not arguing against the mainstream approach *per se*, but against the fact that its dominance is taken for granted in the profession. We are not arguing against mainstream methods, but believe in a pluralism of methods and approaches justified by debate. Pluralism as a default implies that alternative economic work is not simply tolerated, but that the material and social conditions for its flourishing are met, to the same extent as is currently the case for mainstream economics. This is what we mean when we refer to an "opening up" of economics.

The students who have written this proposal are asking for economic students and economists, wherever they are based, who wish to formally and publicly back their proposal to email them at **cesp@econ.cam.ac.uk**, with the following:

"I support the proposal of the Cambridge economics PhD students . . . signed"

Please include university/position if you wish these to be noted. The website www.paecon.net will be regularly updated with the full list of supporters. Other enquiries about the proposal are also welcome, to the same address.

The Kansas City Proposal

(Released 13 August 2001)

An International Open Letter
to all economics departments

Economics needs fundamental reform – and now is the time for change.

This document comes out of a meeting of 75 students, researchers and
professors from 22 nations who gathered for a week of discussion on the state of
economics and the economy at the University of Missouri, Kansas City (UMKC)
in June 2001. The discussion took place at the Second Biennial Summer School
of the Association for Evolutionary Economics (AFEE), jointly sponsored by
UMKC, AFEE and the Center for Full Employment and Price Stability.

The undersigned participants, all committed to the reform of our discipline, have
developed the following open letter. This letter follows statements from other
groups who have similar concerns. Both in agreement with and in support of the
Post-Autistic Economics Movement and the Cambridge Proposal, we believe that
economic theory, inhibited by its ahistorical approach and abstract formalist
methodology, has provided only a limited understanding of the challenging
complexity of economic behavior. The narrow methodological approach of
economics hinders its ability to generate truly pragmatic and realistic policy
prescriptions or to engage in productive dialog with other social sciences.

All economics departments should reform economics education to include
reflection on the methodological assumptions that underpin our discipline. A
responsible and effective economics is one that sees economic behavior in its
wider contexts, and that encourages philosophical challenge and debate. Most
immediately, the field of economic analysis must be expanded to encompass the
following:

1. **A broader conception of human behavior.** The definition of economic man
as an autonomous rational optimizer is too narrow and does not allow for the roles
of other determinants such as instinct, habit formation and gender, class and other
social factors in shaping the economic psychology of social agents.

2.   **Recognition of culture.** Economic activities, like all social phenomena, are necessarily embedded in culture, which includes all kinds of social, political and moral value-systems and institutions. These profoundly shape and guide human behavior by imposing obligations, enabling and disabling particular choices, and creating social or communal identities, all of which may impact on economic behavior.

3.   **Consideration of history.** Economic reality is dynamic rather than static, and as economists we must investigate how and why things change over time and space. Realistic economic inquiry should focus on process rather than simply on ends.

4.   **A new theory of knowledge.** The positive-vs-normative dichotomy which has traditionally been used in the social sciences is problematic. The fact-value distinction can be transcended by the recognition that the investigator's values are inescapably involved in scientific inquiry and in making scientific statements, whether consciously or not. This acknowledgment enables a more sophisticated assessment of knowledge claims.

5.   **Empirical grounding.** More effort must be made to substantiate theoretical claims with empirical evidence. The tendency to privilege theoretical tenets in the teaching of economics without reference to empirical observation cultivates doubt about the realism of such explanations.

6.   **Expanded methods.** Procedures such as participant observation, case studies and discourse analysis should be recognized as legitimate means of acquiring and analyzing data alongside econometrics and formal modeling. Observation of phenomena from different vantage points using various data-gathering techniques may offer new insights into phenomena and enhance our understanding of them.

7.   **Interdisciplinary dialog.** Economists should be aware of diverse schools of thought within economics, and should be aware of developments in other disciplines, particularly the social sciences.

Although strong in developing analytical thinking skills, the professional training of economists has tended to discourage economists from even debating – let alone accepting – the validity of these wider dimensions. Unlike other social sciences and humanities, there is little space for philosophical and methodological debate in the contemporary profession. Critically-minded students of economics seem to face an unhappy choice between abandoning their speculative interests in order to make professional progress, or abandoning economics altogether for disciplines more hospitable to reflection and innovation.

Ours is a world of global economic change, of inequality between and within societies, of threats to environmental integrity, of new concepts of property and entitlement, of evolving international legal frameworks, and of risks of instability in international finance. In such a world we need an economics that is open-minded, analytically effective and morally responsible. It is only by engaging in sustained critical reflection, revising and expanding our sense of what we do and what we believe as economists that such an economics can emerge.

The original 25 signatories of the International Open Letter:

Ricardo Aguado, Universidad del País Vasco, **Spain**
Dr. Stephen Dunn, Staffordshire University, **UK**
Dr. Eric R. Hake, Eastern Illinois University, **USA**
Fadhel Kaboub, University of Missouri – Kansas City, **Tunisia**
Nitasha Kaul, University of Hull, UK, **India**
Peter Kimani, University of Nairobi, **Kenya**
Meelis Kitsing, London School of Economics, **Estonia**
Agim Kukeli, Colorado State University, **Albania**
Joelle Leclaire, University of Missouri – Kansas City, **Canada**
Áine Ní Léime, National University of Ireland – Galway, **Ireland**
Hui Liu, University of Ottawa, **China**
Claudia Maya, National Autonomous University of Mexico, **Mexico**
Dr. Andrew Mearman, Wagner College, USA, **UK**
Jaime Augusto Torres Melo, London School of Economics, **Colombia**
Vassilis Monastiriotis, London School of Economics, **Greece**
Alfred Ng Yau Foo, University of Missouri – Kansas City, **Malaysia**
José Alfredo Pureco Ornelas, National Autonomous University of Mexico, **Mexico**
Jairo J. Parada, Penn State University, **Colombia**
Franziska M. Pircher, University of Missouri – Kansas City, **USA**
David Pringle, University of Ottawa, **Canada**
Dr. James F. Smith, University of Vermont, **USA**
Pavlina R. Tcherneva, Center for Full Employment and Price Stability, UMKC, **USA**
Ermanno Celeste Tortia, University of Ferrara, **Italy**
Eric Tymoigne, Université de Paris – Nord, **France**
Benton Wolverton, University of Missouri – Kansas City, **USA**

The full list of signatories for this petition is maintained at www.paecon.net

Support the Report

Gilles Raveaud, co-founder of Autisme-Économie École Normale Supérieure de Cachan, France

The Fitoussi Report may fail to satisfy some people, especially because it does not acknowledge the existence of a "global alternative" to mainstream economics. Indeed the Report seems to say that nothing really valuable exists outside the "neoclassical–Keynesian consensus," a statement with which we of course deeply disagree. But worse, Jean-Paul Fitoussi, being an "old-fashioned" Keynesian, has apparently not realized that what he believes in is, regrettably, now largely forgotten in most universities. What is taught today in France is not his kind of economics, but "general equilibrium with rational expectations" – a somewhat different approach, to say the least. There seems to be here a sort of "generation gap." Some members of Fitoussi's generation have a culture and an approach to economics that they find hard to believe has disappeared. But it has. And this is why we stress the importance of teaching the history of economic thought and economic history.

Nonetheless, the Report contains strong statements regarding the use and misuse of mathematics and regarding neoclassical economics' oppressive domination. For example:

> One must acknowledge that concerning mathematics and formalization, some excesses have taken place. We sometimes (often?) see an excess of modelization and very little concern for its empirical relevance.

> We must avoid using the teaching of mathematics and statistics (and sometimes microeconomics) in undergraduate courses purely as a tool of selection.

The Fitoussi Report does not, it is true, deal directly with the questions we raised. In particular, it fails to deal directly with the lack of pluralism and the intolerant domination of neoclassical economics. But by proposing a "bottom-up" approach, Fitoussi offers a politically adroit answer to these problems. The Report's method is not to dictate what is to be taught, a method neither feasible nor desirable. Instead, Fitoussi's idea is merely to **take teaching seriously**, something that in economics too few people do. He proposes three ways – these are the teeth of his report – in which this should be done. They entail reforms in the teaching of economics that if implemented (and the Minister of Education suggests that he will see to it that they are) will have the effect of going a long way toward realizing the demands for reform that our movement in France has been seeking. Fitoussi's three primary means of reforming economics teaching are as follows:

1. The organization of a **multidisciplinary curriculum** for at least the first three years. Within this curriculum students will be allowed to choose between disciplines as they progress, and intellectually to confront them with one another. Economics will then find itself in **competition** with other subjects: either it turns to sensible courses or remains as it is and loses students. Furthermore, even if it does not reform, the economics students that remain will, because of their exposure to other disciplines and to real debate in their first three years, be in a much stronger intellectual position than they are today.

2. Fitoussi wants debate on economic issues to be "integrated" into the structure and content of **economics** courses, not only through theory and statistics, but also through institutional and historical facts. There should be no "naked tools" (for Fitoussi these include, alas, the history of economic thought). The Report is categorical on this point. For example, it says (emphasis added):

The debates [in economics] are to be taught, not only for the sake of pluralism, *but because their understanding allows the students better to grasp the concepts*. Economics has always been and will remain the place of debates. It surprises me that people are surprised by this. Can one imagine that problems like unemployment, inequality and poverty could *be treated as physical phenomena*?

3. The shift from silly exercises to the production of essays, oral presentations and student debates, things that are very rare in France. Teachers are to be required to give time to helping their students prepare these projects.

Fitoussi also proposes an **evaluation of teachers**, something that does not exist in the French system. We think that this could be useful for making economics teachers listen to students' complaints, which now, as we know, they usually do not. But we would prefer a system in which students and their representatives would be associated in some way with the evaluation of the curriculum itself, at least as far as teaching methods are concerned.

Apart from this last point, we support the Fitoussi Report, imperfect as it is. We think that if it were implemented, it would make economics in French universities look VERY different to how it does today. The Report's approach could be summed up as an attempt to squeeze mainstream economics from two directions: one from the top with the introduction of multidisciplinarity, and one from the bottom with the stress on debates and "integrated" courses. If implemented, this strategy could be quite effective as a force for the reform of economics both in and out of the classroom.

These are the reasons why we are currently trying to convince economics teachers to join us in support of the Report (at present we are working on an article for *Le Monde*). In fact, it is only the teachers who can now change things. If they will try to do it and succeed then our revolt will turn into a peaceful and quiet revolution, but a revolution nonetheless, where economics teachers will teach and students will learn **economics** at last.

Part II

Teaching

A contribution on the state of economics in France and the world

James K. Galbraith (University of Texas at Austin, USA)

Professor Robert Solow, a distinguished and notably non-autistic economist, has recently entered the debate in the pages of *Le Monde* on the questions of economic teaching raised originally, and now placed before the world community, by the French students. Permit me to underline the important points that Professor Solow acknowledges, while at the same offering a few points of difference where, in my view, the French students have made a stronger case than Professor Solow is willing to concede.

Professor Solow states outright the fundamental issue:

> L'économie est une discipline appliquée. . . . S'il est vrai, comme le prétendent les étudiants, que la composante empirique de l'économie est pratiquement inexistante dans leurs enseignements, alors leurs professeurs ne font pas correctement leur travail. Si l'on enseigne l'économie aux étudiants français comme s'il s'agissait d'une discipline abstraite, axiomatique, ou comme si elle consistait en l'application répétitive d'une seule technique d'analyse élaborée, alors ils ont raison de protester.

> [Economics is an applied discipline. If it is true, as the students claim, that the empirical component of economics is practically non-existent in their instruction, then their professors are not doing their work properly. If one teaches economics to the French students as if it were an abstract, axiomatic discipline, or as if it consisted of the repetitive application of a single technique of sophisticated analysis, then they are right to protest. (Editor's translation)]

This, it seems to me, summarizes the complaint of the French students exactly. Of course, Professor Solow is careful not to comment as an authority on economics teaching in France as it actually is. That would be a subject of which neither he nor I have personal knowledge. But who is in a position to know – other than the students – and their professors? An impartial investigator must therefore turn to the evidence coming from these sources.

This evidence is straightforward. We have, first, the testimony of the students. To quote the English translation of one of their documents:

> ... we are disturbed by the continuous construction of imaginary worlds: that is, the intellectual constructs (the famous models) whose relevance remains to be demonstrated. We have also questioned the manifest lack of pluralism. . . . What we ask for is simple: to have the theoretical and empirical tools which will permit us to understand the world in which we live. Do economics classes discuss business, the state, *or even the market*? No. Do they teach us the operation of the French economy; of Europe; of Japan? No. Do the classes offered enable understanding of the recent Asian crises, of the fluctuations of the Euro. . . ? No.

To an American economist teaching courses on inequality, development and financial crises at a research university – and having just returned from national professional meetings at New Orleans, where a great part of the agenda was taken up by discussions of financial instability, trade conflict, and the misgovernment of globalization – these assertions are extraordinary. I would go so far as to find them mildly shocking. Are they contradicted by any opposing body of students, or by any documentation showing that such issues do, in fact, form part of economics teaching in France? To my knowledge, they have not been.

So, are they contradicted by the professors, whose work they so deeply indict? First, it is worth noting that while the students are united, the French professors are divided. Some support the students; others do not. The latter group admits to this fact, in its counter-appeal lately published in *Le Monde*:

> Un certain nombre de professeurs et d'étudiants en économie ont signé et diffusé un appel demandant une refonte de l'enseignement de l'économie, estimant que celui-ci repose trop sur la formalisation mathématique. Cet appel a le mérite de soulever un authentique problème, celui de la démarche scientifique en économie. Il l'aborde toutefois de façon réductrice, en contestant l'usage (instrumental) des mathématiques et se conclut par une attaque partisane à l'encontre de l'un des corpus centraux de notre discipline, à savoir les théories dites "néoclassiques."

> [A number of professors and students of economics have signed and distributed a petition demanding the reform of the teaching of economics, claiming that it depends too heavily on mathematical formalism. This petition has the merit of raising a real problem, that of scientific method in economics. However, it approaches the problem in a reductive fashion, in questioning the instrumental usage of mathematics and in concluding with a partisan

attack against the body of work central to our discipline, knowledge of the theories called "neoclassical." (Editor's translation)]

The responding professors thus raise two issues, the first being the role of mathematics in economic instruction, and the second being an allegation that the students have launched "une attaque partisane" against the central theories of modern scientific economics.

Professor Solow himself has rightly dismissed the first issue: "Plaider pour ou contre l'usage des mathématiques n'est pas pertinent, comme l'admettent les étudiants dans leur pétition." ["To plead for or against the use of mathematics is not relevant, as the students admit in their petition." (Editor's translation)] The students have not raised an objection to the use of mathematics in economics, and it is beside the point to rebut their complaint on this ground.

It is therefore the second issue – the question of whether the French students may have improperly objected to the core propositions and methods of a scientific economics – that is pertinent, and here Professor Solow expresses his reservations about the movement. And it is this issue that is, indeed, the interesting one, the issue that tends also to preoccupy professional economists who concern themselves in a serious way with methodological questions.

To begin with, Professor Solow points out, rightly and importantly, that applied economics properly consists of a series of particular models, drawn from a variety of intellectual and scientific traditions, which help to structure thinking about empirical issues.

Thus, for example:

- Does the distribution of changes in asset prices or exchange rates follow a normal curve, or one with fatter tails and hence a higher risk of catastrophic deviations?
- Is the market for low wage labor characterized by monopsony power (so that increasing minimum wages may raise rather than reduce employment)?
- Can free international capital movements be justified when information is not equally available to all sides of the resulting transactions?
- Does economic inequality tend to fall, or rise, with economic growth?
- Does unemployment rise when inequality falls, and vice versa (the conventional position), or do more equal societies have fuller employment, as a rule, than less equal societies (my position)?

These are issues all of which can be, and are, contestable using tools that ought to be part of the research training of economists everywhere.

Professor Solow notes that the French students do not make clear that they understand just how much of the terrain of so-called "neoclassical" economics is under such contest these days. But how could they make such a thing clear, if it is not part of their training?

And that brings us to the question, what on earth are the professors teaching? *Nowhere* in the counter-appeal is there the simple acknowledgment that these and similar issues are, in fact, among the most hotly and openly contested questions in economics today. Indeed, the professors do not acknowledge that any issues are contested! Instead, they resort to a characterization of their discipline that is completely at odds with the pragmatic and practical approach described by Professor Solow. Here is how they describe their role:

> L'identification et la définition précise des concepts et des comportements qui caractérisent l'activité économique (consommation, production, investissement . . .) et l'énoncé des hypothèses de base relatives à ces comportements; la formulation de théories ayant comme mode d'expression la formalisation de liens fonctionnels entre les éléments précédemment identifiés; la vérification de ces théories par l'expérience. Jusqu'à preuve du contraire, en économie cette expérience ne peut être constituée que par la confrontation à l'histoire quantifiée par la statistique et l'économétrie.

> [The identification and precise definition of the concepts and the behaviors that characterize economic activity (consumption, production, investment . . .) and the statement of the basic hypotheses relating to these behaviors; the formulation of theories having as their mode of expression the formalization of functional links between previously identified elements; the verification of the theories by experience. Until proven to the contrary, in economics this experiential truth can be reached only through comparisons to history quantified by statistics and econometrics. (Editor's translation)]

In other words, the counter-appeal professors appear oblivious to the high controversy on most important issues of theory, fact and policy into which even neoclassical economics has descended in recent years. They seem unaware of the heterogeneity of models and methods breaking out everywhere in economic research. Truly, if this is a correct perception, then in Professor Solow's words, "ils ne font pas correctement leur travail."[1]

But what about the question of alternative theoretical approaches? Is there anything missing even from the hotly contested domains of modern mainstream economics? I believe there is, and would point to three large areas that have nearly disappeared from the teaching of economics even where that activity is otherwise competently carried out, at very considerable intellectual and social cost.

The first is the history of economics itself. The intellectual roots of our subject – going back in Anglo-American tradition to Smith, Ricardo, Malthus, Marx, Mill, Veblen (not Swedish as *Le Monde* has erroneously reported in passing, but American), Keynes and Galbraith *père*, not to mention such great French figures

as Quesnay, Say, Walras . . . is sorely neglected, and so is the study of the historical relationship between economics and other disciplines, notably physics and the
theory of evolution, as well as the modern philosophy of science (a vastly more
interesting topic than the crude description of method in the French professors'
statement would make it appear). As a matter of intellectual formation, a great
deal of potential creativity is lost when students do not have the origins of their
own subject available to them as an object of study.

Second, there is a tradition of macroeconomic and monetary economics that
has largely been submerged by the neoclassical emphasis on market transactions
between firms and households. A proper understanding of monetary policy, fiscal
accounting, effective demand, debt relations, the operation of banks and credit
institutions, the instability of financial flows and similar subjects forms the core of
a Keynesian and post-Keynesian tradition. To be sure, this tradition has not
entirely disappeared from economics on the American side of the Atlantic. However, it deserves a much more prominent and stable place in the curriculum than
it receives.

Here truly a question of pluralism is raised. For instance, one can view mass
unemployment as a phenomenon of "imperfect labor markets" (the neoclassical
framework), requiring real wage reductions as the principal solution. Alterna-
tively, one can view mass unemployment as mainly a phenomenon of inadequate
effective demand (the Keynesian theoretical position), requiring mechanisms to
support the incomes of those who are not adequately paid in private markets.
Both views are capable of rigorous formulation, but both cannot be correct. The
notion that mainstream economics has somehow demonstrated, as opposed to
having merely asserted, the triumph of the neoclassical over the Keynesian view
is quite wrong.

Third, I would argue from my experience as a teacher of research methods
that the French students are correct in emphasizing the need for instruction in
differing institutional contexts; in political, national and international structures;
in policy histories; and also in methods for collecting economic data and for evaluating the quality of information contained in economic data sets. There are vital
differences, for instance, between the United States Federal Reserve and the
European Central Bank as regards mission, legal charter, accountability and over-
sight. Understanding these differences would form an important part of the back-
drop of a comparative analytical study of the conduct of monetary policy in the
two regions. A textbook caricature of a central bank – which is what one is led to
suspect may be what economics students in France are exposed to – will not
provide a sufficient basis for constructing such a study.

One can multiply examples of this general kind – I might mention my own
research into the measurement of inequalities in the global economy – but the
point would remain the same. A scientific economics, as Professor Solow states
with my emphatic agreement, must be a diverse, pragmatic, applied enterprise

with an open discussion of controversial questions. I go beyond Professor Solow mainly in emphasizing that the core arrangement of theoretical propositions in economics also remains among the questions worthy of debate and therefore of inclusion in the curriculum of economics, since a theoretical framework cannot be debated unless it is first properly taught. The pretense that a single axiomatic framework can be, or has been, built up for all time from first principles and verified by observation – the stated contention of the counter-appeal – merely reveals how far removed from the reality of our profession that statement is.

It also constitutes the best evidence that the French students are correct in their appeal for fundamental reform.

Note

1   One might add that the remainder of the counter-appeal includes an effort to besmirch the motives of the professors and students involved in the protest. This section, with its reference to "conspiracy theory," unsupported by evidence, does not inspire confidence in the scientific disposition of those who signed the counter-appeal.

The Franco-American neoclassical alliance

Joseph Halevi (University of Sydney, Australia)

Solow's and Blanchard's appearances in the two most intellectually oriented papers (*Le Monde*, 12 December 2000 and *Liberation*, 13 October 2000) of France are not random events, but the result of the difficulty in which the French neo-classicists find themselves since the students' movement began in June. At the beginning of Fall a counter-manifesto appeared in *Le Monde*. Its impact has been insignificant and, if anything, it has strengthened the students' position in the eyes of public opinion. The counter-manifesto ignored all the remarks made by the students in their original manifesto and just harkened back on the scientificity of economics. The paucity of their arguments was striking.

Hence the French establishment has resorted to the Americans, initially via Blanchard, who (surprise, surprise), writes with Fitoussi on the French economy. Blanchard is French, but he has been with MIT for more than a decade and is now the chairperson of the economics department. Blanchard's article was as poor and as dogmatic as the counter-manifesto. He claimed that modern mathematical economics has solved the Smith–Walras puzzle of how markets hang together. In this way he highlighted his complete ignorance of Smithian and classical economics, which is a cost-of-production theory of price and value and not a supply and demand story. Furthermore, he maintained that present neoclassical theory is useful in understanding, among other things, the Asian crisis. A very bold statement indeed! Even neoclassically born and bred economists like Joseph Stiglitz would reject such an absurd assertion.

Finally, Blanchard took a typical comprador posture, stating that the research done in the USA is the best you can possibly get. Indeed, this is exactly what the directors of the neoclassical centers in France, such as in Toulouse (home of Laffont), Marseille and Paris, think – they want their own centers just to be MIT/Stanford cells located on French soil. Also, not insignificantly, they want to use their American connections and France's establishment inferiority complex *vis-à-vis* the USA to gain absolute power in matters concerning certification of doctoral programs, research funds, appointments and promotions. These are issues that in France are decided at the national level.

This is why the power of these centers is real only if it is mirrored in the national institutions.

On the whole, the Blanchard piece was even more disastrous than the counter-manifesto. Finally, Solow was brought to the rescue. Behind his pragmatic stance there lay a very imperialistic attitude, blaming the French for being bad teachers. However, MIT itself nurtured the very individuals who stalinistically endeavored to enshrine the monopoly of neoclassicism in France's economics – Laffont and Tirole, to mention just two of them.

These episodes show that the students' perception that *Le Monde* was setting up a straw or false debate is correct. However, the problem does not pertain only to *Le Monde*. It is the coordinated reaction of the establishment that the students are facing. Fitoussi, with his links to MIT and *homme de pouvoir* in France, is fully part of the establishment. In his capacity as the head of the committee entrusted with writing the report, he is not without heavy vested interests. The students are surely aware of this fact.

Plural education

Hugh Stretton (University of Adelaide, Australia)

Just to show that we too can theorize, how about some pure theory of economic education? Here follows a five-step theory of pluralism:

1 Economic life is complex, and some elements of it are easier to know than others. Nobody can know everything about the billions of daily actions and transactions that constitute it. So

2 Any investigation of it has to select what activities to investigate, how far and in what directions to trace their causes and necessary conditions, and how to go about it: what language, identities, categories, collectives and simplifications to employ, and so on. What you hope to use the knowledge for – or, if you are driven by pure curiosity, the aspects of the subject that interest you – should join with technical considerations in shaping your selections. That is another way of saying that your values and social purposes should shape them. Some at least of those values and purposes are bound to be controversial (there are no perfectly unanimous societies). So

3 Your discoveries are likely to be as controversial as the values and purposes that have shaped the search. That does not imply that they must be untrue, or that rival conclusions about similar subjects must necessarily contradict one another. For example: neoclassical economists have explained why substantial unemployment can restrain inflation: Swedes have shown how peak national wage-bargaining can restrain it; Australians have shown how income policies administered by independent institutions can restrain it; John K. Galbraith's first book explained how his US price controls restrained inflation in wartime. In the conditions of their time and place, all four got their facts right and knew what they were doing. Contradictions only set in if one party (the neoclassicists in this instance) insist that theirs is the only true analysis or the only workable policy and the others must be mistaken. (There can also, of course, be any amount of untruth, irrelevance, impracticality or deliberate deception in studies by less competent investigators than those four.) It follows:

4   That democracies that value free thought and speech, and access to government for contending interests and opinions, should encourage similar breadth and disagreement in their economic education. And

5   In democracies that accord expert status to their social scientists, there are critical relations between self-interest and disinterested expertise, both between contending groups and within the minds of their individual members. It is important that these relations be understood, and acknowledged and studied in the education of economists.

The following conclusion regards our present situation. It sketches the role of orthodox neoclassical economic theory in the prevailing (mis)understanding of what causes what in modern economic life.

Conclusion

Consider how you can know what a particular condition or process or event is causing. Sometimes you can observe and understand the causal process itself. For example: a firm's sales decline and unsold goods pile up in its warehouse. To sell the surplus goods the directors have to drop their prices below their costs of production. With the firm losing money, they decide to cut production and dismiss half their workers. The workers happen to have been agitating for higher wages, and stage a one-day strike as part of their campaign. The directors identify that offense as the reason for sacking half of them, and the cause of their losing their jobs. A competent causal analyst will ask what would have happened if they had not staged the one-day strike, and may discover (if the minutes of the directors' meetings are available) or imagine (if they are not) that because of the downturn in sales the workers would still have been dismissed, but on fairer terms. All that their strike lost them was the month's notice and the severance pay to which they would otherwise have been entitled. Honest directors, knowing the real cause of their dismissal, would have given them both. So a causal analyst can reasonably cite some directors' misbehavior as well as the workers' misbehavior as causes of their loss of some pay. In that, as also in arriving at the true cause of their dismissal, the analyst has had to imagine what would actually have happened in the absence of particular causes.

Now consider what the comprehensive axiomatic neoclassical theory does both for its users' selection of causal explanations, and for their necessary imagination of alternatives.

The comprehensive theory models a self-adjusting, single-sector economy. People act in their own interests. Market mechanisms harness that self-interested behavior to the common good in three vital ways: they allocate resources efficiently to maximize the economy's output; they tend to keep the system running in a stable equilibrium; and they pay landowners, capitalists and workers the value of their individual contributions to output. As the sufficient causes of those benign effects, the theory selects some impersonal market mechanisms.

Consciously or not, users of the theory can all too easily assume that if an economy is working well, it must be those market mechanisms that are causing it to do so. So no other causal explanation is needed. Serious investigation is only needed if the system is working badly. Then analysts must discover or imagine what market failure or government interference is preventing the economy from behaving as modeled. (Failing to behave as theorized is the neoclassical definition of market failure.) What the theory actively discourages its users from noticing or understanding is the necessary role of government in the market mechanisms themselves if they are to work efficiently, or in many cases if they are to work at all. The government often needs to be quite intricate, tailored to the peculiarities of particular goods and industries, as it was in most of the developed and fast-developing economies through the mid-twentieth century "golden age" of steady growth and full employment.

Sensible neoclassicists, of course, acknowledge some market failures and some need for public intervention, for example to deter monopoly. However, the very word "intervention" implies an absurd belief in the possibility of an ungoverned market economy. They rarely mention the Companies Acts by which governments create the fundamental powers of the private firm, or the need for continual elaboration of the Acts to prevent the inventive misuse of those powers. (Has any neoclassical theorist ever called the Companies Act an "intervention" in a market economy, or tried to imagine a market economy without it?) There's no space in this newsletter to explore the many effects of neoclassical theory in blinding its users to government's necessarily elaborate role in an efficient mixed economy. (Yes, mixed economy. Except in the blinkered neoclassical imagination there are no pure market or private sector only economies. There could not be.) Or its role in blinding economists to the capital and other needs, and the productivity, of the public and household sectors, which together produce half or more of the advanced economies' material goods and services. Worse: when privatization, deregulation and financial anarchy fail to perform as promised by the master theory, its believers can only imagine that the withdrawal of government has not gone far enough. The proposed Multilateral Agreement on Investment (MAI) and General Agreement on Trade and Services (GATS) are needed to complete the job.

They surely will, if we don't manage to stop them.

Realism vs axiomatics

Jacques Sapir (L'École des Hautes Études en Sciences Sociales, Paris)

In the *post-autistic economics newsletter*, issue no. 4, James K. Galbraith wrote a very interesting and convincing reply to Robert Solow. In the same issue, Joseph Halevi aptly described what he calls a "Franco-American neoclassical alliance," pointing out that Blanchard's reply to the students' manifesto was dogmatic and hollow. I would like to jump into the fray and to offer some points in support of a post-autistic approach to teaching, learning and doing economics.

Before going to my main points, I want to say that I completely agree that teaching (and learning) is the basic issue. I also wish to draw attention to the fact that although some professors have appealed against the students' manifesto, to my knowledge no students have.

My experience in teaching economics began in the late 1970s. After spending four years as a high-school (Lycée) teacher, I taught macroeconomics at the University of Paris–10/Nanterre (where the department of economics is probably one of the least autistic in France), before moving to the École des Hautes Études en Sciences Sociales, a specifically postgraduate institution. I have also taught regularly in Moscow (at the Higher School of Economics and at Moscow University), and at many seminars in the USA, Italy and the UK.

What French students described in their manifesto is the plain truth and the result not of France deviating from "good economics" as taught in the USA, but, to the contrary, of what Robert Solow suggested: the French system converging with the US one.

Now, what is the discussion mainly about? The focus is on the link between teaching and science, and the point is realism vs axiomatism. One of the most important issues raised by this movement is the very fact that you cannot separate tools and contents, teaching and what you are supposed to teach. By engaging the battle on this field, the movement has already won a major epistemological victory. However, even if Solow acknowledges that the discussion is not about mathematics in economics, clearly he does not grasp the meaning of the "realist" requirement. I suspect that some of my post-autistic colleagues do not either.

The real issue is not to know if the realistic content of economics is to be increased just slightly or in a more meaningful way; rather, it is to know if realism is a central requirement or not. This leads to an old but forgotten debate; the one about "natural" or "exact" laws governing economic activities. Without going back to Carl Menger, we have to remind ourselves that if there is something like these laws, then realism is not a requirement for theorizing and a quest for realism is not only not needed but could also even prevent us from reaching a complete understanding of a system obedient to laws.

What has usually been forgotten by people supporting the axiomatist approach, and this is fairly obvious with Solow and Blanchard, is the type of conditions required for "natural" or "exact" laws to exist in economics. Either there must be no creative interaction between economic agents (Robinson Crusoe on his island before the landing of Friday), or an agent's behavioral patterns must be context-independent. The first condition implies that there is no society and no economy, while the second one is a key assumption of neoclassical economics (preferences are supposed to be context-independent, transitive and continuous).

Unfortunately for our neoclassical colleagues, repeated tests have amply demonstrated that preferences are context-dependent (Amos Tversky's framing effect) and are neither transitive nor continuous (see the works of Kahneman, Slovic and Lichtenstein). Unless these tests are proved to have been faked or incomplete or wrong in any given sense, the very Popperian methodology our colleagues are so fond of should have led them to delete this key assumption about behavioral patterns, with the obvious consequence that there are no "natural" or "exact" laws in economics.

It is a well-known fact that very few of them (Kenneth Arrow being the best-known exception) are willing to accept this conclusion. If they were, they would understand why realism is a central requirement in economics. Therefore, it is important for non-autistic economists to understand that it is not just "more realism" that they must fight for, but also (and more importantly) a methodological posture revolving around the requirement for realism.

This last point raises another problem: the all too frequent confusion about the level of abstraction in economics. Having worked for many years on the Soviet and then the Russian economies, maybe I have developed a certain sense on this matter. Going back to James K. Galbraith's contribution, to discuss the market for low wage labor as a specific case of the labor market is not the same thing as to discuss the market for low wage labor in a given country, at a given time and with the given set of institutions governing relationships between the internal market and the world economy.

By the same token, when we discuss the labor market the word "market" does not have the same meaning as when we use it in a discussion about the relative pros and cons of market and central planning. Another extremely dangerous way to do economics is illustrated by Robert Solow when, in his *Le Monde* article, he switches from an highly abstract level to directly operational issues as if concepts were part of real life. Spinoza wrote that the concept "dog" does not bark, but nevertheless, if we understand how to use concepts, "dog" is still useful for understanding life where dogs bark and even bite. Realism is not to be confused with reality. The fight against the misuse of axiomatism in economics (and generally speaking in the social sciences) is not an anti-theoretical turn, but a different approach to theoretical thinking.

Having gone so far in support of the post-autistic approach, I must confess some unease about the widespread use of the term "pluralism" in the PAE Newsletter. First, it is to be understood that I support teaching various theoretical approaches in economics if done in a critical way. Second, I also support the idea that a scientific debate must be held in an open-minded way, particularly when it concerns academic and professional journals. However, and this is no small caveat, no scientific debate is possible without agreed rules about what is correct and what is not. No geographer would teach his or her students the flat Earth theory, except as an historical example of false geographical understanding of the world. No historian of the Soviet Union would now teach students about the 1930s without discussing the 1932/33 famine, whatever the explanation. Anyone in the scientific community pretending that the Earth is flat and Soviet peasants were rich and happy in 1933 would be called a faker or a lunatic. So there are bounds to pluralism.

Reclaiming pluralism makes sense if, and only if, we develop a scientific methodology consistent with the requirements of realism. I understand that among post-autistic economists some still believe that the Popperian approach is worth some consideration. I have my doubts about it, if only because of the logical contradiction embedded in Popper's falsification theory when applied to social sciences, as demonstrated by the late Professor Quine. Here is not the place fully to address this issue, but my position is that without understanding all the realist methodological implications, pluralism could become perverse – that is, the simple addition of conflicting points of view without any means critically to assess them, or even the understanding that some are not compatible with others. Otherwise we will run into big problems, not least that of theoretical inconsistency, and offer a weak flank for autistic colleagues to attack. The so-called patchwork effect I am afraid of is already pervasive among mainstream economists.

I will not spare PAE Newsletter readers this short account of something that happened to me years ago at the IMF. After quite a long meeting with people of the Europe-II department, and a very heated debate about what was really happening in Russia, the chairman of the department wanted to make a point. He then very solemnly declared: "Remember, inflation is, every time and everywhere, a macro-economic phenomenon, as demonstrated by von Hayek." Oooops! You could believe in standard macro-economics, or believe in Hayek, but the fact is that the whole Hayekian understanding of inflation is grounded on a micro-economic process. You can't mix the two.

To return to the issue of individual preference and how economists are to write their model specifications, how can we accept context-independent, transitive and continuous preference functions when we know this is wrong? Daniel Hausman, in his 1992 book *The Inexact and Separate Science of Economics* (Cambridge University Press), wrote a full chapter about how mainstream economists consistently refuse to acknowledge the preference reversals phenomenon, and called that dogmatism. If autism is to be described as an acceptance of fantasy rather than reality, and a withdrawal from reality, then nothing can better describe some of our colleagues' behavior regarding the theory of individual preference. However, to separate ourselves from autistic economists we have to elaborate specific assessment rules to organize scientific pluralism.

This leads me to a short comment about the French PAE curriculum, one I made at the October 2000 meeting in Paris. It's very important to re-introduce the history of economic thought into the core curriculum. It would be even better if backed by the introduction of lectures in methodology and epistemology. If economics belongs to the social sciences, then students who are to be taught economics deserve to learn about the methodology and epistemology of social sciences. I know that students usually don't like methodology and epistemology, mostly because philosophy as taught in secondary school is either boring or has become a complete ideological playground. What's more, the jump to the level of abstraction needed to understand what methodology and epistemology are about is distinctly at odds with the now fashionable posture where teachers and professors are supposed to explain everything from the pupil/student's direct experience point of view. This fallacy now dominates pedagogical practice in French education. Still, I believe that if we could cut the time devoted to math in the curriculum by a half and dedicate a similar amount of time to methodology and epistemology, everybody would be better off.

Teaching economics through controversies

Gilles Raveaud (co-founder of Autisme-Économie, École Normale Supérieure de Cachan, France)

In this article we present the reasons for our discontent as students of economics in France and find that they have a broad cause: the (desperate) quest of economists for scientificity. Our proposal is to turn the teaching of economics in a completely different direction, where teaching of controversies would be given priority. We then explain why teaching through controversies is preferable to current methods, and how to do it.

Reasons for our discontent

I will briefly review here the reasons for our discontent, as expressed in our petition (full text on our website: www.autisme-economie.org):

First, we criticized the construction of "imaginary worlds" by economists – that is, worlds that do not have any link with any plausible mechanism in reality. Such worlds (the famous "models") are just developed for their own sake, because of their tractability. We no longer want to be taught such fairy tales, the aim of which is not to explain "reality" but rather to show the ability of the writer to construct a "nice model." It may be fun for the authors, but we do not want to be part of the game.

Second, we highlighted the excessive use of mathematics in the curriculum. Here, the situation is well known and does not require further explanation. Let me just emphasize the fact that in France the fascination with mathematics is particularly developed, and the level required of students is extremely high in most cases.

Third, we stressed the fact that most "explanations" given in lectures are derived from neoclassical economics. Marxism and Keynesianism, for example, which were living schools of thought in France not so long ago, seem to have completely disappeared.[1] Nowadays, virtually no student has the opportunity to study Marx as part of the common curriculum. Furthermore, the explanations given are not thought of and presented as *possible* explanations of complex phenomena (say, unemployment, or international trade), competing with different approaches; they are supposed to be the only possible economic analysis of such phenomena – even if people do not actually behave according to these views, it is because other elements (social, traditions, imperfections, etc.) blur the picture. However, the proper economic part of their activity is as defined.

As one can see, the situation is disastrous.[2] As so many writers have already given possible reasons for such a situation in economics, we will simply focus on one aspect of the problem: the quest for scientificity for economists. There are two reasons for selecting this problem: first, these are the terms that have been used by teachers reacting to the first teachers' petition, which supported our views; second, we consider it as the central source of our problems, even if this view is only a conjecture and is subject to revision.

The underlying causes: seeking for scientificity

A few weeks after launching our petition in May 2000, we were supported by a petition signed by approximately 140 teachers, with some very famous people among them (Aglietta, Orléan, Boyer, etc.). This text from the teachers stressed the lack of pluralism in economics, and rejected the overall domination of neo-classical economics on courses.

Later on, another text, signed by a dozen economists (nearly all of them important in the Establishment), reacted against both the students' and teachers' petitions. Their purpose was, as they put it, to "preserve the scientificity of economics." This had to be done in the most traditional of ways, following the known recipe. The following principles were insisted upon in this tract:

- First, the "precise identification and definition of concepts and behaviors which characterize economic activity (consumption, production, investment, etc.) and the formulation of basic hypotheses concerning such behaviors";
- Second, "the formulation of theories expressed as formalized relationships between the concepts previously defined";
- Third, "the verification of such theories through experience." This can only take place through confrontation with history, as quantified by statistics and econometrics.

They then denied that there was any illegitimate domination by neoclassical economics: any views are valid, as long as they respect this canvas.

One can note that their reaction did not engage with our criticism: where we talked about *teaching*, they talked about *science*. They did not answer any of our points: imaginary worlds, the excess of maths and lack of pluralism. Instead, they gave us a mythical description of science, where everyone is simply doing their best with their limited means (isn't that rational?). In short, leaving the classrooms, the debate was now entering the field of methodology.

So much the better, as this suddenly gave coherence to our protest. We had focused on specific points which, though related, did not lead to any necessary coherence. Now, with the help of the "counter-appeal," we had more than coherence: we had a common cause. Let's take this case seriously.[3]

In the construction of a "science" so naively understood, one has few options. The phenomena studied, even analyzed as "stylized facts," are so complex that you have to choose among them if you want to produce a "result." From claiming to be global, the analysis in fact turns partial. Then, if your purpose is to construct logical relationships between "objects" (to be defined), you can hardly do without mathematics. But then again, as you progress, things will get just so complicated – leading either to many solutions or none at all – that you'll have to spend your time simplifying your hypotheses. Besides, for reasons that cannot be explained here, the dominant view in neoclassical economics is that everything starts with the individual; you then have to define your "individuals" as narrowly as possible. Actually, you will not deal with "individuals," nor even economic "agents" any more: you simply declare them to be their (unobservable) preference curve, and that's it. You then have a solid basis on which to ground your calculations. Does this lead to any analytical success? We know that it rarely does. Even the logical basis of such a simple phenomenon as the law of supply and demand cannot be established.[4]

The logical consequence is that the whole approach should be re-thought. However, as the "scientificity" of economics is to preserved, this is not an option. You have to follow this road, produce results, refine your hypotheses, in order to "make science progress." You are not going to give up the possibility of constructing a science, are you?

Following the magic scientific recipe has three consequences:

- First, models are not supposed to be realistic: their aim is not to give insights into real phenomena, but to participate in the global and fascinating construction of a science. One can no longer criticize models on the grounds of irrelevance. From the point of view of this major achievement, which is the construction of a general economic science, universally valid, these models are, on the contrary, perfectly relevant. But yes, in a sense they are "imaginary."

- Second, science understood this way has to be mathematical. There is no precise reason for that, apart from the fact that any science is mathematical, isn't it? You would not call sociology a science, would you? As economists, theoreticians deal with quantitative data (inflation rates, balance sheets, etc.), so there is no reason for them not to use them. More fundamentally, their purpose is to construct a general and logical theory on the model of classical physics[5] – so they need mathematics. And, as they need mathematics for research, mathematics needs to be taught.[6] So there cannot be an excess in the use of it; the only possible difficulty is not enough, or inadequate, mathematics; not too much.

- Third, as their aim is (I hope you've understood it by now) the construction of a "science," the idea of competing theories is nonsense. Well, of course you can debate specific problems, propose different tools, but this game must take place on the same field. You cannot play against someone situated on a different pitch, can you? We need common rules, a common language. So you have to learn this language first of all: after that, you will be absolutely free to make any use of it – honest.

The points we highlighted are not here by random selection. Even more, as we hope to have shown, *they are not a problem* for those who subscribe to the line of "scientificity." They are, on the contrary, perfectly coherent. That is, our critics can no longer concern themselves only with teaching: they have to encompass theory and methodology as well.

Looking for controversies

Let's turn back to the image of science insisted upon by those economists: aren't there any competing views on the good in economics? Aren't there completely opposed conceptions of what a society and an economy is among economists? Does everybody agree on the method used to produce scientific analyses of economic problems? To put it frankly, the conception of science those economists have is really naive: many works, written by sociologists studying *natural sciences*, have shown how knowledge is constructed *through* the conflict of theories.[7] Moreover, they've shown how the permanence of such debates is intrinsic to science – is, one could say, its engine. No science is a calm and eternally defined pitch. On the contrary, its lines are constantly evolving, and sometimes scientists do not even agree on the shape of the ball!

Is economics an exception? Fortunately not. Economics has been the scene of terrific fights over the years since its very origin – whenever that was. Moreover, such battles were often over the very foundations of the discipline (the forms of the lines of the pitch), not only its methodology (the rules of the game) and objects (shape of the ball, if any). Such controversies do exist in economics; they are numerous and persistent.

What does "controversy" mean? A strict definition of it could be the following: A formulates a theory, which B criticizes, A replies, and so on. Examples of such controversies are, for example, the "Vining–Koopmans" controversy on the place and role of mathematics and theory in economics. The controversy started with Koopmans' qualifying the Burns and Mitchell (*Measuring Business Cycles*, 1946) notion of "measurement without theory," because it was not based on neoclassical grounds. In his reply, Vining pointed out that Koopmans' judgment relied on a stringent definition of economics, according to which only his approach (neo-classical theory) was valid, although he had no firm results that showed the pro-ductivity of such an approach. The controversy concerned the definition of acceptable theory and the reasons why neoclassical economics should be pre-ferred.[8]

As one can see, this controversy has never been settled: there is no "scientific answer" to the problems raised above, even if the majority of economists support one view rather than the other at a certain time. This is what economics is *really* about: conflicting views on problems and the way to deal with them; competing claims on which policy to support. This is so obvious that one is surprised to have to reiterate it. Newspapers are filled with economists contradicting one another on the policies to be followed, because their theories differ. Everyone knows that there is no such thing as an economic science, at least not in the sense understood above, but the students are required to believe there is. Only economics students are supposed to believe that there is a knowledge about economic facts that is coherent, precise, and leads to clear policy recommendations.

How to teach through controversies

Controversies, even understood in the restricted sense given above, are numer-ous in economics (see the classical debates on value; the question of the nature and measurement of capital; Keynes and Hicks on the IS-LM model; Romer and Solow on growth theory, etc.). However, controversies can be understood in a broader sense: that is, the competing views on recurring problems in economics. Theories of consumption are an excellent example of this: starting with the Key-nesian "consumption function," one can trace back the attempts by Brown, Modigliani and Duesenberry to "save" the Keynesian function. One can then turn to Friedman's radical criticism, with his "permanent income hypothesis," and its revision through the lifecycle model.

All these models should not be presented as trials and errors on the road to an ever better theory: on the contrary, they should be presented as *what they are* — that is, conflicting views on an economic problem of central importance. In particular, such theories (and the differences between them) simply cannot be understood if one is not aware of their consequences in terms of economic policy. These models should be taught quite differently to how they are at present; each theory should be presented on an equal footing, given its chances in the competition of science. In particular, one should focus not only on the "model" itself (if any), but also on three crucial aspects of the problems surround-ing the use of the model: the context of the debate, the role and place of empiri-cal data, and the consequences for economic policy.

As can be seen, teaching is much more demanding in this context, as it is sup-posed to encompass all the dimensions of the problem under consideration. In fact, what we are suggesting here may already exist in some shape or other, but even if this is the case, it is done through various courses that are not linked to one another. Statistics are taught for their own sake, with no or little reference to economic theory; the history of thought very often overlooks the mathematical contents of theories; and economic theory is presented as being autonomous. The complete absence of economics textbooks constructed in the way we propose is a clear indication of this disastrous "division of labor" among researchers and teachers.

As a result of the present state of teaching, students do not acquire any knowledge of the economy they live in, nor of the competing theories that set out to explain it. With what we propose here, it may be hoped that both lacks would be filled: controversies make theories lively and real, and their empirical content gives us knowledge of "facts," as shown below.

Consequences: from tools to knowledge

The very first consequence of our proposal is the *eradication of "micro-macro" lessons*. We no longer want the teaching of economics to focus on *tools*, as if they could be separated from their meaning – the theories and views of the world that use them. We saw above that such "technical teaching" of economics is perfectly consistent with the idea of an "economic science," made up of various techniques, accepted by all, that could be used on any and every subject. However, such a view is completely misleading, *even if one insists on considering economics as a science*. The proper condition of science is precisely its contingency, the uncertainty of its results, and the fallibility of its knowledge. In the case of economics, such uncertainty and fallibility are extreme, as everyone knows.

Teaching should focus on controversies, past and present, and the idea of neutral tools quite simply disappear. "Micro" and "macro" lessons would be replaced by a single and large course on "economic theories," presenting them in the way described above, in historical order. There would then be the time to present Classical and Marxian approaches seriously, spending time on reading texts, and not simply solving silly ready-made exercises. In practice, this implies that neoclassical theory should not be taught in the first year, and perhaps even not in the second year. Besides, we propose a broad course on *political philosophy*, explaining the ethical and political backgrounds and the consequences of the theories proposed.

A canvas would therefore be laid down for a stimulating debate inside economic departments: theories would be presented as being in permanent confrontation with one another, the course on economic theories following their historical development and reasons for success and decline. As stressed above, the purpose of such a course would be to present *both* the historical context of the theories *and* their precise analytical content.[9] This would be completed by the political philosophy course, which would show the permanence of questions such as the role of the State in economic matters, the fairness of the market, the definition of money, etc., and the varying answers given to such questions through history.

Statistics and econometrics would then be taught in close relationship with such lessons. Even if these subjects are necessarily autonomous in the sense that they need to present their own techniques, tutorials (at least) should be entirely devoted to the examination of problems linked with what is presented in the two courses defined above (how does one measure the "natural rate of unemployment"? How did it evolve in the UK or the US or Gambia? What is "purchasing power parity," and how do we measure it? How can one measure the value of the Keynesian multiplier nowadays in a particular country? What is the value of the rate of profit; is it declining? etc.). In particular, it is important that students should work on real data, with imperfections, and not, once again, on artificial sources.[10]

A common and simple consequence of all this is that we would *get rid of all ready-made exercises*. Well, one or two may be tolerated, as they are useful aids to understanding a theory precisely. However, the aim of teaching should no longer be the mastering of such tools. They should remain what they should never have ceased to be, that is, analytical tools with limited relevance. The object and purpose of economics and its teaching is the world outside: what do we know about it? How do we know it? Do we all agree on this knowledge – and if not, why? What do our theories have to say about it? And above all, to be honest, how do we make the world a better place to live in?

Conclusion: science is not technique

This way, we hope to achieve the following aims:

- to make economics interesting, and even exciting again, by showing how lively a subject it is;
- to present a more honest figure of science, with its controversies and provisional results;
- to make students learn about their economic environment, since most controversies are resolved or re-interpreted with contemporary data, as, for example, the Phillips curve, the "natural rate of unemployment" and the theory of international specialization;
- to give students the competencies they need on the labor market. What will be expected from them is their ability to produce a synthesis of complex phenomena that have empirical and theoretical components, and it is not by resolving ready-made exercises that they will acquire such competencies. On the contrary, being trained in the practice and manipulation of theories on *real problems*, they should acquire the general ability to produce critical surveys and original points of views, which is highly valued.

Finally, for the small minority of students who still intend to become economists, we simply cannot imagine a better way to be trained for research than to acquire a "mental map" of the positions and theories in conflict, along with the mastering of tools that can help to choose among them. Once again, this is not done in economics in universities now. We want this situation to change, and do not understand why this should not be possible.

Notes

1 The change was quite brutal: a few years ago, the current author had the chance to read texts from authors like Kaldor, Robinson, Marx, Marshall, etc., *in the first year*, but he no longer has the opportunity to teach them to his students.

2 And to be honest, our protest is fairly incomplete: one could mention for instance the way statistics and econometrics, useful tools as they may be, are taught in France nowadays. That is, students spend hours demonstrating the convergence proprieties of estimators, but we never run real data in tutorials – or discuss the political consequences of the models proposed, etc.

3 What follows may be read as an oversimplified and caricatured synthesis of some aspects of Lawson's (1997) *Economics and Reality* (Routledge).

4 See various books by B. Guerrien (in French only, unfortunately), notably *Concurrence, Flexibilité et Stabilité* (1989, Economica). Guerrien has recently launched a heated debate in the *post-autistic economic review*, starting with his "Is there anything worth keeping in standard microeconomics?," issue no. 2, 15 March 2002.

5 See Mirowski (1989), *More Heat than Light*, Cambridge: Cambridge University Press.

6 And if all the students are not pleased, never mind. As a French teacher put it, "it does not take 15,000 people to build a science."

7 See the program of *science studies*, and in particular works by David Bloor (with Barry Barnes and John Henry, *Scientific Knowledge: A Sociological Analysis* (1996), Athlone and Chicago University Press and Bruno Latour (*Laboratory Life*, 1992, Princeton University Press) (even if their views are themselves quite different).

8 For a full story, see the original texts in *The Review of Economics and Statistics*, 29, published in 1947. Mirowski, (1989), "The Measurement without theory controversy: defeating rival research programs by accusing them of naive empiricism," in *Economies et Sociétés*, 11, 65–87, puts the story in the broader perspective of the conflict between the NBER and the Cowles Commission.

9 One could imagine a course taught by two teachers, one a specialist of the history of thought, and the other a micro- or macroeconomist. It could even vary with the subject, some lessons (on the Phillips curve, say) being done by a statistician and a macroeconomist, others (e.g. theories of value) by an historian of thought and a microeconomist, etc. In France, when we suggest this, everybody laughs: "What? You want to make different people *work together*? What a joke!." Unfortunately, this does not make us laugh. Let's hope that the situation is somewhat better in other countries.

10 In fact, it is hard to understand why it is not already the case, as this is just common sense.

A good servant but a bad master

Geoff Harcourt (Cambridge University, UK)

Edward Fullbrook has asked me to contribute to the *post-autistic economics news-letter*. Since he also told me that my after-dinner speech to the social economists' meeting at Cambridge last year was the irritant that led him, as the oyster, to create this particular pearl of a newsletter, what else could I do but oblige? More importantly, I want to contribute something positive and useful to the ongoing debate in France (and, I hope, elsewhere) on the teaching and scope of economics.

First, the vexed question of mathematics. This is a red herring. My own stance was influenced by Keynes. He argued that in a subject like economics there is a spectrum of appropriate languages, running from intuition and poetry through lawyer-like arguments to formal logic and mathematics. All have a role, depending upon the issue (or the aspects of an issue) being discussed. Mathematics is a good servant but a bad master, that is to say, always pose the economics of an issue first, then see whether some form of mathematics may be of use in solving the problems thrown up. This approach also has the blessing of von Neumann, Michal Kalecki and Josef Steindl, a worthy Trinity if ever there was one.

Second, as a liberal educator, I think teachers have a duty to introduce students to different approaches to economic issues, whether they are in agreement with the approaches or not. A sympathetically critical stance seems to me the least a university teacher can and should take. So I deplore the ruthless hegemony of the mainstream in too many departments around the world, so that clones of the leading mainstream departments in the USA are being created all over the world. Of course, students should be introduced to what the up-to-date main-stream approaches and issues are, but not exclusively. After all, as economists we know of comparative advantage and differentiated products, and to forego these principles in our teaching is both foolish and restrictive. I deplore the existence of zealots in any approach; there are, I fear, too many of them in our trade at the moment.

Third, the failure to teach the history of the subject and economic history is to misunderstand the essential nature of our discipline. Often the same issues and problems arise, and then it will be found that the greats of the past had something of lasting value to say about them. It is not an insult to the greats sometimes to restate their insights in modern terms, provided we are explicitly aware of where and who the essential insights have come from, and that they are a product of their time, place and the personality of the writers concerned. Because economics too often is taught as though the subject has had but a ten-year existence (with a moving peg), again too often inferior versions of older wheels are rediscovered.

Finally, let me put in a plea to students always to be careful not to regard something as irrelevant or uninteresting because it is difficult. To do so is to allow the tough zealots who dominate the trade to have too easy and unnecessary a victory over proper and reasonable demands.

Three observations on a "cultural revival" in France

Joseph Halevi (University of Sydney, Australia)

In March 1999, after a two-year stay, I left France with a rather pessimistic view. It seemed then that on the intellectual plane, barring some isolated individuals, Pierre Bourdieu and his network, flanked by *Le Monde Diplomatique*, acted as the only significant critical force. Today there are reasons for being far more optimistic on both the political and intellectual fronts. The students' movement for the transformation of the economic curriculum toward a pluralistic vision of the discipline is not just part of this cultural revival, but, because it is expressed at a national level, it represents a more advanced step in challenging the ruling orthodoxy. In this context, let me make three observations.

The first concerns the accusation thrown at the students of being mathematical nihilists. It is false and deliberately misleading. This accusation has come from a number of quarters, with *Le Monde* contributing to propagandize it. Alan Kirman – an Englishman teaching at Aix-Marseille, and a tough-minded guardian of the *quality of science* at the economic section of the National Council of the Universities (CNU)[1] – repeated it in the *Newsletter of the Royal Economic Society* earlier this year. Those who started the movement saw quite clearly through the various formalisms. The issues they raised were aimed both at the lack of economic content and at the absence of any contextualization of the models they have to swallow. More specifically, the students' conceptual awareness owes a great deal to the books written and the lectures given by Bernard Guerrien, an outstanding mathematical economist from Paris I-Sorbonne, who has been pointing out since 1989 the economic *non sequitur* embroiling dominant neoclassical theory.[2] The issue of the lack of historical perspectives in the current economics programs has emerged in a number of open debates held throughout France's universities (in Montpellier, the debate held on 16 March 2001 drew 400 students).

If current neoclassical macroeconomics is the ideology for economic policies, microeconomics is the hard core theology of contemporary orthodoxy. Significantly, in a debate held on 10 April 2001 at the Université de Paris X at Nanterre there was no support for the way in which microeconomics is being taught. It seems also that the micro–macro division is being abolished at Paris

I-Sorbonne in favour of a curriculum oriented toward a historical view of economic theories.

The second observation relates to Solow's imperialistic point that the students are reacting to bad teaching. Quite the contrary. French textbooks, when they do not copy the American ones, are more coherent than their US counterparts. For instance, most American macroeconomic texts, such as Olivier Blanchard's *Macroeconomics* (Prentice Hall, 1997), misdirect the students by presenting their material as if it emerged from accurate observations and give an extremely shallow account of the theories and their evolution. Thus the bad teaching occurs on Solow's very turf, and French academics should free themselves from their never-ending inferiority complex *vis-à-vis* the United States and, via the USA, the English-speaking world.

Finally, from the debates held so far it seems that the issue of realism will become a point of contention. At Nanterre, for instance, a prominent academic argued that since facts are created by the theorist (which is essentially true), reality does not exist (totally wrong; the question is, which reality?). Unfortunately, confronted with these statements Solow would have an easy win and the shallowness of his buddy's textbook would carry the day.

Notes

1   The CNU approves/rejects hirings and promotions whenever they fall outside the nationwide bid (concours) for professorships set by the Ministry of National Education. Two-thirds of the members of the CNU are elected on the basis of union-like tickets, and one-third are nominated by the Government, usually from existing tickets. Alan Kirman is a recent non-elected appointee to the CNU for the ticket *qualité de la science*.

2   Bernard Guerrien (1989) *Concurrence, flexibilité et stabilité* (Economica). This book has been followed by a number of others of exemplary didactic clarity, such as *La Théorie Économique Néoclassique* (1999), 2 vols, Paris: la Découverte.

Economists have no ears

Steve Keen (University of Western Sydney, Australia)

Thomas Kuhn once famously described textbooks as the vehicle by which students learn how to do "normal science" in an academic discipline. Economic textbooks clearly fulfill this function, but the pity is that what passes for "normal" in economics barely deserves the appellation "science."

Most introductory economics textbooks present a sanitized, uncritical rendition of conventional economic theory, and the courses in which these textbooks are used do little to counter this mendacious presentation. Students might learn, for example, that "externalities" reduce the efficiency of the market mechanism; however, they will not learn that the "proof" that markets are efficient is itself flawed.

Since this textbook rendition of economics is also profoundly boring, the majority of those exposed to introductory courses in economics do no more than this and instead go on to careers in accountancy, finance or management – in which, nonetheless, many continue to harbor the simplistic notions they were taught many years earlier.

The minority that go on to further academic training are taught the complicated techniques of economic analysis, with little or no discussion of whether these techniques are actually intellectually valid. The enormous critical literature is simply left out of advanced courses, while glaring logical shortcomings are glossed over with specious assumptions. However, most students accept these assumptions because their training leaves them both insufficiently literate and insufficiently numerate.

Most modern-day economics students are insufficiently literate because economic education eschews the study of the history of economic thought. Even a passing acquaintance with this literature exposes the reader to critical perspectives on conventional economic theory – but students today receive no such exposure.

They are insufficiently numerate because the material that establishes the intellectual weaknesses of economics is complex. Understanding this literature in its raw form requires an appreciation of some quite difficult areas of mathematical concepts, which require up to two years of undergraduate mathematical training to understand.

Curiously, though economists like to intimidate other social scientists with the mathematical rigor of their discipline, most economists do not have this level of mathematical education. Though economics students do attend numerous courses on mathematics, these are normally given by other economists. The argument for this approach – the partially sighted leading the partially sighted – is that generalist mathematics courses don't teach the concepts needed to understand mathematical economics (or the economic version of statistics, known as econometrics). As any student of econometrics knows, this is quite often true. However, it has the side effect that economics has persevered with mathematical methods that professional mathematicians have long ago transcended. This dated version of mathematics shields students from new developments in mathematics that, incidentally, undermine much of neoclassical economic theory.

One example of this is the way economists have reacted to "chaos theory." Most economists think that chaos theory has had little or no impact – which is generally true in economics, but is not at all true in most other sciences. This is partially because, to understand chaos theory, you have to understand an area of mathematics known as "ordinary differential equations." Yet this topic is taught in very few courses on mathematical economics, and where it is taught it is not covered in sufficient depth. Students may learn some of the basic techniques for handling linear difference or differential equations, but chaos and complexity only begin to manifest themselves in non-linear difference and differential equations. A student in a conventional "quantitative methods in economics" subject will thus acquire the prejudice that "dynamics is uninteresting," which is largely true of the behavior of linear dynamical systems, but not at all true of non-linear systems. This prejudice then isolates the student from much of what is new and interesting in mathematical theory and practice, let alone from what scientists in other sciences are doing.

Economics students therefore graduate from Masters and PhD programs with an effectively vacuous understanding of economics, no appreciation of the intellectual history of their discipline, and an approach to mathematics that hobbles both their critical understanding of economics and their ability to appreciate the latest advances in mathematics and other sciences. A minority of these ill-informed students themselves go on to be academic economists, and then repeat the process. Ignorance is perpetuated.

The attempt to conduct a critical dialog within the profession of academic economics has therefore failed, not because economics has no flaws but because – figuratively speaking – conventional economists have no ears. So then, "no more Mr. Nice Guy." If economists can't be trusted to follow the Queensberry Rules of intellectual debate, then we critics have to step out of the boxing ring and into the streets. Hence my book *Debunking Economics: The Naked Emperor of the Social*

Sciences (Zed Books, 2001), which describes the many formal academic critiques of neoclassical economics in a manner that I hope is accessible to the interested non-economist and non-mathematical readership. However, it should also prove very useful to those who have come to regard conventional economic theory as autistic, since it clearly and simply explains the source of this endemic autism.

Economics and multinationals

Grazia Ietto-Gillies (South Bank University, London)

Multinationals are everywhere except in economic theories and economics departments. Transnational companies (as I prefer to call them), or TNCs, have been with us for a very long time, but in recent years they have attracted special – often unwanted – attention. They inspire street protests and counter-protests, globalization debates and policy debates – debates that TNCs often shape behind the scenes.

But the reality of TNCs remains largely absent from economic theory and curricula. In fact, I come across many bright young economics graduates who have learned nothing about TNCs and their activities in the course of their studies, though some of them are learning about TNCs from anti (or pro) globalization groups. The more prestigious and highly rated the university that the graduates come from, the less likely they are to have been taught about TNCs.

From the point of view of people in the streets, this situation looks incredible, However, in order to analyze it coolly, let us begin by assuming a world with no national barriers and no frontiers, a single currency and a single tax regime – in other words, the whole world is a single nation state. In this imaginary world there is no theory of international production because there is, in effect, no international economic realm. So here it suffices to use location theory to explain where production is located and to use theories of the firm, business governance and market structure to explain the growth of firms, their boundaries and their behavior *vis-à-vis* other firms. Because the international dimensions to economic reality are assumed away, theories of TNCs and foreign direct investment are redundant.

This is indeed the tacit approach taken in most traditional economics departments. They deal with the international economy at the macro level by teaching and researching issues of international trade and balance of payments. At the micro level, theories of the firm and investment are not usually analyzed in the context of the nationality/transnationality of the investor. Characteristics of companies other than multinationality (such as size or some strategic behavior) are dealt with in the context of oligopoly theory. On the teaching side, multinational companies, their existence, growth, and range of activities may be dealt with in a couple of lectures within a unit on industrial economics. This traditional approach can indeed be justified if one takes the view that the nationality of the investor and the transnationality of operations make no difference to the geographical pattern of investment and production, or to the overall amount of production, or to its impact on the country where the investment takes place.

However, the recent development of separate theories of TNCs and their activities shows that a large number of researchers now think that "nationality" and transnationality do matter. The following factors are regarded as especially relevant: impact on host and home countries; scope for investment; scope for the growth of the firm and the range of its activities; structure and location of production worldwide; international trade; and international capital movements.

Until recently research on TNCs has been confined mainly to "business schools" on both sides of the Atlantic, but the last ten to fifteen years has seen a growing interest in the multinational company on the part of more traditional economists. Two factors have led to this increase. First, there has been a growing interest in "new trade theories" that deal with location and geography issues. Second, the modeling techniques used in these theories can also be applied to the "new trade theories with MNCs" developed by Krugman, Helpman, Markusen, Venables and others. This allows economists, for the first time, to look at MNCs in the context of general equilibrium theories.

However, there are problems with this line of attack, because it is essentially a multi-plant rather than a multination approach. As such, it misses out on the main characteristics of TNCs: their cross- and trans-nationality of operations. This takes us to the arguments in favor of putting the TNCs at the center of economic theory and teaching.

Operating across national borders has three main dimensions. First, there is a *spatial* dimension: the geographical distance between (and within) production sites and markets, and the related transportation costs. Distance, however, is not a cross-border dimension; it is not necessarily linked to nation-state frontiers. The geographical distance between regions/cities of a single nation-state can be as great as the distance between regions/cities belonging to different nation-states.

Second, there is a *cultural* – including linguistic – dimension in cross-boundary operations. Normally cultural differences tend to be greater between than within nation-states, but again this is only a crude generalization. I doubt, for example, whether Milan is culturally closer to Reggio Calabria than to Paris or Brussels.

Third, there is a *regulatory* dimension. Nation-states have different regulatory regimes, including different laws, regulations and customs governing production, markets and the use and movements of resources. Operating across national boundaries gives the TNCs advantages in the following areas, most of them linked to the existence of different regulatory regimes in different nation-states:

1   They confront a fragmented labor force because labor has been unable, so far, to organize across nation-states;

2   They can play national and regional governments against each other in bargaining for incentives;

3   They can spread risks – particularly political risks – across a spectrum of countries;

4   They have wide scope for the manipulation of prices for the internal transfer of products – whether material components or services – between countries.

For all these reasons I believe that operating across national boundaries gives transnational companies advantages (as well as some extra managerial and organizational costs). In particular, it gives them comparative advantages over actors who are unable to do so. So far, transnational companies are the only economic actors who can truly plan, organize and control activities internationally. Other actors, such as labor, national governments, uninational companies and consumers, are as yet unable to do so. This puts TNCs in a very special and privileged position.

This special comparative position influences TNCs' decisions on where and how to produce and sell. It is therefore at the heart of issues of location of production, trade and distribution, including the distribution of production and income across boundaries and between labor and capital, and distribution of the surplus between the private and public sectors and between different nation-states.

Conclusion

Nation-states and their regulatory regimes do matter in the decisions of the major players in investment and production worldwide. Theories of transnational companies and of foreign direct investment are needed because we have nation-states and frontiers. The activities of transnational companies should be an integral part of both micro and macro theory because they shape both micro and macro realities. If we are serious about realism, then let us put the reality of transnational companies at the forefront of our economics both in terms of research agendas and of teaching. The real world out there is doing so. People in the street have understood that the international operations of TNCs matter. We economists do not seem to have awoken fully to this fact.

[These issues are further developed by Grazia Ietto-Gillies (2001), *Transnational Corporations: Fragmentation amidst Integration*, Routledge.]

A year in French economics

Emmanuelle Benicourt (co-founder of Autisme-Économie, École des Hautes Études en Sciences Sociales, Paris)

In May 2000, we – a few students from Parisian universities and *grandes écoles* (mainly l'École Normal Supérieure) – wrote an open letter in which we denounced the way economics was taught in France. Our criticism included three basic points:

1   Most courses deal with an "imaginary world," and have no link whatsoever with concrete problems. Acquiring a sound understanding of economic phenomena is one of the reasons why we have chosen to pursue our studies in this field. Teaching, however, is mainly restricted to presentations of the neoclassical theory (or approaches derived from it). We are rarely confronted either with empirical studies or with historical perspectives and analysis.
2   Formalization dominates our courses. It is also used both to select students and to give a pseudo-scientific proof to theories. Indeed, rather than being a useful instrument of comprehension, formalization has become an end in itself (the more complicated the formulas, the better), and this tends to "eliminate" students with only a basic mathematical knowledge even if they have a sound understanding of economics. Furthermore, formalization is almost always biased so that the "appropriate result" is found, thus "proving" the theory's relevance.
3   Finally, we criticize the lack of pluralism in the economics degree. Generally, courses are limited to teaching – dogmatically – the neoclassical approach, thus excluding other theories and other social sciences. We believe that a plurality of viewpoints is useful in understanding the complexity of the questions we are concerned with (unemployment, inequality, development, etc.).

A few weeks after we wrote our "open letter," articles about our movement, *autisme-économie*, began appearing in French newspapers. Soon our "open letter" had several hundred signatures (more than 500 in July 2000). The consequences have exceeded our expectations and can be grouped into four categories.

First, our letter led to open debate in the academic world about the state of economics and economics teaching. Teachers began publicly to take sides on whether they did or did not support the *status quo*. Following our initiative, over 200 teachers – from all over France – published a text that supported our criticisms of economic studies. On the other hand, a few economists published a "counter-petition" in which they tried to justify the use of mathematics in economics (a point that we had never contested), and in which they expressed their view that it was only mathematical formalism that could make economics "scientific." In addition to this national debate between professors, several famous economists from abroad (including Olivier Blanchard, Robert Solow and Amartya Sen) entered the discussion. In doing so, they demonstrated that the issues we raised were not irrelevant, and that no "consensus" had been reached concerning the way economics should be taught.

Second, the "open letter" – and the many signatures it gathered – led the French Minister of Education (Jack Lang) to ask for a national study on how economics was taught in universities and *grandes écoles*. He appointed a prominent French economist, Jean-Paul Fitoussi, to head up the investigation, and his report is now expected in September 2001. Throughout the year we have met with Fitoussi several times and have discussed the issues we raised in the "open letter." He has listened to our complaints and analysis, and it seems that a certain number of our suggestions (such as more pluralism) will stand in his conclusions. Although he agrees on the "imaginary" content of most courses, he seems unwilling to agree to ending the hegemony of neoclassical microeconomics. However, we have presented him with various texts arguing our case, such as "What is the use of microeconomics" (found on our website www.autisme-economie.org), and, notably, he has been unable to give us satisfying answers.

Third, and closely linked to the above, we have translated our criticism into constructive action. Since some universities were about to devise new curricula, we wrote a petition asking for certain kinds of changes, such as a revamping of the introductory micro and macro courses, a sound use of mathematics, and more pluralism in the economics degree. Concerning this last point, we have asked for a plurality of approaches both in economics (Marxist and Keynesian economics, the French "*école de la régulation*" of Agliett and Boyer, etc.), and in other social sciences (such as sociology, history, political philosophy, etc.). This petition for reform has been signed by over 1,550 students. As a consequence, and in face of the declining number of students in economics, some university administrators have now agreed that economics cannot continue to be taught as it has been. The new curricula are to be decided in June 2001, and we do not yet know if our propositions will be taken into consideration.

Finally, we have organized and participated in numerous conferences and debates in universities across France (including Lille, Reims, Bordeaux, Montpellier, Nanterre and Strasbourg). These have also informed students about the movement, but have also informed us about the state of affairs in other French universities. For example, at the debate in Nanterre three teachers expounded their views on questions we had posed in advance. Over 300 students attended, and some asked the teachers precise questions concerning their studies. Unsurprisingly, one student asked how microeconomics as taught was useful for understanding contemporary economic issues, and got no answer. On a broader scale, these debates were both very instructive and constructive. By sharing their points of view, students expressed their main aspirations and criticisms. On our side, these debates gave us detailed knowledge of how economics was being taught in many universities and helped us to formulate, on the basis of first-hand experiences, more precise suggestions and requests. Also, as we met students all across France, we invited them to participate in the movement.

Since March 2001, we have published a monthly journal. This journal is meant to inform students about what precisely is being done to change the way economics is taught in France. The journal also serves as a means for students to express their opinions on economic issues. Some students have written articles on what is going on in their university; others have critiqued the mainstream approach in economics. We invite anyone to take part in this concrete and theoretical discussion (i.e. how to teach economics and why), either by means of the journal or by going to our website.

So the originally "Parisian" movement now exists on a much broader scale. We hope it will trigger concrete transformations of the way economics is taught in France and abroad. We believe that understanding real-world economic phenomena is enormously important to the future well-being of humankind, but that the current narrow, antiquated and naive approaches to economics and economics teaching make this understanding impossible. We therefore hold it to be extremely important, both ethically and economically, that reforms like the ones we have proposed are, in the years to come, carried through – not just in France, but throughout the world.

These "wonderful" US textbooks...

Le Mouvement Autisme-Économie

Everyone praises the recent US textbooks on "the principles of economics" written by leading authors such as Mankiw and Stiglitz. People praise them for their clarity, for their restrained use of formalism, and for their bright colors, pictures and newspaper articles, which make them visually interesting.

But what is their purpose? It is to convince the student that there is a specific kind of reasoning, called "economic reasoning," that is quite simple to grasp and enjoys universal validity. It has two central pillars. There is the "law of supply and demand," which everyday life supposedly confirms, and there is the proposition that the market is an "efficient" system – i.e. a "mechanism" that generally allocates resources in an optimal way. The efficiency proposition, however, is presented neither as an empirical truth nor as an a priori belief; instead it is offered as a *result* in the mathematical sense, but one too demanding to be shown to the readers. In lieu of proof students are offered various poetic images, including the inescapable "invisible hand."

Everyone knows that economists very often disagree with one another; however, these textbooks try to make the student believe that this disagreement concerns only minor points. Regarding core issues, a consensus is presumed to exist. Stiglitz (1997), for example, offers a list of statements on which all economists supposedly agree. Similarly, Mankiw (1998) builds his first chapter around "Ten principles of economics," which he presents as obvious and, hence, neither needing discussion nor subject to disagreement. In his second chapter, "Thinking like an economist," he presents ten proposals on which everybody agrees. True, both books mention the existence of debates, but they neutralize them epistemologically by characterizing them as due to different "values" rather than different explanations.

Mankiw: "the magical invisible hand"

In its first chapter, Mankiw's book asserts: "in general, competitive markets are an efficient way to organise economic activity." To justify this claim, Mankiw invokes Adam Smith's "invisible hand"

> In his book, *The Wealth of Nations*, the economist Smith remarked (and this is the most famous remark of all economics) that firms and individuals which participate in a market behave as if they where guided by an invisible hand which favours positive results for all. One of the aims of this textbook is to explain *how this magical invisible hand* works. By studying economics, you will learn that prices are the tool through which the invisible hand organises the economy. (emphasis added)

Mankiw, however, never explains how this "invisible hand," for which the prices are supposed to be the "tools," works. Perhaps he has in mind the quite *visible* hand of the walrasian auctioneer, but if so he never says. In the whole textbook one finds not a single reference to the Arrow–Debreu general equilibrium analysis, although generally it is presented by neoclassical economists as the mathematized version of the "invisible hand." Instead, the student must be satisfied with hyperbolic remarks like "the remarkable capacity of the invisible hand to organize the economy."

The "amazement" of Samuelson and Nordhaus, and Stiglitz's "spring"

Samuelson and Nordhaus (1998) also wave the invisible hand when claiming to answer the question, "what's a market?" The "actions and goals" of individuals "are coordinated in an invisible way by a system of prices and markets." Samuelson and Nordhaus, however, prefer miracles and wonderment to Mankiw's "magic." "[T]he true miracle," they write, "is that the whole system functions without coercion nor central direction by anybody." And "most of our economic life takes place without State intervention; this is the true wonder of our society." The market economy may have some "deficiencies," but it is its miraculous feature that matters.

Stiglitz is not so wildly enthusiastic as Samuelson and Nordhaus, but the ideas are the same. His innovation is in the realm of metaphor. In explaining how markets work, Stiglitz substitutes for the invisible hand a "weight attached to a spring," whose movement progressively decreases until it reaches equilibrium. Like Mankiw and Samuelson and Nordhaus, Stiglitz offers no explanation in economic terms of how markets work.

What is a market?

All of these textbooks fail to explain how prices are determined in "markets," and thus how markets work. Where do prices come from? Who determines them? How do they fluctuate? These questions are never addressed, even though it is through the price mechanism that the "invisible hand" is supposed to operate.

When Mankiw wants to give a "concrete" example, such as "the ice cream market in a given city," he cannot explain where the prices come from since he has assumed that buyers and sellers are price takers. So he is reduced to surreptitiously introducing a "current price," through an apparently common sense argument: "a seller has few reasons to sell under the current price, and if he sells above, then consumers will buy their ice cream somewhere else." Isn't it obvious? Economics is so simple . . . But the question of setting the price, even the current one, remains un-addressed.

Samuelson and Nordhaus perform basically the same trick, but with a different metaphor. They write: "on a market, prices coordinate producers' and consumers' decisions . . . Prices are the driving belt of the market mechanism." However, like the other textbooks, Samuelson and Nordhaus sidestep the really big question: how are the prices set?

Conclusion

These textbooks *presuppose* that the market is an efficient device guided by the invisible hand, and then refuse to address the basic questions of how market prices are set and how individual choices are coordinated. It is only when these textbooks deal with market failures (information asymmetries, externalities, public goods, etc.) that they provide a few interesting insights. When dealing with these problems, the authors recognize that there is no obvious "solution." On the contrary, the outcome depends on the factors taken into account, their relative importance and the forces and interests at stake, as well as, very often, the norms and values endorsed by the people. It is striking that these discussions and reflections take place without using any of the famous "tools" of standard microeconomics. However, this is hardly surprising, as these "tools" apply only to imaginary worlds, completely detached from the world we live in.

References

Mankiw, G. (1998) *Principles of Economics*. Dryden Press.
Samuelson, P. and Nordhaus, W. (1998) *Economics* (16th edn). McGraw Hill.
Stiglitz, J. (1997) *Economics* (2nd edn). Norton.

Ignoring commercial reality

Alan Shipman

Consumers confronted with a legal monopoly shop around for cost-effective alternatives. Rival producers innovate around the patent to supply them. They are helped by the monopolist's growing distance from competitive reality, leaving it to churn out, ever less efficiently, products ever fewer people want. If mainstream economists still bought this "Austrian" story, they'd see their own monopoly in a starring role. People seeking to survive in the economy look to journalists for information, financial commentators for advice, and business schools for education. Academic economists, finding little market for their tales of the market, are left chasing shrinking public subsidy – or privately dispensing consultancy and forecasts built on different principles from those they teach in class.

Inside business schools, the research and teaching for which companies and students willingly pay, looks very different from those economists peddle. Management courses and journals mix their economics with sociology, psychology, natural and computer sciences, ethics, and any other discipline whose information and ideas help undertake or understand the running of enterprise. Their presentation ranges from macro- and microeconometrics and statistically strip-mined survey data to cross-disciplinary syntheses, case studies, anecdotes and sectoral straw polls. Their authors are an equally diverse mix of full-time researchers, practicing managers, consultants with a foot in each campus, and gurus with their heads in the sky. They probably resemble the economics departments of 50 years ago, with research posts and products accessible to anyone with informed interest, however convoluted their career path or maverick their method.

Yet while business literature has much to say on the corporate strategy, organizational and consumer behavior, technology choice, expectation and regulation that drive the modern economy, mainstream economists pay it little attention – even when published in journals as rigorously refereed as their own. Dialog has died because neoclassical economists speak an increasingly exclusive language. Like early industrialists, they have found a way of discussing the enterprise by its financial flows, in splendid isolation from human and physical stocks. Accounting made it possible to run a company by numbers, tracking money and materials to avoid touring plants and talking to employees. In the pioneer industrializers (and de-industrializers) Britain and the USA, accountants still outnumber engineers in middle and senior management, and "strategy" offshoots of the big accounting/auditing firms have wrested the consultancy market from those who once practised what they preach.

In the same way, mainstream economists seek knowledge through numbers to stop the messy reality of people, processes and politics dirtying their invisible hands. Missing or hard-to-measure variables are conveniently proxied (e.g. model-consistent predictions for expectations, volatility for risk). Unmeasurable variables, if theory requires them, are hammered into measurable shape (e.g. aggregate capital derived from a whole-economy "production function," bounded rationality recast as rationally chosen rule-of-thumb). More usually, what's not in the National Accounts doesn't count. In the neoclassical division of labor, theorists condense the economy into algebraic symbols, opening its components (firms, households, governments) to much more apparently precise analysis than that of classical theorists, who debated these phenomena in the raw. Applied economists can then "calibrate" the models and "compute" the general equilibrium, their forecasts' correctness to two decimal places somehow forgiving their incorrectness when reality catches up.

A diplomat posted to a new country studies its history, language, political system and social conventions, often taking years to acclimatize before daring to make big decisions. An economist flown in by donor government or multilateral lender studies its national accounts, and is often dispensing expert advice a lunch-hour after stepping off the plane. Just as airline pilots take their cockpit gauges as accurate summaries of external conditions, the more ambitious economists claim to fly an economy by financial newswire – leaving seat-of-the-pants driving to "less developed" social disciplines, and blaming any wrong turns or crashes on faulty statistics, or failure of political passengers' nerve.

Models have helped the mainstream to clarify key concepts (like output gaps and imperfect information), explain away anomalies (persistent unemployment becoming "voluntary"), and turn vague tendencies into quantified causal links. By nailing conflicting approaches to a common framework, they pinpoint deductive mistakes and pare down complex debates ("Keynesian" vs "monetarist," mark-up vs marginal pricing) to disputes over parameter values. They establish a standard reporting style (reassuringly close to that of natural science) that makes papers easy to read and write, for those who've mastered the mathematics. Most importantly, they establish a common debating language. Alternative contributions remain imprecise, incomprehensible and dispensable, until "formalized" into a neoclassical model (and, preferably, estimated from available data).

Thus Marxism can re-enter mainstream debate if formalized as a macro-model with "rational choice" foundations (indeed, Bowles' and Gintis' AER-published model of capitalist labor incentives was one of the foundation stones of orthodox principal–agent theory). March and Simon's "bounded rationality" moved from marginalized management science to mainstream microeconomics once reformulated as a "transaction cost" to be optimized alongside production cost. But such heresies as Austrian economics (tarring the rational expectations model-builder with the same brush as the all-knowing central planner), post-Keynesianism and Sraffianism (with non-marginalist price theories), the Cambridge criticism (dismantling marginalism's aggregate capital), institutionalism (denying that all social structures can be traced to repeated game-play), or classical Marxism (where capitalists' individual rationality sums to collective disaster) fall outside the mainstream's logic, despite tackling its central topics.

Economists' retreat into private language explains their neglect of relevant information and explanation outside their model-based world. Anthropologists, ethnographers, historians and philosophers have much to say about origins and varieties of individualism, altruism, profit maximization; but these are unnecessary interrogations of neoclassicism's a priori assumptions, irrelevant if they support these and inconvenient if they challenge them. Sociology, psychology and politics give equally rich insights into internal and external pressures on (and problems with the outcome of) people's economic choices. But unless (like Jonathan Bendor in sociology, Steve Brams in politics or Kahneman and Tversky in psychology) they spell out their ideas in rational-choice, repeated-game language – so as to publish in mainstream economics journals – they are firmly repelled beyond the disciplinary border.

Instead of engaging with alternatives on their terms, the mainstream tries to refashion them into its own. So where such emerging (and emergent) phenomena as social capital, market-mediating institutions, interdependent expectations and path-dependent technical change appear at all, they do so in selectively interpreted, model-translated, neoclassically-readable form. This complicates the presentation (to anyone unschooled in neoclassical language and its unspoken assumptions), while often oversimplifying the argument by ditching what cannot be distilled to simultaneous equation.

This "imperial" battle has reached its height in the confrontation between neoclassical economics and evolutionary psychology (EP). Like neoclassicism, EP offers an all-embracing explanation for unrestricted individual action having functionally efficient, "natural" outcomes; and for all attempts to guide or manipulate that action being doomed to inflict collective as well as individual damage. But whereas neoclassical "competitive selection" works in the market period, ensuring that behavior persists where best suited to the present time, EP appeals to paleontological periods, resulting in persistence of behavior better suited to pre-historical than post-industrial times. To turn EP from usurper into ally, neoclassicists must assume that the traits "hard-wired" into evolved human minds are fully consistent with individual rational choice and rational expectation. Hence the current quest for game-based models and simulations equating "evolutionary stable strategy" with winning non-cooperative game strategy, ensuring that such EP phenomena as altruism and group selection amount to nothing more than clever manifestations of humanity's universally selfish streak.

While economists play these games, management schools continue capturing staff, students, and research funds from them, because what they teach and publish is what their sponsors and customers want to know. They do so without narrowing the syllabus down to neoclassical nostrums – because underconsumption crises, technological upheavals and panics and persistent disequilibrium are real threats to those working in the economy, even if irrelevant to those working on it, and Marx's assessment is as acceptable as Samuelson's if it helps to steer a way through. Most bookshops have emptied their Economics shelves to make room for a bulging Business section. Business research passes a "market test" that mainstream market champions know they would fail – and so prefer to pass up in favor of "peer review," which judges quality by conformity to accepted method, rather than usefulness of results. The consequent financial rationing helps neoclassical department heads restrict recruitment to researchers in their own image, but it means the mainstream's abstract art is painting itself into an ever more (literally) marginal corner.

[Alan Shipman is the author of *Transcending Transaction: The Search for Self-Generating Markets* (Routledge, November 2001).]

The perils of pluralistic teaching and how to reduce them

Peter E. Earl (University of Queensland, Australia)

Many academics involved in the post-autistic economics movement probably presume that barriers to delivering the kind of pluralistic teaching and doctoral training advocated by the French students and Cambridge postgraduates reduce to politics and infrastructure. They presume it is a matter of having the numbers to get pluralistic policies through faculty committees and of having the necessary teaching resources; resistance from students is not seen as an issue. Certainly, the student petitioning that started off the movement gives the impression that pluralistic teaching modes will be widely welcomed by students who enroll for courses in economics, because such an approach to teaching has greater scientific integrity than the present approach by which the neoclassical hegemony sweeps alternative perspectives aside regardless of empirical evidence.

Such would once have been my own perspective. I had the privilege of receiving my undergraduate training at Cambridge at a time (1974–1977) when pluralistic teaching was the order of the day there. I received contrasting perspectives on value and distribution from Frank Hahn, John Eatwell and Bob Rowthorn. When Ajit Singh, my director of studies, noticed that none of these approaches satisfied me in terms of how they dealt with problems of information and knowledge, he put me on the trail of behavioral economics despite it not being his habitual mode of thinking. My first lectureship was in a department (the University of Stirling, 1979–1984) that both offered subjects that were team-taught by staff with different perspectives and embraced the case study method of teaching management economics and marketing, with all that this entailed in opening the eyes of students to the indeterminacy of economic problem solving in real-world settings. Students at these institutions did not see pluralism as peculiar.

On moving to the University of Tasmania in 1984, I started having to do battle with non-UK-trained neoclassical economists who found it inconvenient to have me delivering post-Keynesian monetary/macroeconomics between their first- and third-year macroeconomics units. Eventually I was pushed out of economics and into teaching marketing and organizational behavior, though not after having had an enjoyable time teaching a first-year unit in Australian Political Economy that had a history of being taught in a pluralistic manner by UK-trained staff. It covered classics by Galbraith, Friedman, Baran and Sweezy, Hirsch, G.B. Richardson, and so on, but it was taken mostly by Arts students, with Commerce and Economics students sticking to orthodox micro and macro papers.

The chance to teach a large pluralistic microeconomics class came when I took up the Chair in Economics at Lincoln University in New Zealand in 1991. I relished this as an opportunity to show non-pluralistic colleagues that it was possible to cover mainstream and behavioral/institutional approaches to business economics simultaneously without diluting their content. However, nothing had prepared me for the resistance I encountered from the students, who had no expectation of being taught in a pluralistic manner. They were used to multiple choice exercises and short-answer types of problems, and lacked experience in essay writing and open-ended problem solving. To them economics was a matter of moving lines on graphs, and the invitation "discuss" meant "describe," as indeed it did to most of my colleagues – something I discovered each time I acted as examinations moderator. The traditional UK-style tutorials in which students discussed economic puzzles were unfamiliar to the New Zealanders and their full-fee-paying Asian counterparts, and many in the class (whether native English speakers or not) were unable to read at the level I expected (that of *The Times*, not the *Sun*). A thinking student's approach to economics, in which students were expected to battle to get to grips with unresolved debates in the discipline, was a shock to the majority of the class. Most were not economics majors, and were simultaneously being spoon-fed marketing and management with overly simplistic texts whose bullet points they could learn and parrot back to their examiners. They had no intrinsic interest in economics as a subject for making sense of the world; it was taken merely as a hurdle *en route* to a degree that would provide better job opportunities.

At the time, I suspected that the problem was that I was working in a third-rate institution, many of whose students really should not have been at university at all. Even so, I taught the subject nine times and turned the teaching resources into a textbook (Earl, 1995), before I lost the political battle and saw it replaced by "intermediate Varian." It was a relief to escape to my present post in a pluralistic department back in Australia – pluralistic, at least, in terms of its approach to research and tolerance of diversity *between* its courses. However, during my first semester I experienced several months of a far more brutal resistance to pluralism *within* a course than anything I encountered in New Zealand.

Students who were used to knowing in advance whether or not they were handing in a high-quality assignment got very aggressive when faced with a lecturer who expected them to read two or three original articles each week and do assignments for which they had no way of knowing whether they had understood the question in the "right" way or used the "right" piece of theory to wrestle with it. The upshot was a petition against my teaching and a steady stream of email complaints about virtually every aspect of the course, which grew into an organized campaign and gave me many sleepless nights, despite the support of a pluralistic head of department (John Foster) who had hired me knowing full well how I was going to teach. (I should add that the final set of grades was thoroughly satisfying; for the first time in ten years, I did not have to dumb my standards down, as most of the class had eventually got to grips with pluralism and open-ended problems – just as I had promised them that they would.)

If this is what happens with a class of able students in an age when most of the class typically consists of business/management students, not economics majors, then those who try to teach in a pluralistic manner risk doing terrible things to their teaching evaluation scores and to their departmental enrolments. Economics done this way looks far harder and more threatening than a typical one-eyed mainstream offering, *even if it contains less mathematics.*

Much of this will not seem surprising to those who have read Pirsig's *Zen and the Art of Motorcycle Maintenance* (Pirsig, 1974), but there are some things that would-be pluralists can do to make their task a bit less harrowing than my first semester at the University of Queensland proved to be. With my new and, on average, far more able body of students, I made one serious mistake right at the start of the subject, exactly as I did when first teaching in New Zealand: I presumed that students were used to the notion that a university is a place where ideas are debated openly and difficult issues are not dodged, rather than a place at which one receives the present state of knowledge in a neatly packaged form without any diversions into the history of the discipline or the personalities and politics that shaped it. Students who are under the latter delusion will naturally be horrified if a lecturer challenges the wisdom of a textbook. When I did so with my 1991 class, they ran crying (well, almost) to the director of the education unit – and as a consequence I was introduced to an essential source for any would-be pluralistic teacher, namely the work of William Perry (1970) on student learning. Subsequent cohorts of my students in New Zealand reacted differently, and this seems in large part to have been due to me teaching them at the start of the subject about Perry's work, and including a discussion of it in the textbook I developed around the course. This was not presented to the Queensland students, who also, due to some accidents of history, were not using my text on that occasion.

William Graves Perry Jr (1913–1998) was an educational counselor and professor of education at Harvard, and he concluded that the presence of different ways of thinking within a classroom is the major barrier to satisfactory teacher/pupil interaction. (I have explored his work in relation to economics at some length elsewhere: see Earl, 2000.) According to Perry, less intellectually mature students operate in a dualistic mode, seeing things in a very black-and-white manner. There is real science versus quackery. Teachers dispense the truth; students are vessels into which it is to be poured, and marks are awarded for showing that one can replicate the material. Dualistic thinkers have a hard time seeing what value student arguments could have in a class discussion, so they keep quiet and wait for wisdom from the teacher.

Perry identified a progression from dualism toward a kind of "committed relativism" in which one has got used to the idea that knowledge is debatable and provisional, but becomes attached to particular theoretical frameworks after thinking long an hard about their efficacy relative to rivals in particular contexts. *En route*, there is a growing awareness that debates exist within a discipline. This is initially seen as reflecting "good" versus "bad" authorities, but is then reframed in terms of "it's not really an issue about whether the scientists are good or bad; they've just not yet got the data that will enable them to resolve things." When students then notice the persistence of debates despite ongoing data gathering, this initially raises questions about whether lecturers can even mark their work: what makes any idea an idea of quality is unclear. However, gradually students come to see that it isn't a matter of scientists simply asserting their position is right but of arguing a case, which is what they realize everyone does in other parts of their lives. It is only by this stage that students will be really comfortable with pluralistic teaching in which they are given contending perspectives and opportunities to test their fit in a variety of contexts, and are then left to make up their minds with mentoring assistance from their teachers.

The transition from one level of intellectual development to another looks, in Perry's terms, likely to be quite painful, but if one explains to students what is going on they seem to be far more receptive, particularly when they can see that in other parts of their lives they do tolerate – even enjoy – debate and ambiguity and can argue cases. The post-autistic economist's task would be much easier if introductory economics at university level broached the dualism / relativism issue by focusing on contending perspectives in a manner different from high-school economics. Unfortunately, the dominance of mainstream economics in the first year locks student expectations into continued faith in dualistic modes of learning about economics, making pluralistic teaching at intermediate and advanced levels much more of a struggle.

References

Earl, P.E. (1995) *Microeconomics for Business and Marketing: Lectures, Cases and Worked Essays*. Aldershot: Edward Elgar.

Earl, P.E. (2000) "Indeterminacy in the economics classroom." In: Earl, P.E. and Frowen, S.F. (eds), *Economics as an Art of Thought: Essays in Memory of G.L.S. Shackle*, London: Routledge, pp. 25–50.

Perry, W.G., Jr (1970) *Forms of Ethical and Intellectual Development in the College Years: A Scheme*, New York: Holt, Rinehart and Winston.

Pirsig, R.M. (1974) *Zen and the Art of Motorcycle Maintenance*. London: Bodley Head.

Democracy and the need for pluralism in economics

Peter Söderbaum (Mälardalen University, Sweden)

The student initiative to challenge the dominance of the neoclassical paradigm at departments of economics in various parts of the world is extremely important. Why is this so? As I see it, the close to monopoly position of neoclassical economics is not compatible with normal ideas about democracy. Economics is science in some sense, but is at the same time ideology. Limiting economics to the neoclassical paradigm means imposing a serious ideological limitation. Departments of economics become political propaganda centers not very different from the many think tanks that we see these days in the USA and Europe. Instead, pluralism and paradigm coexistence are needed for departments of economics. Having more than one theoretical perspective will mean that more than one ideological perspective is represented. Economic Man assumptions imply that human beings are essentially consumers and wage earners. Obviously, this is close to an ideology of consumerism and neo-liberalism. Among alternative ways of regarding human beings, men and women can be seen as Political Economic Persons, meaning that their roles as professionals, parents and citizens are also considered. Furthermore, Economic Man assumptions are tied to utilitarian ethics, which is merely one of numerous ethical theories. Our Political Economic Person, on the contrary, is guided by an ideological orientation that is not limited to one specific ethic.

Rather than the usual "monetary reductionism" of the neoclassical perspective, economics and efficiency can be understood in multidimensional terms. While there are essential monetary impacts connected with road construction, for example, it is not clear that it is "rational" to put a price in monetary terms on all kinds of impacts. If the issues that we face are complex, then thinking in terms of profiles of monetary and non-monetary impacts may be a better idea. If this philosophy, and at the same time ideology, is chosen, then monetary analysis will get the more limited role of a partial analysis.

Cost–Benefit Analysis (CBA), with its connected ideas about "correct prices" for purposes of "resource allocation," is another example of the ideological character of much neoclassical analysis. This approach is built on an idea of aggregation, implying that it is meaningful to add all impacts in one-dimensional terms. It is furthermore built on a closed ideology in the sense that the analyst is able to point out or measure each impact correctly in monetary terms. In this way the analyst can arrive at recommendations about the "best" alternative from a societal point of view. It is not difficult to understand that this role for the analyst of being expert in an extreme sense is attractive. But once more, such conclusions imply that a specific ideology has been applied in terms of ideas about how to arrive at correct prices for each impact. Here again there are alternate, ideologically more open, approaches, such as positional analysis, built on ideas of keeping impacts separate and presenting multidimensional profiles for each alternative considered. The purpose of analysis becomes less one of solving a problem in a final sense and more one of illuminating an issue in relation to possibly relevant value or ideological orientations.

While CBA probably is something that should be abandoned as incompatible with democracy, other parts of neoclassical microeconomics may be more useful. In many ways neoclassical economics plays an important role in public debate. If students want to understand our history and the present situation it is good to learn some neoclassical economics, at least for background purposes. At Mälardalen University, we started in 1995 an undergraduate ecological economics program, where the neoclassical and institutional paradigms are systematically compared right from the first course. In this way an alternative microeconomics is suggested in terms of views of human beings, of organizations, markets, efficiency, development or progress, social change processes, etc. (Söderbaum, 2000). Students are confronted with traditional texts in economics and business management, as well as the alternative microeconomics indicated. In this way students become "free to choose," which is – at least in their rhetoric – also the wish of neoclassical economists.

Readers of the *post-autistic economics review* may wonder how such a program could be designed and implemented. One explanation may be that ours is a relatively young university, which is expected to innovate with respect to interdisciplinary programs and where disciplinary barriers are not so strong. Another is probably that the ecological economics program is connected with a department where business management rather than economics dominates the scene. More important, hopefully, is an understanding among an increasing number of actors that in relation to issues of environment and development, neoclassical economics is today more of a problem than a solution. Interdisciplinary approaches, such as ecological economics, are necessary if we want to reverse trends of environmental and social degradation in Sweden, in Europe and at a global level.

It should be noted that the Bank of Sweden Prize in Memory of Alfred Nobel is part of the problem we are discussing. This award has probably contributed to making economics more "autistic" and to protecting the neoclassical paradigm. However, occasionally economists who stand for a degree of pluralism and interdisciplinary approaches, such as Gunnar Myrdal, have received the award. At a certain stage in his career, Myrdal left neoclassical theory behind and declared openly his sympathies for institutionalism (Myrdal, 1978). In doing so, Myrdal pointed to the role of values not only in economics but in all social sciences, and questioned claims of "value-neutrality" concerning theories, methods or policy recommendations. "Values are always with us" in scientific research, Myrdal argues, and this holds for all steps from problem formulation, choice of theoretical framework, methods to be applied and the way results are presented. Unfortunately, most neoclassical economists (and even some institutionalists) persist with the belief that they can stand outside society and observe it objectively.

I will end this essay by returning to the important role of students as actors in influencing the way economics and business management is taught. At Uppsala University, there is a Center for Environmental and Development Studies, financed by the university but – with the exception of examinations – controlled largely by the students. The students by themselves arrange courses that they find important. Early this year three students made a study of the economics programs at Uppsala University, the Agricultural University Uppsala, two universities in Stockholm and two programs at Mälardalen University. In interviewing those responsible, their starting point was the fact that the mentioned universities all had signed the Copernicus University Charter, implying that they were committed "to the principle and practice of environmental protection and sustainable development." At issue was how this commitment is reflected in the way economics is taught. Is there any systematic attempt to bring environmental issues into teaching and courses? Is there a role for interdisciplinarity and for alternative perspectives in economics? The students found that, with few exceptions, very little had happened. In many cases, those responsible for the programs and courses did not even know about the Copernicus Charter and argued that since there were no difficulties in recruiting new students there were few incentives for change. But the story does not end with this. The students were financially supported by responsible governmental agencies, and the Ministry of Education in Sweden has signaled that a conference will be arranged to follow up these important issues.

References

Myrdal, G. (1978). Institutional economics. *Journal of Economic Issues*, **12(3)**, 771–783.

Söderbaum, P. (2000). *Ecological Economics: A Political Economics Approach to Environment and Development*. London: Earthscan.

Toward a post-autistic economics education

Susan Feiner (University of Southern Maine, USA and The Hawke Institute, University of South Australia)

Taken together, the articles by Marc Lavoie and Peter Earl (*PAE review*, no. 11, 30 January 2002) can be seen as posing a set of interesting, important and inter-related questions. Lavoie asks, "what are the connections between post-Keynesian and feminist economics?," while Earl asks, "how can we understand, and so transcend, the resistance on the part of students to a more 'pluralistic' approach to economics education?"

Lavoie's investigation of the connections between post-Keynesian and feminist economics notes the importance of pedagogy, but his essay does not discuss teaching. Earl's discussion of pedagogy refers to critical thinking, and the development of students' capacity to handle intellectual ambiguity, but his discussion does not mention feminist pedagogy. However, pedagogy reform in economics, at least in the USA, emerged as an organic concern of feminists seeking to develop a new approach to the discipline.

Beginning in 1985 and running through to at least 1997, there were panels at various economics meetings (including the ASSA), conferences, faculty development programs, workshops, seminars, peer reviewed published papers, and a number of edited volumes produced by feminist economists and aimed at deep transformation of the teaching of economics. In the early years, feminist interest in pedagogy was manifest in the papers researching the presentation of topics relating to gender and race in economics textbooks. This work demonstrated the extent to which introductory economics textbooks perpetuated sexist and racist assumptions, reinforced existing biases regarding the perversity of policy aimed at redressing sexual and racial inequality, and basically ridiculed any but the "approved" points of view on these controversial topics.

Quite a number of highly esteemed, mainstream economists were appalled by these findings. With the help of Barbara Bergmann, I recruited such luminaries as Robert Solow, William Baumol, Lester Thurow, Alice Rivlin and Kenneth Arrow to work with me on The Committee for Race and Gender Balance in the Economics Curriculum. My point here is that "autism" and bigotry need not go hand in hand. With a lot of hard work, a great deal of encouragement and helpful support from many quarters, Robin Bartlett (Denison University) and I secured a series of grants from The National Science Foundation to host faculty development programs to help economics professors integrate the new scholarship on women and people of color into the introductory economics curriculum.

Economics pedagogy and the feminist classroom

From the outset, Bartlett and I knew that the standard "sage on the stage" model of college teaching was not appropriate for bringing these controversial topics into introductory economics classrooms. How did we know this? We were both conversant with what was then the cutting edge "active learning," "student centered" approach to teaching that has its roots in the feminist revisioning of education.

As Peter Earl quite rightly points out, students come to college knowing all sorts of things, and one of the things they "know" is that the way to demonstrate "learning" is to parrot back what the teacher said. But when students are likely to disagree with the teacher (as many of them often do on the topics related to sex, race and the economy as seen from the eyes of a feminist), they are going to feel manipulated, brainwashed and angry. When this is coupled with their almost total ignorance, if not complete misunderstanding, of the struggles for women's liberation and racial justice, what was intended as a class discussion can turn into an awful round of name calling, intolerance, and all-round bad feelings (which is why economics professors often choose to avoid these topics).

In *Feminism and Methodology* (Indiana University Press, 1987), philosopher Sandra Harding argues that one of the key distinctive features of feminist research is that the researcher places her or himself and the subject of research "on the same plane." This epistemological position has direct application in pedagogy.

As we were trying to get the economics faculty to rethink the teacher role, we organized the faculty development conferences so that the faculty could re-experience the uncertainty, risk-taking, and mutual support that characterizes classes that are open, non- or minimally hierarchical, and actually welcome free discussion. We knew that the faculty needed to reacquaint themselves with what were hopefully their own best experiences as students, and hoped that the insights gained from this would lead them to realize the need for deep change in the structure of classroom dynamics.

The programs of these conferences had the faculty engage in competitive timed exercises, and then in cooperative, collaborative exercises. We asked participants to reflect on the different feelings these exercises provoked. Here too the recognition that feelings and not just "right answers" are important in learning reflects feminist epistemological commitments. The gulf between this position and the view of personhood (if you can call it that) embodied in Rational Economic Man should be obvious.

Participants also spent a good deal of time reflecting on, and working through, activities designed to highlight the way their own attitudes and histories of sex, gender, race and ethnicity had shaped them as learners. These sessions were invariably highly charged. Emotions ran high as *economists* recounted personal stories of being shunned, or humiliated for who they were; we heard stories about the shame people felt when they realized that their parents were racist, homophobic, or anti-semitic; others told of how they had participated in harassing behaviors; still others revealed that they hadn't known that whiteness was itself a racial identity. I cannot count the number of people who told me that these sessions provided some of their sharpest insights into the problems with the mainstream approach.

Providing a venue for self-reflection is also a hallmark of feminist pedagogy. Feminists have long insisted that social position affects knowledge, and that every view is a point of view. Feminist epistemology is clear on this point; recognizing that power and privilege shape knowledge leads to more – not less – rigor and "objectivity" in scientific inquiry.

The faculty had to recognize that they, too, were marked by the social processes of race, gender, ethnicity and sexual orientation. This self-awareness is an essential prerequisite for creating a classroom where students feel safe enough to self-reveal. All of our students carry a personal history relative to race, gender, class, sexual orientation and ethnicity. Ignoring the emotional underpinnings of their understandings of diversity and the social conflict attendant on diversity virtually guarantees that a classroom discussion will explode with misunderstanding, disrespect or worse.

Another reason why it was important to self-disclose around our experiences is that this placed the participants outside their "comfort zones." The faculty (in general) and economists (in particular) are probably not used to talking about feelings, especially not in relationship to economic concepts. Once they had taken this risk and discovered that the group would support them, they could see for themselves that "the economic is as personal" as the "personal is political."

Only after we had created an atmosphere of trust and community did we turn to the formidable tasks of reinventing introductory micro- and macro-economics. Over the next two days faculty work groups developed creative exercises, all based on active, collaborative learning, which brought questions of gender and race to the center of classroom economic discussions. I recall a simulation exercise in which students were to research and then represent the various people who would be affected if a factory in the southern USA shut down in order to reopen in El Salvador. Another group came up with the idea of holding public hearings on Federal Reserve policy, with students representing a wide range of social organizations. Yet another traced the effects of inflation on different occupational groups. One of my favorites was a skit of a romantic couple using Becker's logic to sort out the decision to marry.

A blind eagle in a blizzard could recognize the connections between this approach to teaching economics and feminist pedagogy. But what is the connection to critical thinking?

The topics of gender and race are especially helpful for introducing competing points of view because everyone "knows" that people disagree. As Peter Earl points out, students often believe that disagreement on such issues exists because the "experts" still haven't discovered the Truth. I will go out on a limb here and insist that you cannot disabuse students of this point of view if your reading assignments are confined to a textbook, regardless of its orientation to economics. That means you need to find articles that students can read – they often need help with this because they are not especially skilled readers – that express different points of view.

Working in small groups during class will help students learn how to read critically. In groups of three to five have them identify the four most important points of each of the articles you've assigned. Make sure they reference each important point to a specific paragraph in the essay. After you've gotten these points on the board (and there should be a goodly number of "most important points," since you have four points per group), the class discussion can focus on which of these are most important and why. By the conclusion of this exercise, every student should understand the articles.

Now you have prepared them for selecting the argument with which they agree. A great homework assignment: "Why I rejected argument X."

Critical thinking requires the ability to recognize and understand what are often complex arguments. In economics, the points of view associated with the heterodox approaches are quite likely to be diametrically opposed to the views of society with which students are familiar. Getting students actually to "think" about these ideas, rather than see this as an attempt to brainwash them, is tricky. So is getting students to do more than parrot back your politics. As I've argued here, feminism informs a pedagogy that is up to the challenge.

[Susan Feiner is the editor of *Race and Gender in the American Economy: Views Across the Spectrum*.]

Steve Keen's *Debunking Economics*

Geoff Harcourt (Cambridge University, UK)

Steve Keen's *Debunking Economics* is a provocative book; deliberately so is my conjecture. The anti-Vietnam war movement in Adelaide dichotomized into either militants or moderates. I belonged to the second group, because I thought it the proper way for academics to play a public role in vital political and social issues. I also thought it would be counterproductive to do otherwise (no prize for guessing the respective weights attached to the two reasons). Steve, I'm sure, would have been a militant – certainly that is his approach here. I worry that this may backfire, for I have sympathy with his aims and many of his arguments and judgments. Time will tell who is right (perhaps I could say that the militants wanted the Australian revolution to occur first, then the troops could be brought home and conscription abolished. The moderates thought it better to get an ALP government elected because these two objectives were core items in Labor's election manifesto).

Keen's object is to go behind what is currently taught to economics undergraduates in order to reveal the conceptual bases of their instruction and the ideological purposes involved. He comes to his task with a thorough knowledge of the classics of the subject, of Adam Smith as well as of Karl Marx, and with considerable analytical skills of the modern sort. He is a graduate of the political economy movement at the University of Sydney, and his PhD dissertation was an amalgam of the theories of Dick Goodwin and Hy Minsky, two modern maverick greats, both alas now dead.

Goodwin was a pupil and then a colleague of Wassily Leontief and Joseph Schumpeter at Harvard, and a pupil of Roy Harrod and Henry Phelps Brown at Oxford. He was much influenced by Maynard Keynes's writings, and by Richard Kahn, Joan Robinson and Piero Sraffa of his Cambridge (England) colleagues in the post-war period. Though he ceased to be a member of the Communist Party by the 1940s, he remained an informed fan of Marx's writings, especially of Marx's deep knowledge of how capitalism works. (Joan Robinson used to say of Schumpeter that he was Marx with the adjectives changed.) This background, together with his love of Wicksell's economics and teaching physics at Harvard during the Second World War, led to Goodwin's pioneering contribution of models of cyclical growth. They incorporated his insight that trend and cycle are indissolubly mixed, not separable and determined by different sets of factors, as usually happens in orthodox economics.

Minsky also knew his Marx. He worked with Oskar Lange as a young man. His great contribution was to show how real and monetary factors interrelated to produce cycles as capitalist economies evolved through time. While he drew on the writings of Keynes and Michal Kalecki, his financial instability hypothesis associated with the analysis of the effects on firms and on the economy of the non-realization of the expected cash flows arising from investment projects is highly original. It has proved of greater and greater value in our understanding in recent years of the financial instabilities and crises in the world economy. Keen's contribution is to put these two strands together to provide a structure for illuminating the malfunctionings of modern interrelated capitalist economies. He does this in a way that not only draws on the insights of our past masters but also employs the most modern of analytical techniques.

With such a background it is easy to understand his horror at the contents of modern textbooks. Increasingly they model the capitalist world as though it were conforming to the dictates of Frank Ramsey's benevolent dictator, choosing optimum paths of accumulation over time for all its citizens. Keynes's long run in which "we are all dead" (well, he's dead and we are in the long run, as an IMF wit recently put it) has returned to dominate our supposed understanding of what is happening. Short-term instabilities are viewed as mere aberrations, fluctuations around this long-period optimum trajectory.

Against this macroeconomic background, modern microeconomics has a bias towards examining the behavior of competitive markets (as set out most fully and rigorously in the Arrow–Debreu model of general equilibrium), not as reference points but as approximations to what is actually going on. Of course departures from them are taught, increasingly by the clever application of game theory. Moreover, the deficiencies of real markets of all sorts are examined in the light of the implications, for example, of the findings of the asymmetric information theorists (three of whom – George Akerlof, Michael Spence and Joe Stiglitz – have just (10/10/01) been awarded this year's Nobel Prize. From Amartya Sen on, the Nobel Prize electors seem to be back on track).

While professional economists increasingly get to know of these and other developments, often through the pages of the excellent *Journal of Economic Perspectives*, the most used undergraduate textbooks are usually light years away from such enlightenment. Moreover, alternative approaches in our subject, economic history and the history of economic thought are either being marginalized in, or driven out altogether from most undergraduate courses. Keen's book is directed against these trends. He examines what is taught in macroeconomic and micro-economic courses, and what their deficiencies and shortcomings are. And he suggests alternatives, some of which come out of the many influences on him and his own contributions.

As I said, I understand his impatience and anger and I applaud his aims. I just worry that the tone of the book and, sometimes, his assertions may allow critics to sidetrack the arguments along byways that may seem plausible but ultimately miss the point – to the detriment of the training of future generations in what Keynes memorably called "our miserable subject."

Nevertheless, if I were given a free hand to design a course, I would urge my pupils to read both Keen's book and Hugh Stretton's marvelous alternative text (*Economics: A New Introduction*, published by Pluto in 1999), as well as the best of the mainstream texts now available. (I would also urge them to read some of the great originals too!) Only then would I feel they had been introduced to the appropriate material with which to make up their own minds regarding what approach(es) to take in their studies. As it is, without the insights of a Keen and a Stretton (and of the past greats), I fear we are likely to produce well-trained but uncritical cogs, the better to fit the needs of our modern industrialized societies. It is not the proper role of university teachers either to be hired prize fighters or produce them.

[This article originally appeared in the *Financial Review*.]

Is there anything worth keeping in standard microeconomics?

Bernard Guerrien (Université Paris I, France)

The French students' movement against autism in economics started with a revolt against the disproportionate importance of microeconomics in economic teaching. The students complained that nobody had really proved to them that microeconomics was of any use; what is the interest of going through "micro 1," "micro 2," "micro 3," etc., using lots of mathematics to speak of fictitious households, fictitious enterprises and fictitious markets?

Actually, when one thinks about it, it turns out that microeconomics is simply "neoclassical theory." Realizing this, I agree with the French students when they say that:

1   In a course on economic theories, neoclassical theory should be taught alongside other economic theories (classical political economy, Marxist theory, Keynesian theory, etc.), showing that it is just one among several other approaches.

2   The principal elements and assumptions of neoclassical theory (consumer and producer choice, general equilibrium existence theorems, and so on) should be taught with very little mathematics (or with none at all), the main reason being that it is essential for students to understand the economic meaning of assumptions made in mathematical language. As they study economics, and not mathematics, students must decide if these assumptions are relevant or meaningful. But for that assumptions must be expressed clearly and not in abstruse formulas. Only if assumptions and models are relevant can it be of any interest to try to see what "results" or "theorems" can be deduced from them.

I am convinced that assumptions of standard microeconomics are *not at all* relevant. And I think that it is nonsense to say – as some people do (using the "as if" argument) – that relevant results can be deduced from assumptions that obviously contradict almost everything that we observe around us.

The main reason why the teaching of microeconomics (or of "micro-foundations" of macroeconomics) has been called "autistic" is because it is increasingly impossible to discuss real-world economic questions with microeconomists – and with almost all neoclassical theorists. They are trapped in their system, and don't in fact care about the outside world any more. If you consult any microeconomic textbook, it is full of mathematics (e.g. Kreps or Mas–Colell, Whinston and Green) or of "tales" (e.g. Varian or Schotter), without real data (occasionally you find "examples" or "applications" with numerical examples, but they are purely fictitious, invented by the authors).

At first, French students got quite a lot of support from teachers and professors: hundreds of teachers signed petitions backing their movement – specially pleading for "pluralism" in teaching the different ways of approaching economics. But when the students proposed a precise program of studies, without "micro 1," "micro 2," "micro 3," without macroeconomics "with micro-foundations" or with a "representative agent," almost all teachers refused, considering that it was "too much" because "students must learn all these things, even with some mathematical details." When you ask them "why?," the answer usually goes something like this: "Well, even if we, personally, never use the kind of 'theory' or 'tools' taught in microeconomics courses (since we are regulationist, evolutionist, institutionalist, conventionalist, etc.), surely there are people who do 'use' and 'apply' them, even if it is in an 'unrealistic', or 'excessive' way."

But when you ask those scholars who does "use these tools," especially those who do a lot of econometrics with "representative agent" models, they answer (if you insist): "OK, I agree with you that it is nonsense to represent the whole economy by the (intertemporal) choice of one agent – consumer and producer – or by a unique household that owns a unique firm, but if you don't do that, you don't do anything!"

There are also some microeconomists who try to prove, by experiments or by some kind of econometrics, that people act rationally. But to do that you don't need to know envelope theorems, compensated (Hicksian) demand or Slutsky matrix! Indeed, "experimental economics" has a very tenuous relation with "theory:" it tests very elementary ideas (about rational choice or about markets) in very simple situations – even if, in general, people don't act as theory predicts, but that is another question.

Microeconomics: "unrealistic" or "irrelevant"?

Most of the time microeconomics is criticized because of its "lack of realism." But "lack of realism" doesn't necessarily mean *irrelevance*; the expression is usually understood as meaning that the theory in question is "more or less distant from reality," or as giving a more or less acceptable proxy of reality (people differing about the quality of the approximation). The idea is implicitly this: "if we work hard, relaxing some assumptions and using more powerful mathematical theorems, microeconomics will progressively became more and more realistic. There are then – at least – some interesting concepts and results in microeconomics that a healthy, post-autistic, economic theory should incorporate."

That's what Geoff Harcourt implicitly says in the *post-autistic economics review*, no. 11, when he writes:

> Against this macroeconomic background, modern microeconomics has a bias towards examining the behavior of competitive markets (as set out most fully and rigorously in the Arrow–Debreu model of general equilibrium), not as reference points but as approximations to what is actually going on. Of course departures from them are taught, increasingly by the clever application of game theory. Moreover, the deficiencies of real markets of all sorts are examined in the light of the implications, for example, of the findings of the asymmetric information theorists (three of whom – George Akerlof, Michael Spence and Joe Stiglitz – have just (10/10/01) been awarded this year's Nobel Prize. From Amartya Sen on, the Nobel Prize electors seem to be back on track).

What is Harcourt saying? He is telling us that the Arrow–Debreu model has something to do with "the behavior of competitive markets;" he is saying that game theory can be cleverly "applied;" he says that there are "findings" made by Akerlof, Spence and Stiglitz. If all this is true, then students have to learn general equilibrium theory (as giving "approximations to what is actually going on"), game theory, asymmetric information theory, and so on. That means that they need micro 1, micro 2, micro 3 (etc.) courses (consumer and producer choice, perfect and imperfect competition, game theory, "market failures," etc.).

I don't agree at all with Geoff Harcourt because:

1   The Arrow–Debreu model has nothing to do with competition and markets: it is a model of a "highly centralized" economy, with a benevolent auctioneer doing a lot of things, and with stupid price-taker agents.
2   Game theory cannot be "applied:" it only tells little "stories" about the possible consequences of rational individuals' choices made once and for all and simultaneously by all of them.
3   Akerlof, Spence and Stiglitz have no new "findings," they just present, in a mathematical form, some very old ideas – long known by insurance companies and by those who organize auctions and second-hand markets.
4   Amartya Sen, as an economist, is a standard microeconomist (that is what he was awarded the Nobel Prize for): only the vocabulary is different ("capabilities," "functionings," etc.).

But, perhaps, all "post-autistic" economists won't agree with me.

It is good, then, that they give their opinion and, more generally, that we try to answer, in detail, the questions: *Is there anything worth keeping in microeconomics – and in neoclassical theory? If there is, what?*

[Bernard Guerrien is the author of *La Théorie des Jeux* (La Découverte, 2002), and *La Théorie Économique Néoclassique. Macroéconomie, Théorie des Jeux*, Vol. 2 (La Découverte, 2002).]

Part III

Practice and ethics

Autistic economics vs the environment

Frank Ackerman (Global Development and Environment Institute at Tufts University)

The unrealistic mathematical models of "autistic economics" would be bad enough if they stayed in the classroom, detached from the real world. Unfortunately, though, the dominant school of economics has itself become a powerful political force: at least in the USA, it is rapidly reshaping public policy in its own image. In the area I am most familiar with, environmental policy, the invasion of abstract economic theory threatens to impose the logic of the marketplace on the very different reality of nature.

Conventional economics has, since Pigou, recognized the importance of unpriced environmental externalities. Even if all the other assumptions of the competitive model are granted, market outcomes are not optimal unless all externalities are internalized – through Pigouvian taxes or, under rare special conditions, through private negotiations à la Coase.

But what is the status of these observations about externalities? Are they one more entry in a long list of ways in which the model of perfect competition fails to describe reality? Or are they the only remaining problem, the last obstacle to be overcome in the pursuit of optimality? The latter, alas, is a very common assumption in environmental economics.

The specific problems caused by the misuse of economic theory in environmental policy include:

1   Reliance on computable general equilibrium (CGE) models. In the realm of mathematical theory, it has been known since the 1970s that the existence of an equilibrium point in a general equilibrium model does not imply anything about the dynamics of the model. The much-discussed static equilibrium point is Pareto-optimal under the usual conditions, but may also be dynamically unstable under small perturbations, rendering it unattainable or unsustainable – and hence irrelevant in practice, even if the model were otherwise a good approximation to reality.[1] However, CGE models have all but conquered the world of American policy analysis. No signs of theoretical uncertainty can be seen; instead, use of the general equilibrium framework is

taken as the mark of good science. The results are no better than the under-lying assumptions: leading CGE forecasts of the effects of the North American Free Trade Agreement (NAFTA) on industrial pollution have been wrong by several orders of magnitude.

2   Mindless monetization. The Pigouvian agenda requires a monetary value for every significant externality. Yet many environmental externalities involve risks of irreversible damages, large but uncertain costs, impacts on future generations, or values, such as human life, that cannot meaningfully be monetized.[2] Economics rushes in, however, where ethics fears to tread: one common figure, used in many cost–benefit analyses, is that a human life is worth $6.1 million (in 1999 dollars). About ten years ago, Kip Viscusi[3] sur-veyed all published studies of the monetary value of a life, many of them done by himself and his co-workers, and calculated the average – which, adjusted for inflation, reached $6.1 million by 1999. There are several tech-nical problems with "Viscusi's number," as well as its obvious ethical and philosophical failures. However, the $6.1 million number appeared, and was treated as an established fact, in a recent US EPA cost–benefit analysis of arsenic standards for drinking water. Based in part on that analysis, EPA set the standard at more than three times the technologically feasible minimum level. With the higher standard more people will die of arsenic-related cancers, but at $6.1 million apiece they (we) just aren't worth saving.[4]

3   Advocacy of *laissez-faire*. Economic theory confronts the world with a tangled mixture of description and prescription. While it seeks to value externalities and thus make markets more perfect, it also critiques taxes and policies that deviate from unregulated market outcomes. Economists are fond of identifying the "distortionary" effects of public policy, measured rela-tive to a hypothetical, perfectly competitive market economy with little or no public sector. The implication is typically that the government is misusing resources that could be better allocated by the market. In particular, too much, or the wrong things, are being done to protect the environment.

There is an urgent need for a more realistic economics of the environment, with theories and analyses that can help to create environmentally sustainable eco-nomic activity. The new field of ecological economics offers promising first steps in this direction, and there is a continuing role for critiques of the misuses of con-ventional theory in the realm of public policy. The struggle against autistic eco-nomics is far more than an academic debate.

Notes

1   Frank Ackerman, (2002) Still dead after all these years: interpreting the failure of general equilibrium theory: *Journal of Economic Methodology*, **9(2)**, 1–21.

2   These issues are discussed further in:
    Ackerman, F. and Heinzerling, L. (2002) "Pricing the priceless: cost–benefit analysis of environmental protection." *University of Pennsylvania Law Review*, **150(5)**, 1553–1584.
    Ackerman, F. and Gallagher, K. (2001) "Getting the prices wrong: the uses and abuses of market-based environmental policy." In: T. Swartz and F. Bonello (eds), *Taking Sides: Clashing Views on Controversial Economic Issues*. McGraw-Hill.
3   Moore, M.J. and Kip Viscusi, W. (1988) The quantity-adjusted value of life. *Economic Inquiry*, **26**, 369–388.
4   See comments by Frank Ackerman on the proposed arsenic regulation at http://ase.tufts.edu/gdae. The issue is also discussed in Ackerman and Heinzerling, *op.cit.* (note 2), and in Ackerman, F. and Heinzerling, L. (2003) *Priceless: Human Health, the Environment, and the Limits of the Market*. The New Press.

Humility in economics

André Orléan (Director of Research, CNRS, École Normale Supérieure, Paris)

Is economics a science? Are there laws in economics as there are in physics? The answers to these questions, which divide economists as well as epistemologists, have important consequences not only for economics itself, but also for the role of economists in society. Take the following example: is it right to say that "An increase in the minimum wage necessarily leads to less employment for the least qualified workers"? The answer is straightforward: no.

The so-called "law of the minimum wage" is an excellent starting point, not only because it has been at the center of the recent (French) debate on low wages, but also because it is one of the very few proposals that can legitimately claim to be an "economic law." According to a survey, 90 percent of economists believe in it. After all, isn't it enough to remark that when the price of a given good rises, its demand diminishes? One could not find a more elementary economic truth. Unfortunately, David Card and Alan Krueger have observed through various North American experiences of increasing the minimum wage that the employment level of the least qualified either remained the same or increased. They did not manage to find the negative effect predicted by the "law." Besides, those who have a bit of memory know that as early as the late 1970s, Malinvaud had proposed a macroeconomic configuration, which he baptized "Keynesian unemployment," in which "when wages rise, so does employment." How is this possible? The reason is that the economy is a complex web of interdependencies that does not allow us to predict the final outcome of a change in a single variable. A rise in interest rates may well lead to an appreciation of the national currency, but the contrary is just as possible. There are no universal laws in economics. Instead there is only a set of highly various mechanisms, such that when analyzing a given situation it is necessary that we take into account economic conditions, institutions and specific histories. "Well, even so," one could say, "don't we simply have to be more precise about the initial conditions in order to predict the final outcome?"

Here we face a second obstacle, even worse than the first. Among the conditions that affect economic fluctuations, one must include the knowledge of persons, their beliefs, and the way they understand their surroundings and justify their actions. As it happens, these beliefs, interpretations and justifications evolve and transform themselves continuously, because they are social objects. And this is because human beings learn and innovate – the future is never a repetition of the past. In the human world, what happened yesterday does not tell us what will happen tomorrow. Which model of the American elections could have predicted that the failure of some machines to punch little holes in ballots would be relevant? Similarly, economic competition constantly creates new and unpredicted situations.

So what conclusion follows for the economist? Humility. In teaching, humility is called pluralism, confrontation with facts and other social sciences, and recognizing the three demands that one finds in the very interesting petition written by the economics students. In political terms, this means that no argument from authority is legitimate. This does not imply that the economist ought to remain outside the public debate; it simply means that the economist must engage him- or herself as a citizen with convictions regarding the public good and ways of treating it, rather than as the holder of universal truth that he or she substitutes for discussion in order to impose it on us all.

Real science is pluralist

Edward Fullbrook (University of the West of England, UK)

Fifty years from now, when historians of ideas write about how economics turned away from scientism and toward science, they may identify the pivotal event as the appearance of Robert Solow's article in *Le Monde* (3 January 2001) (Solow, 2001). This was his ill-fated attempt to calm the growing rebellion of French economics students against the neoclassical *status quo*. Solow's article merely manifests, although with an alarming and attention-getting American imperialist twist, an ideology that has choked the social sciences, economics in particular, for as long as most of us can remember. Let me try to explain.

Recently I wrote a paper concerned with identifying a range of economic phenomena within a theoretical context. It focuses on categories of market behavior that on the one hand are well known, commonplace, completely respectable and increasingly dominant, but on the other hand are excluded from the theoretical core of mainstream economics. One cannot easily imagine a similarly dysfunctional state persisting in a natural science – such as, for example, physics refusing to consider microphysical phenomena because they don't observe the metaphysics of gravitational theory. But of course such states of affairs in economics are the rule rather than the exception, and it is worth considering why this is so. I am going to filter this brief inquiry through the ideas found in a short passage by Roy Bhaskar.

In *The Possibility of Naturalism*, Bhaskar (1979) writes as follows:

> . . . one has in science a three-phase schema of development in which, in a continuing dialectic, science identifies a phenomenon (or range of phenomena) [that's phase one], constructs explanations for it and empirically tests its explanations [that's two], leading to the identification of the generative mechanism at work [that's three], which now becomes the phenomenon to be explained, and so on. [and that's the dialectic] [p. 12]

My view is that, with one notable exception, this dialectic largely failed to function in twentieth-century economics, and that this breakdown resulted from the discipline's refusal to enter into Bhaskar's phase one.

Instead of identifying phenomena which it then seeks to explain, economics avoids the dialectic by only considering phenomena consistent with existing explanations. In recent decades, this upside-down "science" – this choosing what one sees in order to justify a theory and its ontology, rather than using theory to understand intransitive realities – became hegemonic as economics construed support for this behavior from new narratives of scientific practice, especially Thomas Kuhn's. I want to outline the negative role that I think philosophy of science, in spite of Bhaskar's illuminating work, has played in economics.

This requires me to say a few things about the philosophy of science, especially its relation to historical events. The last century's fascination with this previously obscure corner of philosophy seems to have been triggered by the acceptance of Einstein's theory of relativity. This event fits well with several narratives of scientific progress, including Bhaskar's. Unlike Bhaskar's, however, Popper's and Kuhn's narratives of *The Logic of Scientific Discovery* (Popper, 1959) and *The Structure of Scientific Revolutions* (Kuhn, 1962) respectively also fitted the meta-narrative that dominated geo-political perceptions from the 1940s onwards – that is, that of global powers and ideologies battling it out until one gains total victory over the other. Popper indirectly, and one assumes unconsciously, brought this narrative structure into play by shifting the epistemological focus from scientific theories themselves to their dramatic encounters with tests designed to discredit them. The stylized exemplary case for Popper's narrative became the falsification and overthrow of Newtonian physics by means of tests devised through the competing and victorious theory of the cosmos, Einsteinian physics. This story had instant appeal for an intellectual population accustomed to global conflict and submerged in Cold War mythology. It offered a simple winners and losers story-line worthy of Hollywood, and echoed the major traumas and neuroses of the latter half of the century. So it was no wonder that by the 1960s even people who had never opened a science book could chatter about falsification.

The popularization of the putative ins and outs of scientific advance accelerated with the appearance in 1962 of Thomas Kuhn's *The Structure of Scientific Revolutions* (Kuhn, 1962). It was really this book that made philosophy of science big box-office. It also, with its multi-faceted concept of the paradigm, provided economics with a rationalization for its worst practices, especially its head-in-the-sand approach to major kinds of economic phenomena. Recently, rereading Kuhn's book after a space of many years, it was a shock to be forced to re-engage with the paranoid, polarized rhetoric and logic that throughout the 1950s and 1960s shaped most public discussion in Kuhn's America. Kuhn himself is open about locating his book in this historical framework. In his preface to the original 1962 edition, he writes that his book was conceived of and written over a period of fifteen years – in other words, from the heyday of McCarthyism to the Cuban Missile Crisis and the height of the Cold War.

And it shows. The scenario that Kuhn so skilfully sketches regarding scientific endeavor is, in the main, the same as that which structured the more intemperate, more right-wing accounts of what was billed as the struggle between Communism and the Free World. Kuhn's book methodically transposes the Cold War narrative onto the competing theories narrative of science. This transposition extends even to his vocabulary, with a heavy use of Cold War jargon and expressions like "subversive," "polarization," "crisis" and "crisis provoking," "techniques of mass persuasion," "allegiance," "commitment," "conversions," "total destruction" and "total victory," and, of course, "revolution." Others of Kuhn's most favored expressions echoed then current geo-political equivalents. For example, "adherents" translates as "patriots;" "incommensurability" as "no peaceful co-existence;" "different world view" as "different ideology;" "pre-paradigm" as "third-world;" "rival theories" as "rival powers;" and so on.

Kuhn also repeatedly foregrounds a parallel between paradigms and political institutions. For example, he writes, "Like the choice between competing political institutions, that between competing paradigms proves to be a choice between incompatible modes of community life." It is this emotionally charged us or them, all or nothing mentality that Kuhn's book seems to legitimate as the ethos of science. "After the pre-paradigm period," writes Kuhn, "the assimilation of all new theories and of almost all new sorts of phenomena has in fact demanded the destruction of a prior paradigm and a consequent conflict between competing schools of scientific thought" (p. 96). Kuhn's narrative makes the defense of one's paradigm community through the elimination or marginalization of rival ones, the scientist's over-riding goal. And it makes the identification of new sorts of phenomena, the first phase in Bhaskar's schema, something to be avoided like nuclear war.

Kuhn's paradigmatic, that is *anti-pluralist*, science does, however, make one fundamental concession to the notion of science as a pursuit of truth. Although Kuhn condones all manner of evasions and closed-mindedness, he posits a limit beyond which empirical realities count for more than loyalty to a community of belief; where, in his words, scientists "can no longer evade anomalies that subvert the existing tradition of scientific practice," and where in consequence a scientific revolution takes place (p. 6).

However, in social sciences conditions rarely, if ever, exist for a revolution in the way Kuhn describes. Here paradigm changes are more likely to result from changes in socio-political forces and their concomitant world views than through any logic of scientific discovery. Unlike natural scientists, social scientists seldom come up against reality's hard-edged recalcitrances. With rare exceptions – like The Great Depression – the links between the social scientist's paradigmatic beliefs and the intransitive world around him or her are both conceptually tenuous and unconnected to the possibility of objective tests. Consequently, difficulties thrown up by external reality can – when the paradigmatic (that is anti-pluralist) ethos prevails – be brushed aside or charmed away by rhetorical and formalistic devices or – better yet – by wilful disregard for all phenomena inconsistent with one's beliefs.

For these reasons, Kuhn's narrative becomes, in the hands of economists, a formula for supporting an eternal *status quo*, for the cessation of all significant change. It excuses exclusionary devices in defense of the dominant paradigm community, and it subordinates the advancement of economic knowledge to the upholding of a system of belief tied to a vast network of patronage.

Kuhn's narrative, however, fails as a generally fair description of development in the natural sciences, which in general are not opposed to registering awareness of new ranges of phenomena. Bhaskar's narrative, as encapsulated in the paragraph quoted at the start, is a vastly superior account of scientific practice – superior both as a description of actuality and as an ideal. The competing theories narrative of scientific advance, in its various forms, builds its case primarily on the basis of examples drawn from physics. Yet even here it is easy to show, once one has escaped from the spell of Kuhn's intoxicating Cold War rhetoric, that the now traditional view both fails to account for and runs counter to major developments. This holds especially true for Kuhn's version, which turns on the notion of irreversible *gestalts*.

For several generations, fundamental research in physics has been focused primarily on "unification." Various schemes exist for characterizing "the unification process," but all describe a state of affairs incomprehensible in terms of the traditional competing theories, anti-pluralist narrative of scientific development. Stephen Hawking, for example, in *A Brief History of Time* (Hawking, 1988), explains the quest as follows (p. 13):

> Today scientists describe the universe in terms of two basic partial theories – the general theory of relativity and quantum mechanics. They are the great intellectual achievements of the first half of this century. . . . Unfortunately, however, these two theories are known to be inconsistent with each other – they cannot both be correct. One of the major endeavors in physics today . . . is the search for a new theory that will incorporate them both – a quantum theory of gravity.

Reading this passage through the lens of competing theories, as offered by Popper or Kuhn, invites total misunderstanding. Physicists perceive relativity and quantum mechanics not as competing theories championed by warring camps of physicists, but rather as different and complementary conceptual approaches to the fundamentals of physical reality. These two narratives illuminate separate ranges of phenomena in what unification physicists see as ultimately the same domain of inquiry, but which, until some more fundamental structure or generative mechanism is identified, cannot yet (if ever) be reconciled with each other. Rather than behaving paradigmatically, that is, ignoring the existence of micro-phenomena because they contradicted both relativity and classical theory, twentieth-century physics proceeded *pluralistically*. It got on with the difficult work of progressively identifying this range of phenomena and then constructing and testing new explanations. The physicists' dream of unification, with its implicitly deeper level of understanding than that of existing theory, arises directly out of physics' *pluralistic approach*. It allows for the peaceful coexistence of the two narratives, the heuristic significance of each being enhanced by the existence of the other. Physicists seek to discredit neither relativity nor quantum mechanics, but rather to create, in Hawking's words, "a new theory that will incorporate them both."

Hawking's view of twentieth-century physics also contradicts Kuhn's narrative in another way. The central plot device in Kuhn's story of paradigmatic, anti-pluralist science is his portrayal of natural scientists as *gestalt*-bound – that is, as capable of thinking only within single conceptual systems. He identifies this intel-lectual incapacity as a sort of negative force that necessitates taking an anti-pluralist approach to science, which then creates blockages to the advancement of knowledge, thereby creating pre-revolutionary states. But are scientists really so conceptually inept? Was John Stuart Mill really so wrong when he characterized the scientific imagination as the faculty for "mentally arranging known elements into new combinations" (Mill, 1893)? Are scientists really incapable of shifting back and forth between seeing the world in different combinations – between, if you like, seeing the duck and seeing the rabbit?

If natural scientists were as *gestalt*-bound as Kuhn repeatedly alleges, then twentieth-century physics could never have taken place. Shifting between narra-tives with radically different conceptual systems can be a daily occurrence for twentieth-century physicists. For them conceptual agility – that is, the ability to move freely between conceptual *gestalt*s – is imperative. Unlike theory replace-ment, unification of theories demands the ability to jump back and forth between conceptual systems. And even to become a physicist, one must learn to think within the conceptual frameworks of both relativity and quantum mechanics. All the rest of modern physics is derived from one or the other of these two theories, whose "basic concepts," notes the physicist David Bohm, "directly contradict each other" (Bohm, 1983). General relativity conceives of matter as particulate; of physical objects as having actual properties; of all physical reality as determinate; and all events as, in principle, having a causal explanation. Quantum theory, on the other hand, conceives of matter as a wave–particle duality; of physical objects as having only potential properties within the given physical situation; of the existence of indeterminacy; and of the existence of events incapable of causal explanation. Conceptual differences and theoretical inconsistencies greater than these are scarcely imaginable. Yet for nearly a century these two metaphysically dissimilar narratives have worked not in competition but in tandem to produce what are arguably the greatest advances in the history of science.

Unlike Kuhn's narrative, Bhaskar's three-phase schema of scientific development sits comfortably with this history. It also suggests a way of advancing radical reform of economics. Taking Bhaskar's view of science, the question becomes how, in economics, do you kick-start the dialectic, when in the main it has been stalled for decades, and when powerful institutional forces work to keep it from starting up again?

As previously indicated, my view is that the blockage of the first phase – the identifying of phenomena – has stalled economics. Here Bhaskar's verb "identifies" must be given a robust interpretation. Passive identification of economic phenomena not covered by existing theory is, for the reasons stated above, insufficient for getting economists to take them into account. To get from phase one to phase two – that is, from identification to construction of explanations – reformers must find a way through the defense mechanisms, mis-education and indifference with which, by tradition and Kuhnian anti-pluralist ideology, the profession encases itself. This, I believe, argues for two kinds of initiative, both directed at the identification of economic phenomena, but by different means.

First, economics will be resuscitated and made relevant to the urgent needs of the new century, only if roused from its ontological slumber. Wittgenstein characterized his kind of philosophy as "not a body of doctrine but an activity," whose "work consists essentially of elucidations" (Wittgenstein, 1974). Because economic ontology has been forbidden territory for so long, much elucidatory activity regarding economics' concepts and the nature of economic reality, as in the work of Lawson and Stretton, is now called for. Economists and students must be led to a practical awareness of the open nature of economic existence and of the importance of internal relations, and of how these dimensions of economic reality mean that the deductivism of traditionalist economics excludes the identification of most economic phenomena from within the context of explanation. The ontological preconceptions and methodological pieties of traditionalist economics both mask from view the larger part of economic events, and block inquiry into the structures that generate them.

In economics, the first stage of Bhaskar's schema has been trumped by devotion and obedience to an obscurantist metaphysics. The re-education of economists to attend to these exclusions and to the possibilities that they imply will, it is hoped, coax the discipline into engaging with a larger range of economic reality. Such elucidations not only create an intellectual space in which members of the post-autistic vanguard can operate, but also provide respectability and justification for traditionalists contemplating post-traditionalist, post-autistic pursuits. Such work provides ordinary economists with the conceptual means of articulating their misgivings and intuitions, and in general of liberating the repressed awareness of all those phenomena whose relevance the anti-pluralism of their elders denies.

These elucidations serve to identify economic phenomena in a broad ontological way. Through a form of applied philosophical analysis they explain why vast tracts of unexplored economic territory exist, and at the same time the reasons behind the notorious failure of traditionalist methods. But they identify the general nature and scope of socio-economic reality, rather than particular phenomena or ranges thereof.

So a second type of initiative for the identification of economic phenomena is also required. Compared to the first it is less glamorous, but it is at least as important. As a lure away from autistic economics, philosophical enlightenment is most likely insufficient for the rank-and-file economist. He or she must also be enticed with concrete possibilities for research. To this end, conceptual frameworks must be developed that bring into view ranges of economic phenomena that enter strategically into economic outcomes, but that are unrecognized by traditionalist conceptualization. That a surfeit of such possibilities exist is self-evident to the post-autistic economist. That their successful realization – the development of effective understandings of the these phenomenal realms – is now crucial to human welfare is, outside the economics community, accepted fact.

References

Bhaskar, R. (1979) *The Possibility of Naturalism*. Hemel Hempstead: Harvester Press.

Bohm, D. (1983) *Wholeness and the Implicate Order*. London: Routledge.

Hawking, S. (1988) *A Brief History of Time*. London: Bantam Press.

Kuhn, T.S. (1962) *The Structure of Scientific Revolutions*. Chicago: University of Chicago Press.

Mill, J.S. (1893) *A System of Logic: Ratiocinative and Inductive*. London: Longmans, Green and Co.

Popper, K.R. (1959) *The Logic of Scientific Discovery*. London: Hutchinson.

Solow, R. (2001) L'économie entre empirisme et mathématisation, *Le Monde*, 2 janvier.

Wittgenstein, L. (1974) *Tractatus Logico-Philosophicus*. London: Routledge.

Books of oomph

Deirdre McCloskey (University of Illinois at Chicago and Erasmusuniversiteit, Rotterdam)

I think the best way for you to grasp what upsets me so much about modern economics is for you to read a little bit in other fields of the intellect. After looking into scientific history or paleoanthropology or literary criticism or Latin literature or astrophysics, I'll bet you'll join me in being upset about the scientific deadend that economics has wandered into. *Seriously*, stomach-wrenchingly upset. You and I can go together to the gastroenterologist and get some pills.

The first indigestion-producing book I read last year was Jered Diamond's *Guns, Germs and Steel: A Short History of Everybody for the Last 13,000 Years* (W.W. Norton). Diamond is, of all things, *not* qualifying one to write the economic history of the world since the last Ice Age, a professor of physiology at a medical school. He's an evolutionary biologist, trained as (of all things) a botanist. The economic historian Joel Mokyr told me that he approached Diamond's book on page 1 the same way I did: "Who's this fool? He's claiming to talk about economic history. *I'm* the expert in economic history around here." Joel says that by page 50 he was converted. It took me only 20 pages, which just shows that Joel has higher intellectual standards than I do.

Diamond argues that the reason Europe ended up so powerful is that it was the inheritor of a biological accident – that plant and animal species, only a small percentage of which prove suitable for domestication, are especially numerous in the great East–West swath of land from China to Spain. And that's why the middle of the swath – Mesopotamia – was the first to get socially organized in a big way. The North–South places, such as Africa and America, were broken up by ecological barriers to spread of cows, wheat, that sort of thing – the Isthmus of Panama, for example, and anyway the barrier arising from varied growing conditions by latitude.

Interesting. But my point here is that in making his arguments Diamond does science. He doesn't do what economists, without acquaintance with any alleged science but their own, persist in imagining is science. Diamond is not big on phony, existence-theorem mathematics or phony, significance-testing statistics. (The temptation to be so must be considerable, since the neighboring field of population biology, like economics, is in love with the cargo-cult techniques perfected after the Second World War, axiomatic and significance-test game playing: autistic economics.) He is big on quantitative arguments based on factual matter, arguments that have "oomph."

For example, in arguing the case for New Guinea as a test of how important food production is in causing societies to flourish he uses new linguistic evidence on the origins of Micronesian and Polynesian languages, such as their crop vocabularies. The philosopher of history, R.G. Collingwood, himself a historian of Roman Britain, once defined "scientific" history (by contrast with "scissors-and-paste" history) as studying problems, not periods, asking questions *about the world* and *seeing one's way to answering them*. He notes that a scientist is neither a theorist–philosopher speculating about whether an endogenous-growth model has equilibrium solutions under assumptions x, y, or z, nor a scissors-and-paste econometrician rummaging in bad data for significant coefficients. She is, on the contrary, a maker of testable arguments about real worlds, like a detective.

Diamond does science, I say. He's a detective. At a session of the Economic History Association last year in Los Angeles I heard him talk about his book. After Diamond spoke, our own Jeff Sachs gave a similar presentation of his new ideas about geography and underdevelopment. Sachs, like Diamond, is a detective, a scientist. So can we all be, if we'll stop spending our valuable time on the non-scientific talk about things "existing." (So I commend the French students in open revolution against Cartesian–Samuelsonian–Arrovian economics; *Aux barricades!*)

Or take a professor of English, Jane Tompkins, in her elegant book on the genre of the Western in American literature, *West of Everything* (Oxford University Press, 1993). What? An *English* professor? Surely *they* (or I should say "we") aren't "scientists"! Well, Tompkins is. She's a Collingwoodian detective. She asks a question about the world and sees her way to answering it. Why is it, she asks, that the Western was invented rather suddenly by Owen Wister in 1902 (*The Virginian*), became immensely popular in novels read mainly by men (Zane Grey), and then popular with everybody in the movies (my multilinguistic Dutch friends find the dubbing of John Wayne just hilarious in the German TV stations)?

And then why rather suddenly in the 1970s did it die? Why are women characters so clueless in Westerns? Why is talking so devalued? Why are horses and cattle ubiquitous, but so strangely neglected (considering that the business of these lads was supposed to be animal husbandry)? Indians, too (considering that their other business was supposed to be killing them)? And then for the answer she marshals the detective's case (the hardboiled detective story, by the way, has a similar history). The Western (and detective story), she argues, and shows, and illustrates, and tests beyond reasonable doubt, was a reaction to the feminization of American culture in the nineteenth century. The anxiety about Women Stuff (religion, for example) that her father's and grandfather's generation (I should say *our* fathers' and grandfathers' generation) felt could be assuaged by basking in *High Noon*.

Observe that Diamond is "just" a botanist and Tompkins is "just" an English professor. Not physicists. Not mathematicians. Not a significance test in hundreds and hundreds of well-written pages (not that physicists use those: my students and I have shown by examining the magazine *Science* that it is only economists and population biologists and medical scientists who misuse statistical significance). Not a theorem in sight (not that the physicists care about theorems). Yet both Diamond and Tompkins are really serious about knowing things *about the world*. So the issue is not "science vs the humanities" or some other British simpleton's philosophy of knowledge; what we seek is *science* in the usual French sense: "inquiry."

Get with it, oh my beloved fellow economists. Read, and get that queasy feeling in the pit of your stomach. Read the linguist Merritt Ruhlen's *The Origin of Language* (John Wiley and Sons, 1996). Read the literary critic Stanley Fish's *Surprised by Sin* (Harvard University Press, 1998). Read, and compare what these scientists do in discussing language families and Milton's epic poems with the pseudo-science that makes nonsense of even the best articles in our splendid field. And if your stomach really comes to bothers you, get Howard Spiro's great book, *Clinical Gastroenterology* (Macmillan, 1993), beautifully written (about bowels), steadily quantitative (about ulcers), a detective's guide to gut science.

Back to reality

Tony Lawson (Cambridge University, UK)

In recent months a number of French students, joined by some of their lecturers, have initiated a debate on the state of modern economics. The debate turns on the question of which research methods are appropriate for the investigation of economic reality. As so often in the past, a French debate has provoked an international response. Because of the importance of this debate to the future of economics, it is essential to be clear about what is at issue, especially in these pages where the debate began.

Simply put, the message from the students is that there is insufficient pluralism in the modern economics faculty. In particular, there is a widespread insistence on the use of just one set of methods: those of mathematical modeling.

A standard response to this observation, one that is also found in recent pages of *Le Monde*, and the one I would like to address here, is that this emphasis is unavoidable just because economics needs to be scientific, where being scientific necessitates the use of mathematics. When stated as starkly as this I think it will be seen that the response is inadequate. Most clearly it begs the question as to why economics needs to be scientific, but actually its central deficiency is to presume unquestioningly that a science necessarily uses mathematics. Such a presumption is false. What is more, a little reflection on the nature of natural science suggests that there is every reason to suppose that even an economics almost devoid of mathematics can yet be scientific in the sense of natural science. Thus the heading in *Le Monde* of 31 October 2000, "Les mathématiques, condition nécessaire mais pas suffisante aux sciences économiques," is actually quite wrong. Let me briefly elaborate.

I take it we all agree with the French students that illuminating social reality is the primary objective. Certainly I find few, if any, commentators rejecting this goal explicitly. The point here is that mathematical methods of the sort used by economists are (as with any methods) useful to the task of illuminating reality only under certain conditions. Specifically, the usefulness of the sorts of mathematical procedures in question is restricted to systems in which event regularities (deterministic or probabilistic) occur. Thus for those who suppose that science means using mathematics, the assertion that economics can and ought to be scientific is in effect a claim that event regularities prevail in the social realm.

Maurice Allais, one of France's great economists, formulated this claim explicitly when he wrote (Allais, 1992):

> The essential condition of any science is the existence of regularities which can be analyzed and forecast. This is the case in celestial mechanics. But it is also true of many economic phenomena. Indeed, their thorough analysis displays the existence of regularities which are just as striking as those found in the physical sciences. This is why economics is a science, and why this science rests on the same general principles and methods of physics.

However, Allais is actually quite wrong in both aspects of his claim. Econometricians repeatedly find that their supposed correlations are no sooner reported than they are found to break down; social event regularities of the requisite sort are hard to come by. And, more to the point, it is just not the case that event regularities are essential to science. Let me defend this claim.

Actually, although the successes of natural science are widespread, event regularities of the requisite sort are rather rare even in the natural realm; outside celestial mechanics they are mostly restricted to situations of well-controlled experiment. Furthermore, most of the results of well-controlled experiments are successfully applied outside the controlled experiment, where event regularities are not at all in evidence.

We can make sense of these observations only by realizing that the aim of the controlled experiment, and of science more generally, is not the production of an event regularity *per se*, but the identification of an underlying mechanism that can account for it. Gravitational forces may give rise to an event regularity in an experimental vacuum, but gravitational forces continue to act on autumn leaves wherever the latter may fly, and help us to send rockets to the moon.

It is an understanding of the mechanism, not the production, of an event regularity that is the essential goal here. The controlled experiment constitutes a human intervention aimed not at producing an event regularity for its own sake, but at empirically identifying (or testing a theory about) an underlying mechanism.

Medical researchers are not interested in correlating the temperature of a patient with the intensity or location of spots on the patient's body, but with identifying (and counteracting) the virus or cause behind the symptoms.

In short, *if* there is a unifying feature of (pure) science, it is the search for causes behind phenomena regarded as of interest. If there is an essential component common to all successful science, it is this movement from phenomena at one level to their explanation in terms of causes lying at a deeper one. Mathematics is useful in the few (typically experimental) cases where surface phenomena are correlated, but science goes about its work of uncovering causes even where correlations in surface phenomena are not to be found.

So science is quite feasible in economics. It entails identifying the causes of phenomena of concern – say of high levels of unemployment or poverty. If mathematical methods are useful to this process, then so much the better. The central point, though, is to recognize that, whether or not they are useful, mathematical modeling methods are not necessary for any research process to qualify as being scientific in the sense of natural science. My Cambridge colleague, Professor Amartya Sen was correct when recently in *Le Monde* (31 October 2000) he observed that mathematics is not a unique foundation of economic science. *In fact it is not a foundation of economics-as-science at all.*

Actually, it is my own view that we can go further than this. We have good reason to suppose that the scope of relevance of mathematics is very limited indeed in the social realm. For example, it can be demonstrated that not only the poor success rate of modern economics, but also the phenomenon of modern economists repeatedly making assumptions known to be wildly false, are due to mathematical methods being employed where they do not fit. These are amongst the assessments I defend at length in *Economics and Reality* (Lawson, 1997). But they are not essential to the points being made by the French students, and I put them aside here. The students' "complaint" is only that, in modern academic economics departments, mathematical modeling is pursued for its own sake. They argue, and I agree, that we should start with (or at least not neglect insights concerning) the nature of reality. The point is not to reject mathematical methods a priori, but to use such methods as and when appropriate.

One final point. I have set out a conception of science that some will contest. It is possible indeed that it will prove inadequate, or time may show that my pessimism about the relevance of mathematical modeling for economics is unfounded. All knowledge is fallible, after all. But to recognize that any argument or claim can turn out to be wrong is to acknowledge, at the same time, a need for a non-dogmatic, indeed more pluralistic, approach in the academy.

This, of course, is just the first and most fundamental point of those of us who are unhappy with the state of modern economics. The objective is not to replace one dogma by another. Certainly it is not an a priori rejection of the use of mathematics in economics. Even less is it a rejection of the possibility of economics as science. And nor is anyone suggesting an abandonment of standards of rigor in the return to relevance. Rather, the goal is simply to open up the economics academy to a more intellectual orientation, allowing, in particular, the combining of high standards of research with a return to variety and greater (albeit critically informed) pluralism in method.

[Excerpts from this essay appeared in *Le Monde*, 21 March 2001.]

References

Allais, M. (1992) "The economic science of today and global disequilibrium." In: Baldassarri, M. et al. (eds), Global Disequilibrium in the World Economy, Basingstoke: Macmillan.

Lawson, T. (1997) Economics and Reality. London: Routledge.

The relevance of controversies for practice as well as teaching

Sheila C. Dow (University of Stirling, UK)

One of the important PAE arguments put forward by Raveaud in the March 2001 *Newsletter* ("Teaching economics through controversies") is that economics should be taught in terms of controversies instead of as an agreed body of thought. In effect this means teaching the dynamic development of ideas over time, i.e. an historical approach, since controversies involve sequential developments. If theory is context-dependent then we can learn much, not only from controversies among contemporaries in different contexts, but also from controversies between economists working within different contexts in history. Controversies reveal a range of possible ways of theorizing about the economy, drawing out the different understandings of the subject matter, the different meanings attached to the same terms and the different methodologies employed. By getting a sense of the range of possibilities, students can develop the capacity for judgment necessary for deciding how best to develop theory to address future contexts.

But what is the role of controversy for the practising economist? It is perhaps helpful to think of controversy in terms of Kuhn's paradigm framework. Each paradigm is pursued by a community of economists who share foundations, in terms of understanding of reality, meaning of terms, methodological approach, and so on. There is considerable scope for controversy between paradigms in that each will approach similar problems quite differently. There is also much scope for talking at cross-purposes, since the nature of the problem may be understood quite differently, similar methods may be part of very different methodologies, and similar terms may have very different meanings. In other words, paradigms are incommensurate; there is no neutral ground on which to stand. Kuhn made much of agreed methods within the paradigm. The significant controversies are the province of extraordinary science, which puts the focus on the foundations of paradigms.

If most economists are likely to engage in normal science, then what is the relevance of controversies that refer to fundamentals? First, the Kuhnian framework is helpful for putting the focus on the scope for incommensurability between paradigms, but requires careful consideration when applied to a discipline like economics where there are coexisting paradigms. Kuhn's framework originally referred to the physical sciences, in terms of succeeding paradigms. In economics the paradigms have never been mutually exclusive; it has simply been helpful to think in terms of the clear differences between "representative members" of different paradigms. Increasingly there are efforts to promote synthesis, particularly between heterodox paradigms, thus blurring the distinctions. Synthesis of course means the emergence of new paradigms, but the picture of what will emerge is not yet clear. Within orthodox economics there have also been developments that call attention to fundamentals; but here the developments are more ones of fragmentation than synthesis.

In the current state of flux in economics, therefore, extraordinary science comes to the fore. In order to make sense of these processes of synthesis and fragmentation, it is important to be aware of the foundations of new theory developments. Indeed, it could be argued that those developments in economic theory that have proved pivotal have arisen at the margins of paradigms, within extraordinary science. New developments in thought can always be traced back to some extent to previous history of thought (within some paradigm), but at the same time require new connections to be made and new meanings to be employed. A prerequisite for such a development is exposure to different possible approaches. This is an argument for methodological awareness, which can be most effectively acquired through engagement with controversies past and present. Without such awareness, which promotes alertness to differences in understanding, methodology and meaning, the different protagonists in controversies will be misunderstood and opportunities for new connections lost. As James Galbraith points out in his contribution to the January 2001 *Newsletter*, there is a notable lack of awareness within orthodox economics of the challenges it faces.

The argument for methodological awareness as a prerequisite for engagement has most force in periods, such as the present, when economics is in a particular state of flux. But what about more stable periods? Methodological awareness can be promoted by study of past controversies. However, there is a second case for methodological awareness that is different in that it rests more heavily on the benefits of tolerance. Tolerance means allowing a range of approaches to develop to maturity, so that when new challenges arise there is a diversity from which ideas may be selected (just as in biology diversity is important for adaptation and survival). When a discipline is stable, there is a danger of thinking of the dominant paradigm as being not just preferred by the majority, but as being preferable in some absolute, extra-paradigmatic, sense. Such a state of affairs can breed intolerance to any other paradigm. Not only does this limit the scope of the dominant paradigm, but it also encourages institutionalized constraints on alternative paradigms. There is further an asymmetry in that paradigms that adopt a methodology unified around mathematical formalism applied to a shared set of axioms (as in orthodox economics) are more likely to have a closed-system theory of knowledge than paradigms that embrace some form of pluralism. However, without some prior knowledge of pluralism it is hard to see how the judgment in favor of a monist (i.e. anti-pluralist) methodology can be justified. It is a matter of choice as to the methodology we employ in order to understand a complex reality. No one methodology can reasonably claim any absolute superiority, yet choices have to be made for policy issues to be addressed. No one approach can be justified relative to the others without an informed comparison.

We have come back full circle to the value of a pluralist education in economics.

Revolt in political science

Kurt Jacobsen (University of Chicago, USA)

The following article describes an important off-shoot of the PAE movement in the USA. There are tactical lessons to be learnt from its quick success. Various documents relating to these events, including a long article from the New York Times, *have been posted on* www.paecon.net *On the home page, click on* **The Perestroika Movement***.*

In the USA the post-autistic economics movement has reverberated most power-fully in political science departments. There, as in economics, it increasingly is the pure elegance and artificial neatness of models, not their relation to real world activities, that reap the greatest rewards. Every other kind of scholar – and there still are many kinds – has gotten the disturbingly clear message that there is one right way and they need not apply. There was ample tinder for a spark to ignite.

One might imagine that the American Political Science Association (APSA) preaches that the best governing system, despite all its faults, is a democratic one, but APSA luminaries obviously display grave doubts as to how far democracy ought to be allowed to go. From inception, the Association never entertained the wildly radical notion of conducting internal elections. What rules is a cozy arrangement whereby a committee chosen by the president nominates its succes-sor members, who pick the next governing council, who pick the next president, and so on. Disgruntled political scientists link the absence of democracy in the organization to the suffocating disciplinary dominance, especially in the last decade, of formal models and rational choice theory.

Rational choice theory derives from neoclassical economics, which (ambitious political scientists cannot help but notice) grabs lots of Nobel Prizes. The theory deploys a set of assumptions about behavior that boil down complicated lives and societies to prioritized "rational" choices in any given situation. In short, political science is sanctifying a chalkboard universe inhabited by "*homo economicus*," which, in the name of utility maximization, tries to erase all trace of culture, history, personality or any quirky quality that might smudge the one-size-fits-all model. Rational choice undeniably has its merits when used with a bit of humility, especially in studies of collective action. For many scholars, however, it also dangles the tantalizing appearance of a skeleton key to open everything, although ensuing explanations, critics find, are usually trivial, obvious, or require psychiatric treatment to restore contact with recognizable reality.

Rational choice modelers quickly became notorious in political science for forming potent self-promoting coteries, partly because they wield a common catechism. The APSA of late has been run by rational choice exponents or sympathizers, and its flagship journal, *The American Political Science Review*, reflects their unbending bent. David Pion-Berlin and Dan Cleary report that over 1991–2000, the *Review* offered 225 articles using statistical methods, 88 articles featuring mathematical models, and only 5 pieces of qualitative work. Only counting evidently "counts," inasmuch as mathematics conveys a glittery and illusory sense of precision. Dissidents complain that rational choice modelers cannot admit that equations are metaphors just as much as any literary image deployed by a supposedly "soft" social scientist. Giandomenico Majone, a mathematically trained political scientist who lectures in the USA and Europe, suggests the problem lies less with formal models than the excesses of undereducated enthusiasts: "You should know more than the tool you use." Indeed.

It is dismayingly common for modelers to take a framework derived from a Western context and apply it elsewhere with remarkably little care. In an egregious example, a graduate student in the *perestroika* web discussion site recalled a faculty modeler who incorporated India into his rational choice analysis without any knowledge of its complex history or culture. "Isn't Delhi the national language of India?," the undaunted chap asked. Another (and more typical) example I examined is a recent paper by a pair of academics who impose their homogenizing conflict framework upon Northern Ireland where, among other howlers, they assert that the Irish Republic can pressure the good Reverend Ian Paisley to join the peace process, if only it tries. One searched in vain for any hint that they knew or cared what was going on "on the ground." Everything looks like easy prey if you've never tried to capture it – or just want to look as if you have.

The political science revolt erupted in November 2000 with a mass emailing by "Mr. Perestroika" – probably a junior faculty member or members aware of French events – who excoriated "poor game-theorists who cannot for the life of me compete with a third-grade economics student" yet crush the "diversity of methodologies and areas of the world that APSA 'purports' to represent." (Perestroika, according to its – ahem – original sponsors, promoted the "vital creativity" of society's members; development of democracy; "initiative and independence," and "the widening of criticism and self-criticism in all spheres of social life.") In a single month a two-tiered movement of insurgents crystallized, divided between those who could and those who could not afford to reveal their identities. It speaks volumes that young scholars fear to reveal their identities in a profession that purports to prize vigorous and open exchange. By January, 222 senior faculty, including 24 named chairs, signed a reform petition, drafted by Professor Rogers Smith. "It is about getting pluralism back into political science," said Susanne Hoeber Rudolph, Distinguished Service Professor at Chicago University. "Why does the [Association and the Journal] seem so intensely focused on technical methods at the expense of the great substantive political questions?"

In a response that fanned the flames, APSR editor Ada Finifter asserted that all was well so long as scholars provided "high-quality work using methods appropriate to the research problem." Finifter categorized work outside formal methods as "interpretive" – clearly second-class citizens. Perestroikan Greg Kasza of Indiana University beheld the peculiar logic: "One scholar works inductively from diverse sources of empirical data to develop a qualified middle theory of how some aspect of politics has worked in particular conditions. His work is interpretive." Another posits assumptions about human behavior observed nowhere, and deduces from them a grand scheme of theoretical axioms. She is providing us with "systematic and reliable knowledge." About what? If the former is "interpretive," might we call the latter "imaginary." APSR editor Finifter was succeeded by Lee Seligman in 2001, who promised to heed many perestroikan complaints. The first two issues of APSR under Seligman's watch displayed no change in content, but perestroikans point out that Seligman inherited a large backlog of articles.

APSA Council member James Scott of Yale University vowed in 2001 to push the perestroika platform. A conciliatory APSA Council soon selected a perestroika-backed candidate as President for 2002–2003, Harvard's Theda Skocpol. "A discipline that is 'methodologically dexterous' is bound to advance more effectively," said Skocpol, "than one becoming overly specialized in narrow or fixed techniques." In a 2002 New Year message to the *perestroika* web discussion site, Skocpol invited nominations so as to "put together a pluralistic slate of about 100 nominees for service on dozens of APSA standing committees, including awards, publications, and nominations committees, service committees, and committees concerned with the representation of minorities." Later, however, Skocpol, perhaps displaying what she took to be presidential impartiality, chided *perestroika* as being an unrepresentative force that ought to come out in the open as a formal grouping.

Still, a sign that reform was rolling ahead was the selection last February of Chicago's Susanne Rudolph as President for 2003–2004. Dissidents hope Skocpol and Rudolph will help carry out, as Mr. Perestroika put it, a "dismantling of the Orwellian system that we have in the APSA." (APSA deputy director Robert Hauck, presumably a student of the way power really works, expressed surprise that anyone needed to shield themselves in a profession where an appointment can be killed by the right word in the right ear.) Rudolph heartily agrees that diversity of methods must be encouraged, and favors "the transparent and competitive election of officers and the council by means that are compatible with demographic and institutional minority representation." Several electoral proposals are kicking around, including a proposal by an *ad hoc* perestroikan committee. In Spring 2002 the APSA's official committee, headed by Gary Jacobsen of the University of California at San Diego, rejected elections, but the APSA council was careful to "receive" the latter's report only as a discussion document, which perestroikans regarded as a minor victory. Perestroikans are also looking into National Science Foundation and Social Science Research Council funding practises, which, to the degree they are in the hands of opponents, back the increasing quantitative hegemony. There is attention trained as well on the permanent, non-elected, bureaucracy of the APSA, which, as perestroikan Ido Oren finds, has an interesting history of links to the national security establishment.

Perestroikans surely agree that the scholarly objective is "high-quality work using methods appropriate to the research problem," but echo the PAE movement in arguing that "the problem dictates the method," and not vice versa. Perestroikans certainly aim to improve democracy outside their profession too. These increasingly otherworldly methods "in the social sciences make it difficult to communicate with and make our work relevant to the wider public," argues Chicago University politics professor Lloyd Rudolph. "We have to know and live with differences within our profession as well as in the world."

Ironically, however, when the September 11 attacks occurred a heated debate erupted which was quickly herded onto other websites. Many perestroikans are (perhaps wisely) shy of provoking underlying splits within their mélange of methodological approaches and political leanings. By contrast, Chris Howell of Oberlin believes that over-reliance on quantitative methods is only a symptom and that the "real goal is a critical and engaged political science that does not readily conform to what the powers that be want of it." Tim Luke of Vermont notes the familiar disturbing pattern that "formally inclined rational choicers look down on others as story tellers and journalists." No epithets are more damning. (One political science department in North Carolina contemptuously discarded a young academic over a decade ago as a mere journalist – just months before he was awarded a Pulitzer Prize for a biography.)

Mr. Perestroika summarizes the debate in mid-2002 about the nature and organizational form of the insurgency as opting to retain "the amorphous character of this movement and list group. However, we will form working groups in Democracy, publishing, future initiatives to broaden intellectual base. In the same vein, *perestroika* as it stands needs to make a real effort to draw in people of color and other oft-marginalized communities if it is to make any valid claims to representativeness." Skocpol, and especially Rudolph, were strongly supported by minority caucuses within the APSA. Yale University Press recently commissioned a book of essays on the *perestroika* phenomenon. Meanwhile, there is always a danger of rifts among a delicately constructed coalition who are up against cohesive opponents. And there is room for a sobering bit of modesty all around too. "I rarely encounter any political scientist," said University of Pennsylvannia Professor Rogers Smith in an online chat, "who is 100 percent versatile in all the methods that are employed within political science." What methodological pluralist would say otherwise?

Beyond criticism

Paul Ormerod (Volterra Consulting, UK)

I welcome very much the debate initiated by the PAE community about how economics is taught and to what extent mathematics is appropriate to the discipline. I sympathize with many of the aims. Overall, I stand very firmly by the criticisms which I made of conventional economics in the *Death of Economics* (Faber and Faber) in 1994. Economics needs a awful lot of special assumptions to apply before it is able to give a good description of how the world operates.

Too often, economics loses sight of the fact that formal modeling skills are not the only thing that matters in the social sciences. Awareness of the social and institutional setting in which a problem is being analyzed is often essential, as is a knowledge of economic history. Social science is *harder* to do successfully than are the natural sciences. The idea that people respond to incentives – to prices – is as close to a universal law as we have got, but the strength of the response to a given set of incentives is emphatically not universal. It varies with the social and institutional setting, and with the historical context.

We must abandon the wholly unrealistic claim of mainstream economics to have discovered a general rule of agent behavior – namely maximizing behavior – which applies in all circumstances. We know the enormous amount of evidence from the cognitive sciences about the limited ability of agents to process information, which undermines the concept of maximization except in very special circumstances. The appropriate rules of agent behavior will be shaped by the institutional setting in which agents operate.

But the excellent debate on economics which has been started is weak on a key issue. The principal strength of economics is that it trains people to think analytically. There is great value in this, and we must now move beyond criticism. The more effective and widespread the criticisms are, the greater the responsibility on critics of orthodoxy to produce better accounts of how the world operates. So far, it is only a distinct minority of critics of mainstream economics who appreciate that there is a responsibility to provide not just criticism but also better analysis. As Alan Kirman, a highly innovative economist based in Marseilles, has remarked: "In the long list of those who have signed the petition, there seem to be very few who are actually making an attempt to model the economy."

My own work over the past few years has been concerned with trying to use the new approaches of complexity theory to produce models that are more general than those of orthodoxy, that need fewer assumptions to be valid in order to understand the world better than existing models. I must stress that I am not being in any way prescriptive. Other approaches may prove to work as well or even better, but unless we make the effort, the mainstream will simply ignore us.

To repeat again, to avoid misunderstanding, I am not saying that formal models are the only thing that matters. The world is a very complicated place, but an important way in which we can make sense of it is by using models that are simplifications, often drastically so, of reality. The advantage that those of us in the critical community have over many in the mainstream is that we are constantly aware of the fact that these *are* simplifications. Far too many economists have been socialized into believing that rational maximization is the only conceivable way in which agents can operate.

It seems to me that the most restrictive assumptions of orthodoxy – restrictive in that it severely limits its capacity to illuminate many real world problems – is the assumption that the tastes and preferences of agents are fixed. Individuals and firms in standard economic theory can process huge amounts of information in exceptionally complicated ways, but the one thing they are not allowed to do is to alter their behavior in the light of what others are doing. They respond to the decisions of others only in so far as these affect the prices of the goods and services that the individual buys and/or sells. They do not want a Teletubbie, say, or a hula hoop or, much more seriously, a 30-year US government bond rather than a French one, simply because other people do. But in the real world this sort of behavior is pervasive. From fashion markets to financial markets to the degree of optimism or pessimism that firms feel about the future, the opinions and behavior of others affects directly how individuals behave.

These are examples of what I believe will be the future of theoretical analysis in economics. Other examples that I give in *Butterfly Economics* (Faber and Faber) include the choice of restaurants, the success and failure of Hollywood films, the evolution of crime, how family structures change, and the American business cycle. We are now in the position of being able to create micro foundations of macro-phenomena, computer-based models in which individual agents following rules of behavior interact with each other. And the macro-properties of the system emerge from these interactions.

Orthodox economics claims to be able to do this already. Indeed, it *can*, but only under very special circumstances. Conventional theory permits the behavior of others to alter the behavior of any given individual only *indirectly* via the price mechanism. Agents may convey information to others, but this does not alter their tastes and preferences. This assumption is essential to the mathematics of conventional theory, which remains rooted firmly in the nineteenth century. It enables the behavior of the system as a whole to be characterized by the "representative agent," and enables macro-properties to be derived from individual behavior – the so-called "micro-foundations of macro," the Holy Grail of conventional theory.

This has been a powerful stick with which to beat dissidents, from the lowly post-graduate student right up to Keynes himself – after all, where *were* the micro-foundations of his so-called General Theory? But now I believe the wheel has turned full circle.

Relaxing the assumption of fixed preferences opens up the possibility of a much better understanding of how the world operates. Conventional theory can be thought of merely as a special case of this far more general approach: it has its greatest validity in circumstances in which fixed preferences offer a reasonable approximation to reality, like the shopper in the supermarket.

Until recently, it has not been possible to relax this central assumption. The growing ability to begin to understand systems in which agents can alter each other's behavior directly is, in my view, by far the most important methodological development in economics for many years. It will eventually change completely the way in which economics is done.

Methodologically, this approach enables a more scientific testing of theories. The key properties at the aggregate level of the system being examined are identified. Time-series econometrics consists of no more than curve-fitting around such properties. In this approach, individual agents are given behavioral rules. The properties of the system as a whole *emerge* from the interaction of these rules. The macro-properties that emerge from micro-behavioral rules can then be compared with the actual macro-properties.

So I find this very exciting. Here is a development that enables orthodox economics to be undermined on its own terms. Yes, conventional economics does have micro-foundations of macro-behavior, but these are only applicable in special circumstances, and the claim of orthodoxy to generality, to general rules, collapses.

The approach also calls for very careful consideration of the framework in which the model is set up – the institutional setting. In trying to understand the possibilities for the exchange rate, for example, a world of free capital movements implies a different set of behavioral rules for the micro-level agents than a world in which capital is controlled.

It is not so much that orthodoxy is dead or useless; it's more a case of keeping the whole construct in a box to bring out on the occasions when it is relevant. In the twenty-first century, economics really can be re-born and give us a much better understanding of the world.

How did economics get into such a state?

Geoffrey M. Hodgson (University of Hertfordshire, UK)

I greatly applaud the recent initiatives of the movement for a post-autistic economics in France and the petition for reform from economics graduate students at the University of Cambridge. They are two great rays of hope in an otherwise largely disturbing intellectual scene. It is to be hoped that these initiatives can help to reverse the narrowing and over-formalization of economics that proceeded apace in the second half of the twentieth century.

In 1903, Alfred Marshall established one of the first economics degrees in Britain at the University of Cambridge. It had a much broader curriculum than is typical in the year 2001. If he were still alive, would Marshall get a job at the University of Cambridge or any other leading Department of Economics in the world today? Probably not. First, there is very little mathematics in Marshall's writings, and he saw mathematics as no more than an auxiliary tool.

In his letters, Marshall explained that he had "little respect for pure theory." He declared: "Much of 'pure theory' seems to me to be elegant toying." Along very similar lines, Marshall wrote to Francis Edgeworth in 1902: "In my view 'Theory' is essential. . . . But I conceive no more calamitous notion than that abstract, or general, or 'theoretical' economics was economics 'proper'" (Whitaker, 1996).

Sentiments like these would not help Marshall get a job in a top economics department today. Concerning pluralism and tolerance in economics, much has changed for the worst in the last 100 years. Economics today is much less concerned with the history of economics, the history of ideas, the study of real and relevant social institutions, and the detailed practicalities of policy formulation and implementation.

How has economics got in its present state? The ideological polarization of the Cold War period cannot on its own explain why economics took a wrong turning. To some extent it may explain why Western economics was increasingly dominated by pro-market ideology from 1948 to 1991, but it cannot explain the degree of narrowing and impoverishment of the standard economics curriculum in the last 50 years.

Several economists have suggested that the growing mathematicization of economics has been the key impetus behind the narrowing of economics since 1950. Formalization feeds on itself. It creates a peacock's tail process of positive reinforcement, in which all that matters is that which can be put in mathematics: all else is marginalized or rejected. The curriculum is thus narrowed. In time, the selection criteria of enticing and innovative formalization come to dominate the leading journals and the professorial appointment processes. In ratchet steps, the economics profession as a whole becomes progressively dominated by the formalists. And so it goes on, in a narrowing, accelerating, inescapable spiral.

The positive feedbacks involved with formalization do much to explain why economics got into the state that it is. But I do not think that this is the whole story. Formalization does not provide a complete explanation of the travails of the social sciences, especially when we glance outside economics.

Look at sociology. It is in deep trouble. Its central theoretical project of relating agency to social structure is in virtual chaos. Its discourse is frequently confounded by fashionable but deliberately obscure intellectual bandwagons that never should have been taken seriously. In addition, having abandoned former theoretical presuppositions, many sociologists are now embracing a version of utility maximizing "Economic Man" and proclaiming this as the "new sociology," whereas it has little to differentiate itself from Gary Becker-type neoclassical economics. Sociology is in such a mess that it no longer has any apparent ability to define its own identity.

I do not ignore the fact that some good work is being done within sociology and elsewhere; however, ironically, much of the best work in sociology in the last twenty years has addressed topics and phenomena that used to be under the purview of the economist.

In the case of sociology, in contrast to economics, formalization has not played a significant role in causing its recent distress. Considering the social sciences as a whole, something more than formalization has been at work. I am now of the opinion that something even more awesome and worrying is at work in modern academia. There are global forces in operation that threaten the intellectual integrity of all the academic disciplines, and the two leading social sciences have been an early casualty.

My tentative explanation of these global developments would rely on a theme that is central to the third part of my book *Economics and Utopia* (Hodgson, 1999): the scenario of growing complexity, knowledge intensity and specialization under capitalism. In the competitive process, capitalism creates ever more products, technologies and wants. Although deskilling exists in some sectors, modern capitalism also relies on an increasing variety of skilled specialists. The global workforce divides between the skilled professionals and the unskilled underclass. Under specific institutional conditions, the level of required skill among the skilled population is pulled upwards by the expanding frontiers of science and technology, and by the rising managerial burdens of growing social and organizational complexity.

Clearly, this scenario has several consequences for modern universities. First, the growing corporate demands for highly skilled labor have brought the needs and concerns of the corporate world into the center of the academic arena. The knowledge economy has expanded the hold of commercialization inside the bastions of knowledge. While a good dose of real worldliness in stuffy ivory towers can often do a power of good, it can also corrupt and undermine. The risk is that the universities will lose their aura of detached enquiry. The commercialization of learning and enquiry can threaten the ancient institutional function of universities as centers of relatively detached enquiry.

In the social sciences, a recent effect of this commercialization has been the relative decline of student recruitment into economics and sociology in favour of the business schools. Economics has reacted in an attempt to maintain its position and prestige, by reaching for its feathered head-dress of formalization. This accelerated a process of mathematicization that has its own independent institutional logic, as described above. Meanwhile, sociology as a whole has imploded in an orgy of self-doubt. Some have escaped the sociology departments to pursue (sometimes excellent) case studies of business organizations in business schools, but the theoretical core of sociology has become an abandoned battlefield.

This is only part of the story. The accelerating process of specialization and the growing volume of knowledge – as described in *Economics and Utopia* – have equally serious effects on academic life. The number of scientific journals and other publications has exploded. At the same time, science itself is subdividing endlessly into a growing number of subdisciplines. As a consequence, it is increasingly difficult to keep up to date in any subdiscipline, let alone in a whole subject. The crucial result is that wide-ranging critical reflection and interdisciplinary conversation are increasingly impaired. It is ever more difficult to take a more general view, and make an impact across the disciplines. Generalists of the orientation of Marx, Mill, Marshall, Durkheim, Pareto, Weber or Schumpeter would find it difficult to obtain a foothold in the modern university. Today, as the grand view is more difficult to obtain, the big questions fall out of favor. The disciplines narrow down on relatively minute technicalities. Sadly, the grand vista is lost.

I believe that the causes of the ills of economics are not confined to economics alone. Accordingly, its restoration to health will be all the more difficult. The modern university may require a Humboldtian reform similar to that which made the nineteenth-century German universities the envy of the world. A key feature of this academic revolution was that philosophy replaced religion at the apex of all enquiry; the pursuit of truth remained the purpose of the university, and all students were required to understand the philosophical problems of truth and explanation. The faculty of philosophy received full equality of status with the other faculties. We now take it for granted that every scientist should have some training in mathematics and statistics, but today an induction in philosophy is the exception rather than the rule.

Philosophy should take a similarly general and prestigious position, in both the natural and the social sciences. Philosophy is a skill that is transferable to multiple fields of inquiry, and hence it can enable communication between disciplines. It encourages a critical frame of mind and can help locate the big questions. Scientific development is facilitated by a common philosophical awareness of problems of truth, meaning, testing, modeling, explanation, prediction, unification and progress

In addition, I would suggest that every student scientist should have some training in the history of at least his or her own subject. There should be a widespread awareness of historical precedents for successful or failed innovation in science. The contemporary development of science can be guided and inspired by knowledge of its own history.

In sum, just as the requirement of mathematics is now virtually universal, so too should be some philosophy, and relevant parts of the history of ideas. All three should be part of the compulsory core curriculum of every science. I do not know how this second Humboldtian revolution can come about. Perhaps, at least in Paris and in Cambridge, it has already begun.

[Prof. Hodgson's latest book, *How Economics Forgot History: The Problem of Historical Specificity in Social Science*, has just been published by Routledge.]

References

Hodgson, G.M. (1999) *Economics and Utopia*. Routledge.

Whitaker, J.K. (ed.) (1996) *The Correspondence of Alfred Marshall*, vol. 2. Cambridge University Press, pp. 256, 280, 393.

An extraordinary discipline

Ben Fine (School of Oriental and African Studies, University of London, UK)

Whether in absolute terms or by comparison across the social sciences, economics is an extraordinary discipline by a number of criteria. First, it is astonishingly ignorant of its own history and traditions. As if to prove as well as to proclaim the point, long ago David Gordon (1965:123–126) argued that:

> [Adam] Smith's postulate of the maximizing individual in a relatively free market and the successful application of this postulate to a wide variety of specific questions is our basic paradigm. It created a "coherent scientific tradition" (most notably including Marx) and its persistence can be seen by skimming the most current periodicals ... I conclude that economic theory is much like a normal science and that, like a normal science, it finds no necessity for including its history as a part of professional training.

Matters have since only got worse.

Second, in part a corollary, the discipline is systemically – in appointments, journals, textbooks and teaching – intolerant of alternatives. They might just as well not exist.

Third, methodologically, ignorance and incoherence are endemic. Economics continues to rely, at least in principle, on axiomatic models tested by externally given data. Such a stance has long been abandoned by the natural sciences and sorely exposed by social scientists and others working on methodology. In addition, the "let us assume," *ceteris paribus*" forms of argument have long been notorious for their total lack of attachment to material reality.

Fourth, economics relies upon the optimizing individual, with the calculating mind of a machine and the base motives of a beast. It is not simply that no humanity is displayed as far as the individual is concerned but rather, on a deeper logical plane, the presumption is that the social can be derived from the individual and not vice versa.

Fifth, despite these glaring deficiencies, economics proclaims itself as the only true, rigorous and scientific social science. It contemptuously dismisses anything without formal models and/or statistical testing as unacceptable.

Sixth, whilst from outside economics can be seen to be built on an intellectual pack of cards — mainly jokers and no aces — its inner strength as a discipline has never been greater. Heterodoxy and self-doubt have been eliminated, and "Americanization" of the discipline reigns supreme.

Seventh, despite all these shortcomings, economics imperialism, or the colonization of the other social sciences by economics, is stronger than ever before. On the basis of the new information–theoretic economics, a whole new flush of fields have sprung up — the new institutional economics, the new political economy, the new development economics, the new economic geography, the new economic sociology, etc. Unlike the "old" economics imperialism, most notably associated with Gary Becker, for whom the world in all its aspects should be treated as far as possible as if it were a perfect market of costs and benefits even where a market is not in place to make valuations, the "new" economics imperialism treats the world as if it is riddled with market imperfections. In this way, the "social" is reintroduced into mainstream economics despite its dependence upon an extraordinarily narrow version of methodological individualism. History, economic and social structures, customs, culture and so on are all the rational path-dependent responses to market, especially informational, imperfections.

Taken together, these features of mainstream economics paint a depressing picture, not least as far as alternatives are concerned. However, locating them in a wider intellectual setting suggests otherwise. Currently, across the social sciences as a whole, there are two discernible trends. One, in which economics has participated to some extent, is the retreat from the extremes of neoliberalism. Academics peddle originality, and it is only so often and in so many ways that it is possible to repeat the mantra — "leave everything to the market." So now there is much more interest in how the economic and the non-economic, and the market and the non-market, interact with one another. Hence, the success to some degree of the new phase of the-world-as-if-market-imperfections economics imperialism.

The other broad trend across the social sciences, also a retreat from excess, and also uneven and faltering, is from the influence of postmodernism. The latter has been concerned with the meaning of objects, with identity and subjectivity. Necessarily economics has been unable to participate in the retreat because these were no-go areas for it in the first place, as both individuals and the material world were unproblematic as in the idea of given utility functions and factor inputs or objects of consumption. The other social sciences, however, are now increasingly concerned not only with how our world is understood but also with how it is created. Most notably this is revealed in the rapid rise to prominence of notions, however problematic, such as globalization and social capital (that have scarcely figured in economics).

The result is that the other social sciences are developing a strong interest in the economic. They do so in part from a position of ignorance, in part intimidated by the formalism and technical virtuosity – or the authority – of mainstream economics, and in part with a healthy skepticism with, and contempt for, its methods and theory in light of their own intellectual traditions. In short, there is a tension across the social sciences in its growing attention to the economic – should it be seduced by the unsubtle charms of a colonizing mainstream economics, or revitalize itself in the traditions of classical political economy?

The prospect is that there will be considerable debate over the economy in the coming period. However, it will not be within economics in the first instance, although there will be feedback effects. Rather, debate over the economy will take place across the other social sciences, in which economics imperialism will be a participant. The outcome remains open, and is likely to be uneven from discipline to discipline and from topic to topic. Teachers, students and researchers within and against the authority of mainstream economics must not only welcome these developments, but also promote and participate in them.

[The themes of Prof. Fine's article are explored in depth in his recently published *Social Capital versus Social Theory: Political Economy and Social Science at the Turn of the Millennium* (Routledge, 2001) and in his forthcoming *The World of Consumption: The Cultural and Material Revisited* (Routledge, 2002). Also see http://www.2.soas.ac.uk/Economics/econimp/econimp1.html for his work on economics imperialisms.]

Reference

Gordon, D. (1965) The role of the history of economic thought in the understanding of modern economic theory. *American Economic Review*, **55(2)**, 119–127.

What we learned in the twentieth century

Frank Ackerman (Global Development and Environment Institute, Tufts University, USA)

Is the traditional form of general equilibrium theory, and the neoclassical framework that supports it, still worth talking about? Or is the subject too old and outmoded to bother with? When confronted with criticisms of general equilibrium, many economists claim that the discipline has moved on. No one, it is said, still relies on the old Arrow–Debreu framework. Instead, *avant-garde* economists describe themselves as being involved in all manner of new, sophisticated theoretical analysis. The old, idealized, textbook model of competitive markets is said to be uninteresting, yesterday's news, no longer representative of the leading edge of theory.

As intriguing as this sounds when announced in seminars, it is hard to find published evidence that supports the hypothesis of brave new theorizing. Scanning recent issues of the top mainstream economics journals turns up very few examples of a new paradigm, or of sharp departure from traditional models. The great majority of articles still appear to be applications or minor extensions of standard theories, sometimes experimenting with relaxing one of the standard assumptions to see how much difference it makes.

Where, then, are these innovative new theoreticians hiding their work? One of the few high-profile statements of new theoretical approaches is a group of three articles in the November 2000 issue of *Quarterly Journal of Economics*. The *QJE* editors solicited essays on what we have learned about economics since the days of Alfred Marshall, paralleling Marshall's own retrospective essay on the economics of the nineteenth century. For the *QJE*, Olivier Blanchard (2000) reviewed the field of macroeconomics, while microeconomics is covered in one essay by Sam Bowles and Herb Gintis (2000), and another by Joseph Stiglitz (2000).

Blanchard's useful summary of trends in macro-theory describes an eclectic field, increasingly certain that market imperfections are among the causes of macroeconomic fluctuations, but divided on the questions of which imperfections to focus on, and how much they matter. Fortunately, the profession has lost interest in the strong form of rational expectations theories, a delusion of the

1980s in which business cycles result only from random shocks to a perfectly competitive economy. However, there is no obvious new synthesis or alternative theoretical framework emerging from the work surveyed by Blanchard.

Bowles and Gintis, and Stiglitz, present overlapping critiques of standard microeconomics, drawing heavily (though not exclusively) on their own work. For Bowles and Gintis, there are two crucial innovations in microeconomic theory: modeling of endogenous preferences, and of the incompleteness of contracts, both undermine Walrasian general equilibrium.

Neoclassical economics, as embodied in general equilibrium theory, assumes that individual preferences are formed outside the economic system (exogenously) and are not influenced by economic interactions. The unreality of this assumption is hardly news, having been the subject of eloquent and sweeping critiques by Thorstein Veblen at the beginning of the twentieth century, and by John Kenneth Galbraith at mid-century. What is new in the Bowles–Gintis account is a recent strand of literature in experimental economics and social psychology, amply confirming that social norms and memories of recent interactions influence individual choices even in the simplest, most contrived laboratory settings.

Yet there is a trade-off; in exchange for "scientific rigor" the new literature has apparently retreated from the broad political and social analysis of Veblen and Galbraith. For Veblen, conspicuous consumption was a cornerstone of an unequal, hierarchical, consumerist society. For Galbraith, the ability of advertisers to create consumer demand for their products was a key mechanism creating the problems of the "affluent society" of American capitalism. The new, experimental research on endogenous preferences and social norms has yet to achieve any such broader interpretation of its significance; it is at best a provocative body of data on which interesting theories could be based. To date, there is little evidence that the new endogenous preference literature is influencing economic theory as written by the majority of economists, let alone communicating with a wider audience.

The second point raised by Bowles and Gintis is that contracts are necessarily incomplete, giving rise to strategic interaction or principal–agent problems surrounding market exchanges. For example, efficiency–wage theories argue that employers often pay more than the market-clearing wage in order to create incentives for greater effort on the job. On this point, Bowles and Gintis overlap with the more comprehensive treatment of similar issues by Stiglitz.

Among the three *QJE* articles, the one by Stiglitz comes the closest to presenting an alternative new theory. For Stiglitz, the fatal flaw of the Arrow–Debreu model is its assumption of perfect information, costlessly and symmetrically available to all. In fact, perfect information is impossible; a reasonable economic theory needs to assume that information is limited, costly, and frequently asymmetrically distributed. Neither the characteristics of goods and services, nor the behavior of market participants, can be fully known or specified in advance. Among other things, this implies that contracts are necessarily incomplete, the point made by Bowles and Gintis. Even small imperfections of information can lead to large deviations from the Pareto-optimal outcomes of general equilibrium theory; in an imperfect-information economy there is no reason to expect markets to reach or even approach Pareto optimality. Indeed, the very existence of a market equilibrium is in doubt in an economy of limited information.

Prices cannot, according to Stiglitz, simply convey information about scarcity. In the context of limited information, prices must also address the selection problem, communicating about unobserved characteristics of goods and services (as when the price of an unfamiliar bottle of wine, say, is interpreted as a sign of its quality), and the incentive problem, influencing the unobserved or unmonitored behavior of market participants (as in the efficiency wage story). These multiple, often conflicting, roles for prices imply that the standard theories of producer and consumer behavior are inadequate, and that the standard solution to the problem of scarcity will not always be achieved, even in a competitive market.

This analysis leads to the well-known problems of adverse selection (e.g. if insurance is available to all, accident-prone people are the most likely to buy it) and moral hazard (insurance reduces the cost of accidents, and thus may make people more accident prone). Stiglitz sees these problems as pervasive, and shows how the limited-information paradigm explains many practical puzzles and policy debates. Intervention in the market often leads to welfare improvements, particularly when public policy is crafted to increase access to information or remove asymmetries. In some cases, new institutions are needed to overcome information problems.

Does this constitute a new theory, replacing neoclassical models, general equilibrium, and the Arrow–Debreu results? Yes, in a narrow sense; but no, in a larger and more important sense. The good news is that Stiglitz provides a richer, more complex picture of market interactions, and explains a way in which the traditional neoclassical view is inadequate. His emphasis on the multiple meanings of prices creates space for the systematic exercise of unequal power in market transactions, a point that is developed more fully by Bowles and Gintis. Politically, Stiglitz recognizes the importance of the traditional general equilibrium results, particularly the presumed optimality of *laissez-faire* outcomes; he repeatedly demonstrates that his analysis overturns the traditional theory and justifies intervention.

Yet the bigger picture of economic theory is surprisingly little changed by this handful of innovative brush strokes. The normative and evaluative apparatus of neoclassical economics, including the utilitarian standard of individual welfare maximization and the focus on Pareto optimality, survives unchanged. That is, the market no longer gets an A+ on every exam, but the exam questions are the same. The presentation of results in contrast to traditional general equilibrium theory is both a strength and a weakness: Stiglitz does well in highlighting where the traditional theory goes wrong, but by the same token is less successful in developing and presenting a coherent alternative.

The political agenda that flows from the economics of limited information mirrors the strengths and weaknesses of the theory: it fails to present a frontal challenge to contemporary capitalism, but justifies frequent government interventions in the market on specific issues. It is the agenda of Clinton-style "New Democrats" in the USA (and in fact Stiglitz served in the Clinton administration), or Blair's "New Labor" in Britain. Both in politics and in economic theory, we have done much worse in recent memory – but we should aspire to do much better.

The economics of limited information, as presented by Stiglitz, offers intriguing and valuable insights into the meaning and functioning of markets, as does the story of endogenous preferences and the analysis of incomplete contracts offered by Bowles and Gintis. However, these do not yet add up to a complete new perspective; at most they are building blocks that should be used in a new theory. They are hardly new enough, and hardly accepted enough, to support the claims of a bold departure beyond neoclassical traditions, on the part of the economics profession as a whole. Anyone who finds out where the innovative new economic theorists are hiding should be sure to tell the rest of us.

References

Blanchard, O. (2000) What do we know about macroeconomics that Fisher and Wicksell did not? *Quarterly Journal of Economics*, November, 1375–1400.

Bowles, S. and Gintis, H. (2000) Walsarian economics in retrospect. *Quarterly Journal of Economics*, November, 1411–1439.

Stiglitz, J. (2000) The contributions of the economics of information to twentieth century economics. *Quarterly Journal of Economics*, November, 1441–1478.

Rethinking economics in twentieth-century America

A political–economic approach to the history of thought

Michael A. Bernstein (University of California, San Diego, USA)

What came to be known as the "new economics" of the post-Second World War era and the interventionist fiscal and monetary policies pursued by the American government after 1945 did not simply arrive in the published text of Keynes's General Theory, and nor did they emerge *de novo* from college and university seminar rooms, faculty offices, and typewriters. They came with military mobilization and war in particular, with power and global authority in general. This "new economics" could not, in fact, subsist without national power. On the one side, American hegemony in the American century was crucially linked with the expansion of the scope and size of government activity, and with a significant commitment by the government to wielding the means (diplomatic, political, military and economic) of that power. It was, as well, dependent upon an apparent political consensus tied to a constellation of social and cultural forces that made anti-communism, global intervention and militarization policies appeal across dimensions of class, ethnicity and gender. For all these reasons, a political–economic approach to the history of economic thought, especially in its American contexts, offers a great deal of enlightenment for our understanding of the emergence of the neoclassical "consensus" in our field.

History shows that it was the Second World War that most decisively laid the groundwork for the participation of the American economics profession in the Cold War of the 1950s and later years. That involvement in the affairs of state insured the triumph of neoclassical perceptions over alternative points of view, and furthered the emergence of a "mainstream" economics as the dominant discipline of the social sciences. Indeed, future Nobel Laureate Paul Samuelson commented in 1945 that "the last war [i.e. the First World War] was the chemist's war . . . this one [had been] the physicist's. It might equally be said that this [had been] the economist's war."

The usefulness of economics to the American war effort in the 1940s was demonstrated in two broad areas of endeavor – mobilization and resource allocation, and strategic decision-making. It was on matters of allocation that economists made some of their most significant contributions, and with which they (collectively as a profession) had their most important wartime experience. Conversion to defense production had created virtually intractable problems of materials scarcity for government officials. How to choose efficiently the timing and distribution of various productive activities necessary for the war effort became a major concern. With American entry into the war, allocation problems became only more intense. Not surprisingly, the American armed services and allied government agencies were quite eager to develop allocative techniques for wartime production, transportation and distribution that would minimize costs and extravagance, and that would have as their corollary the maximization of some objective such as output, frequency or endurance. The investigation of such "linear programming problems" had a tremendous impact on the future course of research in mathematical economics in particular and economic theory in general – as demonstrated, for example, by the invention of algorithms to maximize particular functions subject to sets of "linear inequalities." In other words, scholars sought to establish techniques by which specific goals, such as output-maximization or cost-minimization, could be met with reference to specific constraints such as fuel supply, labor availability, raw material bottlenecks, and national (indeed international) transportation capacities.

It was with the development of game theory, however, that the intellectual evolution of American economics and the concerns of a burgeoning national security state truly melded. On a strictly mathematical level, the development of both linear programming and game theory depended on advances in the understanding of linear inequalities in constrained maximization or minimization problems. In this sense, the mathematical techniques used in both areas were the same. However, game theory had a powerful appeal for strategic analysis because of its focus on conflict and decision-making. Not surprisingly, the theory of games was also a field greatly stimulated by the Second World War years – but in certain ways it did not achieve its full stature until the coming of the Cold War.

The 1940s work of John von Neumann and Oskar Morgenstern signaled the entrance of game theory as a major part of economic analysis. Their demonstration that it was possible to derive definite results from mathematical simulations of complicated scenarios of conflict and uncertainty was revolutionary. They showed that under certain conditions and assumptions, game participants (that is to say, those involved in competitive situations that approximated a contest of some sort) could implement strategies that would secure at least certain minimum gains (or their parallel, incur at most certain predictable losses). While it was immediately clear that their findings would be useful in conventional microeconomic theory – especially with regard to estimating pricing outcomes in contested markets – over time it also became obvious that they would be applicable to strategic choice problems and national defense planning.

Game–theoretic approximations and simulations of two-person conflicts seemed appropriate scenarios in which to investigate the implications of the nuclear duopoly, between the USA and the Soviet Union, of the early Cold War era. The dramatic intellectual impact of the work of von Neumann and Morgenstern among academic economists was thus, not coincidentally, paralleled by the willingness of the federal government to support the continued evolution of this line of inquiry. Research funding, distributed by the US Department of Defense and affiliated agencies – most notably the US Office of Naval Research – was rapidly made available to those economic theorists, in particular mathematical economists, whose work in game theory and linear programming seemed to have potential value for the missions of the national defense and security establishment – all this at a time when the mission of the American defense agencies expanded in novel and indeed global ways.

The United States Navy and Air Force proved most eager to lend support to the work of game theorists and linear programming specialists. The Navy in particular supported much of the work in mathematical economics – in large part done by Kenneth Arrow and Gerard Debreu (both future Nobel Memorial Prize Laureates) – that, during the 1950s and early 1960s, propelled the field into great visibility and prominence. Official publications of both the Office of Naval Research and the Air Force Office of Aerospace Research claimed, in the late 1960s, that the Arrow–Debreu project was exceptional for its "modeling of conflict and cooperation whether it be [for] combat or procurement contracts or exchange of information among dispersed decision nodes."

Crucial support, both financial and logistic, was also given to these activities by the RAND Corporation. During the 1950s, what had been the US Air Force's Project RAND (an acronym for Research and Development), and what later became the non-profit RAND Corporation known today, underwrote much of the work on linear programming that had been stimulated by the 1940s work of people like George Dantzig (now Emeritus Professor of Economics and Operations Research at Stanford University) and Tjalling Koopmans (the late Professor of and Nobel Laureate in Economics at Yale). It was at RAND that Dantzig refined his simplex techniques (with the enormously important contributions of mathematician Richard Bellman), and RAND employees began the systematic application of game–theoretic principles to war planning and simulation. Government officials were often participants in RAND conferences and workshops geared toward helping them prepare for crisis management. Indeed, the presidential administration of John F. Kennedy, according to available RAND records, was evidently most engaged by and committed to this sort of experience for its officials. (It was, by the way, no idle exercise, as Herbert Scarf – a former RAND investigator and now Sterling Professor Emeritus of Economics at Yale – noted in an oral history interview, for colleagues at RAND to relax over games of "Kriegspiel" and "Liar's Poker" while taking a break from their investigations of strategic choice and conflictive outcomes.)

Under the auspices of RAND, continued research in game theory and operations research flourished throughout the 1960s and 1970s. The Corporation funded what it called "Defense Policy Seminars" at UCLA, Columbia University, Dartmouth College, Johns Hopkins University, MIT, Ohio State University, Princeton University, the University of Wisconsin and the University of Chicago. In 1965, RAND created a graduate fellowship program to support relevant training in economics and international relations. In that year, such fellowships were distributed among the Universities of California, Harvard, Stanford, Yale, Chicago, Columbia and Princeton. Not infrequently, talented graduate students and postdoctoral investigators received major support from RAND (and through RAND from the federal government) for their work in economics that touched upon matters of strategic decision-making. (One such individual for whom this was true, whose career as a "cold warrior" would take many twists and turns, was a Harvard University graduate student in economics, specializing in game theory, who later became a prominent figure in the 1971 "Pentagon Papers" scandal surrounding the Vietnam War – Daniel Ellsberg.) The authority and legitimacy of the new work in economic theory that had been, in large measure, an outgrowth of the war years, carried over to the post-war era and the years of the Cold War. In a wide array of activities related to the defense establishment and the new global power of the USA, economic analysis came to play a significant role. From defense cost minimization, to budgeting techniques and strategies, to transportation and logistical-support scheduling, to shadow-price estimation of the burdens of military–industrial procurement, the research of the Second World War years paid off. Even in the private corporate economy, not to mention in the civilian activities of government, what came to be known as the operationally-useful methods of economists came of age. And with these successes, the prestige of those engaged in such research (along with the governmental and private-foundation support for their scholarly activity) were powerfully enhanced.

More than all this, what the war-inspired development of such things as linear programming and game theory served to do was to legitimize a transformation in the object of economics research that had been in the making for some 70 years. Ever since the so-called marginalist revolution in the latter part of the nineteenth century, American economists had been very much part of this redefinition of the science. No longer the study of "the nature and causes of the wealth of nations" (as Adam Smith and other classical theorists had claimed), nor "a critical analysis of capitalist production" (as Karl Marx had suggested), the discipline became, in the twentieth century, the formal study of what Lionel Robbins had so deftly called in his 1932 book *Essay on the Nature and Significance of Economic Science* "the adaptation of scarce means to given ends." While the work of marginalist theorists had gained increasing respectability since the 1870s, earlier (and quite famous) works in this tradition had had a distinctly polemical, usually anti-Marxist quality. (I have in mind here the work of Eugen von Bohm-Bawerk, for example, in the European case, and that of John Bates Clark in the American.) That tone was sharply distinguished from, and ultimately displaced by, the ostensibly objective, apolitical and elegant formulations of mid- and later-twentieth-century mathematical economic theorists. The fundamental ingredients of the hegemony of neoclassical thinking in the economics discipline were thus secured.

The ascendancy of particular points of view is not, of course, simply a matter of scholarly debate or pedagogy. A real environment of wealth distribution, corporate control, diplomatic pressure and military force also plays a crucial role in distinguishing between, and differentially empowering, dominant and oppositional ideologies. It is appropriate, therefore, that we turn our attention to the role of both political–economic processes and of ideas in structuring the history of economic theory itself. One very promising way to do this, as I hope I have conveyed to you, is by rethinking economics in twentieth-century America.

[Prof. Bernstein's new book, on which this article has been based, *A Perilous Progress: Economists and Public Purpose in Twentieth Century America*, is now being published by Princeton University Press.]

Why the PAE movement needs feminism

Julie A. Nelson (Global Development and Environment Institute, Tufts University, USA)

What can feminist economics contribute to the post-autistic economics movement? Anyone familiar with both of these will have noticed that the two have much common ground. Both seek to put at the core of analysis the economic and social problems facing women, men and children. Both protest the definition of the economics discipline around a single, narrow set of methodological tools. Both are international and pluralistic movements, incorporating participants from many countries and many schools of economic thought.

I would like, in this essay, to bring to the attention of PAE participants what I believe is one of feminist economics' most unique and fundamentally important contributions to the discussion of the potential transformation of our field. This newsletter has carried articles examining materialist, institutional, geographical, political and intellectual explanations for the current abysmal state of economics research and teaching. Feminist analysis brings to light other important dimensions of the story of how economics got into its current autistic condition, and why it is so resistant to change. I believe that PAE will to some extent misunderstand its own historical dynamics, and be less effective as a force for change, if it neglects the insights that come from a gender-sensitive analysis of the value system underlying contemporary economic study.

I invite you to do a three-part thought exercise with me. First, think about the characteristics held in highest esteem within the contemporary hegemony of mathematized rational-choice modeling. You will probably come up with a list that includes characteristics like rigor, precision, detachment, quantitative analysis, abstraction, self-interest, autonomy, rationality, etc. Next, think about the flip side of each of these terms. You will probably come up with a list something like this: pliability, vagueness, connection, qualitative work, concreteness, generosity, interdependence, emotion. Lastly, consider the gender connotations of each list. Most people raised in Euro-American cultures will immediately recognize that the first list is culturally coded as "masculine" and is associated with toughness and power, and the second as "feminine" and associated with softness and powerlessness.

What is at issue, then, for PAE is not simply changes at the level of methodology, but a sea change in the underlying value system of contemporary economics. A long and intricate history of relations among gender, social organization, science and conceptions of knowledge formed these values. At the time of the Enlightenment, the world – and the economy – came to be seen as clockwork and mechanical. This image of the economy, and an epistemological image of the knower as radically separate from the subject of study, encourages the primacy of mathematical modeling. Feminist scholars have pointed out how this epistemology reflects a fantasy of achieving solid security through the control of nature by our minds, and a denial of all connection, embodiment, vulnerability or flux. An early Secretary of the British Royal Society (Henry Oldenburg, 1620–1677), for example, stated that its scientific purpose was to "raise a masculine Philosophy . . . whereby the Mind of Man may be ennobled with the knowledge of Solid Truths." (Note the absence of feminine, body, women and contingency.) The autism of contemporary economics reflects the cultural sexism in which it historically developed – with a vengeance.

What is needed, much feminist theory suggests, is not a flip-flop into an image of humans as totally powerless and fragmented, but rather an overcoming of the whole either/or understanding of the relations of humans to each other and to the world. An authentic recognition of natural and social connection leads to an understanding of the human knower as both part of the reality to be studied, *and* being able to reflect on that reality. The fantasy of detached control can be replaced by the knowledge of lived experience.

Participants in the PAE movement should therefore be aware that whenever we call for more connection to social problems, whenever we call for more concreteness, for more flexibility or for more embodiment, we are asking a lot. We may think we are shaking a disciplinary branch, but in reality we are rattling a very big emotional and socio-cultural tree. We should not be surprised when defenders of the *status quo* often fail to engage with us at an intellectual level. The fact that we are generally much more reasonable than they are (in the broad sense of human wisdom) is almost beside the point. Our calls for change will often be perceived as calls for the emasculation of economics, for making economics soft, for making economics impotent. Our calls for change demand that our listeners "think outside the box" in a radical way that will, at the least, feel unfamiliar and uncomfortable to many, and be perceived as profoundly threatening by some.

That said, it is important to clarify the roles of actual men and women in the perpetuation of sexist gender constructs at the core of economics. Common misperceptions about feminist economists include beliefs that it is concerned only with "women's issues," is only done by women, advocates a purely qualitative and emotional alternative to contemporary thinking, or treats men as the enemy. Those who hold these views display their ignorance of contemporary feminist work. A number of men challenge the sexist beliefs at the core of the value system, and many women do not. The reason that women have tended to take the lead in the feminist push within economics is not because we "bring something different" (via our genes or brain functions), but because the biases are far more obvious to those who start somewhat outside the system. Fish, it is said, do not notice they are swimming in water. Other "outside" groups, characterized as "other" by way of race, sexual preference, age, disability, nationality or class *vis-à-vis* the dominant culture, also bring important perspectives. The PAE movement will be self-deluded if it looks for accomplishments largely within a debate among Euro-American professional men. It will miss its mark if it ignores the problems suffered – and contributions offered – by those who have long been labeled as non-rational and dependent, by a culture that elevates mind and autonomy above all.

As I write this essay, in October of 2001, the events of September 11 are fresh in everyone's mind. To readers who may still think of feminist concerns as "just" women's issues, and of no concern to them, I offer one last reflection. The Taliban, and its variety of fundamentalist thinking, has been the most controlling and oppressive regime with regard to women in contemporary times. Contemporary academic economics, and contemporary global economic policies, are gripped by other rigidities of thinking – what George Soros has dubbed "market fundamentalism." Fantasies of control are operative in both phenomena, and gender is far from irrelevant to understanding their power, and their solution.

[Julie A. Nelson is the author of *Feminism, Objectivity, and Economics* (Routledge, 1966) and (with Marianne A. Ferber) *Beyond Economic Man: Feminist Theory and Economics* (University of Chicago Press, 1993).

For more about feminist economics, visit http://www.facstaff.bucknell.edu/jshackel/iaffe/]

An International Marshall Plan

Geoff Harcourt (Cambridge University, UK)

It is necessary that those who masterminded the attacks on Tuesday, 11 September should be brought to justice, but parallel with the steps needed to achieve this should be international efforts to remove the injustice and poverty that provide the conditions that create such despair in persons that they are moved to take such awful actions in the first place.

In the early post-war years, the USA rightly received praise for implementing the Marshall Plan to help Europe recover from its wartime devastation. This was an example of the best of American virtues. What is needed now is an International Marshall Plan to tackle injustice and poverty in the Middle East, Africa, the poorer parts of Asia and Latin America. The funds should come from the USA, Europe, Japan and the wealthier economies on the Pacific Rim. The administration of their use could be monitored by the World Bank and the IMF. The aid should be immediate, and then a sustained flow of funds over several years. *Quid pro quos* would be necessary; for example, Israel should again allow Palestinians into Israel to work, and should allow the development of social and industrial infrastructure in the Palestinian areas themselves.

The altruism implied by these suggestions would not be without benefit to the altruists. The expansionary forces unleashed by the measures would be a welcome offset to the contractionary forces (probably soon to be reinforced by reactions to last week's horror) at present sending the advanced economies into recession or, in the case of Japan, worsening its recession of the last ten years. If such a cumulatively virtuous process could be started, it would not only bring economic benefits to the poorest citizens of the world, but would also serve to lay a base on which democratic institutions could be erected.

People of good will are desperately needed to float ideas, to offset the understandable reaction to the happenings of Tuesday, 11 September 2000 that warlike actions are the only possible ones.

The war economy

James K. Galbraith (University of Texas, Austin, USA)

An economic calamity

In a war economy the public obligation is to do *what is necessary*: to support the military effort, to protect and defend the home territory, and especially to maintain the physical well-being, solidarity and morale of the people. These may not prove to be easy tasks in the months ahead.

We are facing what is not only a terror attack, but also an economic calamity. The impacts of the strikes at the World Trade Center now include a 14.4 percent drop in stock prices in the first week following the attack, and a collapse in those sectors related to travel and leisure – notably airlines, hotels and resorts. As these events cascade through the economy, they will shatter fragile household balance sheets and precipitate steep cuts in consumer spending. The ensuing recession could be very deep and very long.

This is not merely a shock to a healthy system, requiring only limited measures to restore confidence and stimulate spending. Household finances have been badly out of balance since 1997, as the household sector financed consumption above income by borrowing, largely against capital gains. But capital gains turned negative after April 2000. Once that happened, large cuts in consumer spending could be delayed but not avoided, without major policy changes. What has happened since September 11 consolidates, advances in time, and also intensifies a decline that was already well under way.

By way of a rough order of magnitude, my Levy Institute colleagues Wynne Godley and Alex Izurieta estimated last summer that unemployment would have to rise to 7.4 percent just to bring household expenditure into line with income. Unemployment would rise as high as 9.0 percent, they estimated, if households were to try to return to *normal* post-Second World War saving levels. And that was on a smooth trajectory involving a gradual but not catastrophic slowdown – namely, before the events of September 11. Now it is possible that households will try even harder to restore depleted reserves, driving unemployment higher still.

There is thus no chance that events will right themselves in a few weeks, or that we will be saved by such underlying factors as technology and productivity growth – as Chairman Greenspan professes to believe – or by lower interest rates or the provisions of the recent tax act. Rather, we are in for an economic crisis; the sooner this is recognized and acted upon, the better.

Normally during wartime large-scale support of the domestic economy is not needed, because of vast increases in military spending. However, what we face so far is not the reality of wartime mobilization, but a veneer of military action over a worldwide diplomatic and police offensive. The $20 billion already appropriated for the military may cover the costs of near-term operations, but neither that nor the $20 billion allocated for relief and reconstruction in New York City is nearly enough to deal with the larger economic problem.

In total at this moment, federal spending measures of $55 billion are being considered, including the airline bailout. A further program of perhaps $100 billion may soon be proposed, including expanded unemployment insurance, extended tax rebates, and payroll tax relief. This movement in Congress to lift the "budget constraint" is a welcome revival of Keynesian instinct, but proposals so far have been based on numerical guesswork and not on the objective of maintaining full employment. As their advocates will usually acknowledge, proposals in the $100–200 billion range still involve accepting a severe recession, loss of tax revenue and, no doubt, falling government spending at state and local levels no matter how much federal spending expands.

In these circumstances, the concept of "stimulus" should be discarded in favor of the larger objective of *economic stabilization* – a sustained effort commensurate with the crisis as it unfolds.

Business tax cuts, whether temporary or permanent, are useless in this situation. Without profits, reduced taxes on profits have no effect; without sales, investment is pointless even if the tax regime favors it. Both the logic and the motives of those proposing such measures are to be suspected. All wars attract profiteers; public morale will be destroyed if they succeed. For this reason, the shocking proposal to reduce capital gains taxes in the crisis was rightly shelved, for a few days at least.

A further dilemma emerges when one considers that personal tax cuts, even if temporary and targeted properly at working households, may not stimulate spending by much in a time of crisis. If households are determined to increase their financial reserves, and as they are flush with durable goods after a long expansion, increases in cash on hand may translate weakly into increased spending; such a situation could last for years. Of the available tax cuts, payroll tax rate reductions are the most likely to prove effective at stabilizing spending, because they would target households that are income-constrained.

Averting collapse

Cautious men are in charge of the economy at the moment, but this attitude can only bring disaster. There is no longer any danger of overdoing fiscal policy; demand–pull inflation is not even a remote threat. The danger, at the moment, is collapse. To avert this, an initial program could be up to three times as large as that so far proposed.

Increases in federal spending on public health, education, transport and other areas are also absolutely needed, and should be funded liberally. But the option of revenue sharing is perhaps most readily created and implemented on a large scale, most likely to have early direct and indirect effects, least likely to be dissipated in saving or imports, and also the most non-partisan in concept. Direct purchases by state and local governments now constitute nearly 10 percent of GDP; they have been rising rapidly in the past few years and could fall rapidly if revenues are curtailed. Preventing this, and creating new capacity for state and local action in many areas (including direct job creation), should be a very high priority at this time.

In activity on a grand scale, the federal government might extend revenue sharing to cover as much as one-fourth of total expenses this fiscal year – $300 billion – with a provisional follow-through of 20 percent in the second year and 10 percent in the third. The numbers can be adjusted as events and more refined calculations dictate, but they should be large enough to stabilize budget and service provisions at all levels of government.

In the realm of financial issues, it is now clear that Federal Reserve policy has completely lost domestic effect. Cuts in interest rates on 17 September had no impact on the largest one-week decline in stock prices since 1933, and none on underlying economic activity.

History and the dollar

Here, the analogy to Second World War mobilization is misleading. After the First World War, the USA was the world's creditor nation and held a near-monopoly on the gold stock. With the collapse of world trade in the 1930s, global economic interdependencies receded sharply; meanwhile, the USA in the late 1930s was energy self-sufficient and did not run a large trade deficit. None of these conditions now holds. In historical terms, the US position today much more closely resembles that of the Great Powers in Europe in 1914 than that of the USA in 1939. As a result, a high-order Keynesian response will have global financial repercussions. To finance either a major military or a major domestic economic effort (or both) on world capital markets could very well unhinge the dollar and shift the balance of financial power – presumably to Europe.

Lower interest rates worldwide – beginning on 17 September – have so far staved off a major fall in the dollar. However, that situation could change, particularly if the brutality of actual hostilities or the outbreak of famine in Afghanistan or a similar calamity leads to a global shift of opinion against the USA. Oil and gas prices will follow demand downward in the short run and the recession will cut imports, improving the current account so long as exports do not continue to slump. But uncertainty over the war aims of the administration is likely to curtail activity worldwide and so add falling exports to our miseries; moreover, oil supplies could be disrupted in a wider war, and imports will rise again if large-scale Keynesian policies take hold.

Any of these scenarios could destabilize the dollar, causing a decline far greater than the 20 to 25 percent that is probably needed for current account adjustment. There are vast public and private dollar holdings overseas – all substantially contingent on confidence that other actors will hold on to their holdings. In this crisis, they may not stand firm; a run on the dollar cannot be ruled out. This is the classic scourge of war efforts and "populist" expansions. Unless prevented, the natural reaction of the Federal Reserve would be to raise interest rates, thereby deepening the slump. An economy with high unemployment and high inflation is a very possible, even likely, result in this case.

Cars and the global financial architecture

What is to be done about this risk? An old truism in global finance holds that debtors cannot run wars – or economic recovery programs – without the organized assistance of their friends and allies. Such assistance will surely not be forthcoming, on a sustained basis, unless it involves a commitment to a more stable and successful global financial system afterward. The further reality is that the USA needs the sustained support of the world community for diplomatic, intelligence and military purposes. This support cannot be assumed to be available free of cost, especially from poor countries that have not benefited at all from the modern global order. Therefore, like it or not, a new and more just and stable global financial order will have to emerge from the present crisis, or we will eventually become mired indefinitely in fruitless and unending military struggles, aided by fewer and fewer reliable allies. Comprehensive debt relief for cooperating countries (Pakistan is a key example) would be a good place to begin.

The modern system of floating exchange rates and unregulated international capital markets – just 30 years old – has never been tested on the present scale. It could easily fail now. This being so, planning for a transition in the global financial system toward an effective multilateral regulatory and stabilization system should begin quietly, but soon. It is time to examine a return to a Bretton Woods framework of fixed but adjustable exchange rates among the major currencies, backed by a multilateral reserve. This task is simplified by the creation of the euro; it would be easier now than at any time in decades to fix parities for the industrial world, allowing first for a substantial dollar depreciation. Beyond this, we will need new, perhaps regionally decentralized, exchange stabilization and liquidity facilities for the developing world

Further, the current crisis offers compelling reasons to examine the structural sources of the US trade position. Here, oil is a major factor: cutting imports totally would reduce the deficit by a quarter. Cars are a larger factor still. In the medium run, reconstruction of our transportation networks and housing patterns in a way that would rely far less on oil and automobiles (and airlines) may be the necessary domestic adjunct of real security abroad.

The issues of global financial architecture and our national monoculture of oil and cars lie behind the present emergency; they have helped to translate a terror attack into an economic crisis. In the end, our ability to address these issues effectively will prove central to ultimate success in the quest for both physical and economic security. The immediate response should include a planning process in which these issues can be discussed freely by competent experts and without domination by partisan views or special interests.

If mass unemployment or inflation cannot be avoided by pre-emptive means, then the entire experience of the New Deal and the War Economy will have to be called upon in due course. But there is no point in going into all that now.

[With the author's permission, this article has been excerpted from a longer version available on the website of **The Levy Economics Institute** at http://www.levy.org/docs/pn/01-8.html. James Galbraith is the author of *Created Unequal: The Crisis in American Pay* (University of Chicago Press, 1998) and the editor (with Maureen Berner) of *Inequality and Industrial Change: A Global View* (Cambridge University Press, 2001).]

The globalized economy

Jeff Gates (Shared Capitalism Institute, USA)

Finance-driven phenomenon

Globalization is a finance-driven phenomenon. Its operations are geared to a key assumption advanced by neoliberal economists: "maximize financial returns and – trust us – everything will turn out fine." As I will show, that naively mechanistic model is dangerously dysfunctional. Its unbridled operations are a key reason wealth is being redistributed worldwide – from poor to rich, from poor country to rich country, from the future to the present – with the unflinching support of rule-making crafted by the World Trade Organization (WTO).

The problem with globalization is *not* the corporate entity, as some insist. Nor is globalization a problem *per se*. The malady lies in the combination of: (a) the narrow bandwidth of values to which the corporate entity mechanistically attunes its operations (i.e. financial values), and (b) the current state of corporate owner-ship – abstract, remote and concentrated. The result is a globalizing economy that is experienced by most as disconnected, speeded-up and dumbed-down. The solution lies in evoking a policy mix insistent that business methods mature so that ownership patterns quickly become more personalized, localized and human-sized. In a private property system, that is the only sensible way globalized private enterprise can attune its operations to the legitimate concerns of those influenced by its operations.

Globalization has the potential to be a positive force. However, under neoliberal-informed rule-making, globalization instead has emerged as a capital markets-led, government-backed process that radically redistributes wealth (from *weal* or "well-being"), as I chronicle below.

Rather than integrating the world economy, today's dominant economic model divides people (both within and between nations), plunders natural resources and imperils posterity. Instead of fostering free enterprise democracies, today's globalization attunes its operations to such a cramped range of values that the "financially fit" are viewed as sufficient unto themselves while the rest are not worth the bother.

Wealth redistribution trends

This finance-obsessive rendition of globalization guarantees results that are inequitable and unsustainable. Left unreformed, WTO rule-making is destined to evoke hostility and instability as its operations are often associated with oppression, exploitation, domination, corruption and disrespect. To become sensible and sustainable, globalization requires a counter-force to today's wealth-redistribution trends:

1 *From the bottom to the top.* As the US is the leading advocate for the neoliberal model of globalization, the trends emerging there are instructive. The wealth of the *Forbes 400* richest Americans grew an average $1.44 billion each from 1997–2000, an average daily increase in wealth of $1,920,000 per person ($240,000 per hour or 46,602 times the minimum wage). The financial wealth of the top 1 percent of US households now exceeds the combined household financial wealth of the bottom 95 percent. The share of the nation's after-tax income received by the top 1 percent nearly doubled from 1979–1997. By 1998, the top-earning 1 percent had as much combined income as the 100 million Americans with the lowest earnings. The top fifth of US households now claim 49.2 percent of national income, while the bottom fifth gets by on 3.6 percent. Between 1979 and 1997, the average income of the richest fifth jumped from nine times the income of the poorest fifth to roughly fifteen times. The average hourly earnings for white-collar males was $19.24 in 1997, up from $19.18 in 1973.

2 *From democracies to plutocracies.* Today's capital markets-led "emerging markets" development model is poised to replicate US wealth patterns worldwide. For instance, 61.7 percent of Indonesia's stock market value is held by that nation's fifteen richest families. The comparable figure for the Philippines is 55.1 percent, and is 53.3 percent for Thailand. Worldwide, there's now roughly $60 trillion in securitized assets (stocks, bonds, etc.), with an estimated $90 trillion in additional assets that will become securitizable as this model spreads.

3 *From the future to the present.* Unsustainable production methods are now standard practice worldwide, due largely to globalization's embrace of a neoliberal-inspired financial model that insists on maximizing net *present* value (that's largely what stock values represent). That stance routinely and richly rewards those who internalize gains and externalize costs (such as paying a living wage or cleaning up environmental toxins).

4 *From poor nations to rich.* Today's version of globalization assumes that unrestricted economic flows will benefit the 80 percent of humanity living in developing countries as well as those 20 percent living in developed countries. Yet the UN Development Programme (UNDP) reports that 80

countries have per capita incomes lower than a decade ago, and 60 countries have grown steadily poorer since 1980.

5 *From families to financial markets.* How is globalization affecting OECD countries? The work-year for the typical American has expanded 184 hours since 1970. That's an additional 4½ weeks on the job for about the same pay.

6 *From free-traders to protectionists.* OECD nations channel $326 billion a year in subsidies to their own farmers while (a) restricting agricultural imports from developing countries, and (b) insisting that debtor nations repay their foreign loans in foreign currency, which they can earn only by exporting.

7 *From law-abiders to law-evaders.* Roughly $8 trillion is held in tax havens worldwide, ensuring that the most well-to-do can harvest the benefits of globalization without incurring any of the costs.

8 *From personal freedom to financial freedom.* The free enterprise component of democracy is founded on the notion that free markets provide an opportunity for free people freely to express their free choices and thereby enjoy the dignity of self-determination, democracy's most treasured freedom. Though terrific in theory, the map fails to match the territory. To equate markets with expression of the common will is misleading, even deceptive. Markets don't respond to people, but to people *with money.* Embrace a policy mix, like today's, that concentrates income, and that mix is destined to undermine both self-determination and markets – the moral foundations of free enterprise democracies.

9 *From education to incarceration.* Since 1980, US prison budgets have increased at a pace six times that for higher education. Florida now spends more on correction than on colleges.

10 *From the real to the abstract.* Today's neoliberal-dominated perspective on progress insists that globalization has helped the US achieve two decades of unprecedented *financial* prosperity. Yet social, fiscal, cultural, political and ecological indicators confirm that the world's "richest" nation is experiencing a steady twenty-year decline across a broad array of quality-of-life indicators, and in numerous living systems.

Conclusion

Globalization's "guidance system" is designed to scour the globe for shareholder value, with financial value a proxy for shareholder value. If that value "shows up," the neoliberal model signals success, and this self-reflective process repeats itself *ad infinitum.* Only with a component of personalized "up-close capitalism" will privately owned enterprises become "re-wired" so that their operations adapt to the more complex, diverse and multidimensional concerns of people, place and pace. Tyranny becomes structural when a model enforces behavior attuned to too narrow a bandwidth of values.

In "systems-eze," the challenge lies in how best to smarten up free enterprise by re-wiring its signaling systems into more robust patterns so that it learns ongoingly and, ideally, trans-generationally. At present, the corporate entity has no designed-in means for taking into account the values of those whose lives it affects. Though envisioned as a self-organizing model, it's missing a key component: locale-imbedded ownership, the essential feedback-generating relationship required for locale-sensitive self-correction. Regulation becomes the alternative when those affected have no property-empowered right to have their voice heard. Yet the WTO routinely rejects regulation as a restraint of trade. If the maladies that accompany globalization are re-framed in terms of property relationships, it is clear that components of localized ownership offer a hopeful way to rationalize today's dysfunctional, finance-myopic paradigm.

Given the nature of the threats that sovereign nations now face – global, systemic, multidimensional, interdependent, transgenerational – the best risk-management strategy lies in a multilateral commitment to prove the truth of an age-old axiom: "If you want peace, work for justice." Today's immature and mechanistic model generates results that alternate between disappointing and appalling. The solution lies in a paradigm that evokes property relationships able to reflect a broader spectrum of values – social, economic, cultural, political and ecological. At a minimum, *globalization requires a model that stops today's radical redistribution of wealth*. In that direction also lies the only sensible strategy for long-term national security.

As presently practiced, globalization urges that nations ally to make the world secure, not for the forces of democracy, but for the forces of finance. That fanciful stance is founded on the neoliberal assumption that the free flow of global capital will evoke free enterprise democracies that are robust, just and sustainable. Instead, insistence on that naive prescription has ravaged the natural world, ignored the legitimate needs of the poor, and fed the greed of a privileged few. Any economist not actively crafting a paradigm to reverse these trends is lending support to a globalized form of finance fundamentalism.

[This article is based on Jeff Gates's testimony to the United Kingdom Parliament's Select Committee on Economic Affairs on 8 October 2001. His full testimony, including documentation of his statistics, is available at http://www.btinternet.com/~pae_news/Gates-testimony.htm. Jeff Gates is President of the Shared Capitalism Institute (www.sharedcapitalism.org). Former counsel to the US Senate Committee on Finance, he is the author of *The Ownership Solution* (Perseus Publishing, 1999) and *Democracy at Risk* (Perseus Publishing, 2001).]

Some old but good ideas

Anne Mayhew (University of Tennessee, USA)

As post-autistic economics moves beyond criticism and on to the task of building a more relevant and robust economic science, one challenge is to develop a theoretical framework that will guide pluralistic borrowing from a variety of disciplines and approaches. Some useful guidelines for development of such a framework may be found in the history of American economic thought as it developed and flourished in the first half of the twentieth century. During the first five decades of that century, a group of economists who taught at a number of the major American universities created the reasonably coherent, pluralistic and non-autistic approach to the study of economies and economic issues known as institutionalism – an approach that dominated American economic thought during the interwar years.

Four basic themes characterized this approach:

1   Regularities in the organization of both production and distribution are the same as all other social regularities in that they are human creations and are subject to change by human intervention. In other words, there is no "natural economy" and there is no reason to assume that an idealized market system is historically or morally prior to other social systems. This perception was rooted in American pragmatic philosophy that saw individuals as recipients of inherited ideas, but also as active agents capable of perceiving problems and imagining new possibilities. The basic autistic assumption of isolated individuals interacting from the beginning of human history through exchange, but little changed by it, was rejected in favor of the notion that humans are always social beings. Mind, thought and consciousness are products of active processes of human interactions, processes that do not end but evolve through time.

This understanding of the social and inquiring nature of humans is crucial to two tasks that must confront post-autistic economic analysis: the understanding of variation in economic organization across time and space, *and* variation in human understanding and behavior across the lifetime of individuals. The idea that we all start with a set of inherited ideas and perceptions is crucial to explaining economic and all other forms of social behavior. A simple example: young American children learn at an early age that food can be acquired by spending money, and that money is acquired by "hard work and thrift." They may learn that beggars without money for food are victims of hard luck; they are as likely to learn that such beggars are undeserving of receiving money because they have not worked hard or been thrifty. In this process, the idea of a market economy with justified and even desirable income inequality is instilled. Young children in other times and places have learned different things, and have a different understanding of distribution and its relationship to production.

What the pragmatists and institutional economists also stressed is that all people are capable of questioning the ideas that they inherit. We all know that many Americans come to question the conventional wisdom that the poor have earned their own economic fate, but note that the questioning itself is via a social process of questioning, of contact with others with different ideas (contact that is now global as well as local), and of formal learning. In the process, ideas of what constitutes justice and injustice are changed, as are ideas of how to achieve justice. It is this active process that produces the evolution of thought and consciousness, and that leads to change in human culture and organization.

2   It follows from the above that as humans create their economies, they can change those economies to solve perceived problems. A central part of economic analysis should therefore be the identification of problems, which is to say to patterns of production and distribution that do not accord with the goals of society. This analysis should lead to reasoned advocacy of reform through normal political and social processes. This aspect of pragmatism underlay the reform activities of the 1920s and 1930s in the USA, activities that included creation of the Federal Trade Commission, the Social Security Act that provided income security to the elderly, unemployment compensation, regulation of securities trading, and much, much more.

3   While the institutional economists saw their role as one of criticism and advocacy, they did not purport to offer permanent solutions or design of Utopias. They were reformers, not revolutionaries who could advocate permanent solutions. Instead, the pragmatic solutions to problems were offered with the sure knowledge that these solutions would create new problems, and that as science and technology changed the interaction of humans with the physical world, so too would that alter the relationship of humans with each other. Central to institutionalist thought was the perception that the advent of industrial as opposed to craft production had altered the relationship of producers to products and of producers to consumers. New rules, regulations and patterns of interaction were required, and those very

rules, regulations and patterns themselves created new conflicts that would lead to more change via a process of cumulative causation. Not only was the path of change difficult to predict, but it was also impossible to formulate an ideal toward which such change tended. In other words, it was also futile to speculate on the conditions that would prevail in an ideal economy.

4   In order to understand the processes of ongoing change, and in order to understand the human organization of production and distribution, a variety of tools were found to be useful. Wesley Mitchell, one of the most active of institutionalists and founder of the National Bureau of Economic Research, was a strong advocate of descriptive statistics and of statistical analysis as a way of discovering the actual (as opposed to idealized) patterns of economic behavior. Others borrowed the methods of anthropology and sociology to discover patterns of behavior through rough observation and participation. Study of the legal system as a working system of evolving human rules was central to the approach taken by John R. Commons and his students. The study of economic history was vital for understanding patterns and processes of change. In all of the institutionalist work, the tools were just that: ways to achieve the goal of understanding the patterns of human behavior and how they changed. The tools did not define the discipline.

There is much to be learned about the early twentieth-century American economy from reading Thorstein Veblen, John R. Commons, Wesley C. Mitchell, John Maurice Clark, Rexford Tugwell and the others who brought the pragmatist approach to the study of economics. What is more important is that these authors and others offer rich examples of how to build an economic science that would, in the words of Tony Lawson, describe and explain event regularities. They can teach us much about how to do non-autistic economic science.

Against: a priori theory. *For:* descriptively adequate computational modeling

Bruce Edmonds (Centre for Policy Modelling, Manchester Metropolitan University Business School, UK)

Introduction

Autistic economics is rightly held in disregard by an increasing number of people. Unfortunately, it has sullied the reputation of all kinds of formal social modeling by association. On the other hand, there is sociology and discursive social theory, but here there is a huge gap between its thorough and detailed observation and its abstract theoretical terms. I suggest that the way forward is *not* to abandon all types of formal modeling, but rather to use expressive computational systems to build *descriptive* models of observed dynamic processes. This aims to combine the relevance and realism of social observation with the rigor of formal computational models (Moss, 1999). This is a bottom-up attempt to bridge the gap and move towards a science of social phenomena (see Moss *et al.*, 2001) for a discussion of this). This is a consequence of accepting that economics will have to be more like biology, which employs lengthy observation and description before modeling, than physics (or, at least, than the economist's perception of physics). This is what some of the researchers in the new field of social simulation are attempting to do (for an insight into this field see *JASSS*[1]).

Modeling complex systems

Complex systems are precisely those for which it is extremely difficult to deduce behavior from first principles. For example, it is extremely unlikely that one would be able to predict the behavior of a particular animal purely from a priori principles; rather, one would have to spend a lot of time observing and describing its actions to get a hold on the intricate contingencies of its actual behavior. With complex systems observation and description must come first, and only much later (when the detailed behavioral mechanisms are well understood) is it *sometimes* possible to encapsulate some of these in a predictive model. It seems likely that much economic behavior is complex in this way. This is not surprising, since it arises as the consequence of the intricate interactions between members of a species that is characterized by the variety and contingency of its behavior.

But if we are to give up the chimera of numerical predictive models built using a priori principles, doesn't that mean we have to give up formal models and rigor? I would say that we do not. What it does mean, however, is that we have to use formal and computational models that are capable of capturing the detailed behavior as it is observed. We then need to constrain these models *as much as possible* using observations of the relevant phenomena, both in terms of the trajectories of the causal processes *as well as* the outcomes; in terms of qualatitive information (such as anecdotal accounts) *as well as* quantitative data. Pinning down our models using only validation from predictive outcomes and an insistence on formal simplicity will not be enough; we will need to capture the workings of the processes *stage by stage* as they are observed.

In order to perform this feat we will need systems that are up to the task of expressing the qualitative cognitive and social processes that economic phenomena are rooted in. These more expressive systems come at a price; they are not simple and they allow for multiple representations of the same outcomes. However, there is no need for them to be any less formal than a set of differential equations.

I am suggesting that we should attempt to construct models of quite specific sets of observations that are more akin to a description than a theory. It is, of course, impossible to lose *all* assumptions in the construction of any model, but the point is to move towards using fewer and less drastic a priori assumptions and more qualitative and quantitative constraints derived from observation of the processes under study. The purpose is to provide an unambiguous framework for the exploration of the possible processes within these constraints so as to inform the direction of further observation and modeling (see Edmonds, 2001). This is not merely static description, for we are not concerned with static phenomena, but dynamic description of particular sets of observations using the techniques of computational and cognitive modeling. The extent to which such models are generalizable to other phenomena will only become apparent when compared with other descriptive models, just as the general characteristics and markings of a species of animal may only become clear when several descriptions of the animals are compared.

To many my position will seem too pessimistic. They may be still hoping for some brilliant short cut to a predictive model that will allow them to avoid the laborious business of observing and describing the underlying processes. However, I would point out that the science of biology has become enormously successful using the methods I am suggesting and, once we have accepted the amount of field work that our subject matter entails, equal success might be achieved in economics.

Using agent-based models

The move to agent-based models in economics can be seen as part of a transition to a more descriptive style of modeling. An agent-based model must, by its very nature, model a real actor with a computational agent (in some way), so there *should* be a one-one correspondence between actors and agents. It is not necessary to assume that the law of large numbers will iron out the messy details. The model can allow the global properties to emerge (or not) without having to *assume* these details away. Real economic actors are (almost always) encapsulated, i.e. they will have an inside, where the decision-making is done, which is largely hidden from view, and a series of ways in which they interact with the outside environment that are more easily observable. The agents that are used to model these actors are encapsulated in a directly analogous way.

However, many agent-based modelers do not see the need for any greater descriptive accuracy than this. Thus when inspecting the learning, inference and decision-making processes that an agent uses in such a model, one often finds something as unrealistic as a simulated annealing algorithm or standard genetic algorithm. These are algorithms that have been taken from the field of computer science, regardless of their descriptive appropriateness for the actual economic actors being modeled. Now it is possible that in some circumstances such algorithms will give acceptable results for some purposes, but at the moment we can only guess whether this is the case. It is not only that we do not know the exact conditions of application of each algorithm, we do not know of even a *single* real circumstance where we could completely rely on any of these "off-the-shelf" algorithms to give a reasonable fit.

To be clear, I am not criticizing looking to computer science for ideas, structures and frameworks that might be used in modeling – being a bounteous source of possible types of process is one of the computer science's great contributions to knowledge. What I am criticizing is the use of such algorithms without either any justification of their appropriateness or modification to make them appropriate.

Thus many agent-based models fail to escape the problems of more traditional models. They attempt to use some ensemble of interacting agents to reproduce some global outcome without knowing if the behavior of the individual agents is at all realistic. The wish for the "magic" short-cut is still there.

Constraining our models

Clearly what is needed is some way of modeling the behavior of economic actors by computational agents in a credible way. As noted above, real economic actors are probably complex in the sense that it is unlikely that we will be able to deduce their actions using a priori principles. What we can do is to constrain our models as much as possible from what we do know. There are several sources of such knowledge. We can:

1   *Ensure that the global outcomes of the model match the global outcomes of real actors in the standard way.* This is a start, but when one is using a more expressive formal system (like an agent-based computational one) then this is unlikely to sufficiently constrain the possible models. In other words, there are likely to be many computational models that produce the same global outcomes.

2   *Ensure that the actions of the individual actors match those of our agents' behavior as they learn and interact.* Axtell and Epstein (1994) set out some criteria for the performance of multi-agent simulations. In this: *level 0* is when a model caricatures reality at the global level through the use of simple graphical devices (e.g. animations or pictures); *level 1* is when the model is in qualitative agreement at the global level with empirical macro-structures; *level 2* is when the model produces qualitative agreement at the agent level with empirical microstructures; and *level 3* is when the model exhibits quantitative agreement at the agent level with empirical microstructures. The constraint I am suggesting corresponds to their *level 3*, with an emphasis on the agreement over time.

3   *Look to the emerging guidelines coming from cognitive science as to the sort of learning and decision processes humans might use.* Now the task of the cognitive scientist is difficult, but such scientists are able, at least, to exclude some mechanisms for modeling behavior and make suggestions for the mechanisms derived from a lot of observation. It is notable that many successful sciences take their ultimate grounding for the behavior of their components from outside their discipline (e.g. chemistry is grounded in physics).

4   *Simply ask the actual actors why they made the decisions they did and how they learnt what they learnt, i.e. use some of the techniques of business history.* This method has its known drawbacks, but can be successfully used, especially when confirmed by other methods. In any case, it is likely to produce more useful and accurate information about the real behavior of actors than is implicit in many of the assumptions used in economics. Edmund Chattoe has recently written a more thorough catalogue of the ways in which we can collect social data to constrain our modeling properly (Chattoe, 2002).

Conclusion

Bad science starts with a technique and changes the problem to fit it; good science starts from the problem and chooses the appropriate technique. With the advent of cheap computational power and flexible modeling software, we have the appropriate techniques for performing that essential abstraction task called description. In this case it is a description that captures the dynamic, emergent and complex cognitive and social processes we observe to be involved in economic exchange. "High theory" may eventually emerge, but only when there are sufficient intermediate, more descriptive models to inform and support it. Our complex subject matter means that there is no short cut to success, but that this will require a lot of hard work.

Note

1 *Journal of Artificial Societies and Social Simulation* (JASSS), http://jasss.soc.surrey.ac.uk.

References

Axtel, R.L. and Epstein, J.M. (1994) Agent-based modelling: understanding our creations. *Bulletin of the Sante Fe Institute*, Winter, 28–32.

Chattoe, E. (2002) Building empirically plausible multi-agent systems – a case study of innovation diffusion. In: Dautenhahn, K., Edmonds, B., Bond, A. and Cañamero, L. (eds), *Socially Intelligent Agents: Creating Relationships with Computers and Robots*, Chapter 13. Kluwer.

Edmonds, B. (2001) Towards a descriptive model of agent strategy search. *Computational Economics*, **18**(1), 118–133. http://www.cpm.mmu.ac.uk/cpmrep54.html.

Moss, S. (1999) *Relevance, Realism and Rigour: A Third Way for Social and Economic Research*. Centre for Policy Modelling, Manchester Metropolitan University. http://www.cpm.mmu.ac.uk/cpmrep56.html.

Moss, S., Sawyer, R.K., Conte, R. and Edmonds, B. (2001) Sociology and social theory in agent-based social simulation: a symposium. *Computational and Mathematical Organization Theory*,. **7(3)**, 183–205.

An alternative framework for economics

John Nightingale (University of New England, Australia)
and Jason Potts (University of Queensland, Australia)

The award of the Nobel Prize in Economics for Information Economics gives an opportunity to illustrate why this form of economic analysis is a dead end. The theories advanced by the prize winners, Akerlof, Stiglitz and Spence, are *ad hoc* auxiliary assumptions tacked onto the neoclassical, and neowalrasian, hard core. The work of these auxiliaries is mainly ex-post-rationalization rather than prediction or explanation.

Is modern economic theory just a morass of special cases? It is important that some alternative framework be found to allow valid generalization once again to characterize economic theory and, this time, not fail to provide robust empirical results in the absence of *ad hoc* auxiliaries. Is there such an alternative? We can report that there is, and that it promises all that is missing from orthodoxy.

The autism of orthodoxy stems from its treatment of the human agent, who is mindless and does not interact with other agents. The broad solution then is to develop a framework in which agents carry knowledge and interact with other agents to use and create knowledge. This is the essence of the new evolutionary economics (e.g. Loasby, 1999). In *The New Evolutionary Microeconomics*, Potts (2000) argues that all heterodox thought shares a common ontological foundation in the view that the dynamics of evolving economic systems are in the space of connections. An economy is a complex system of interactions, and the dynamics of an economic system involve change in the connective structure of the system. Three main themes can be found to share this common foundation.

The first is the evolutionary economics revived by Nelson and Winter (1982). This builds on Book IV of Marshall's *Principles*, and on Schumpeter's theories of cycles and innovation, creative destruction and greed for monopoly profit. Market capitalism is a restless system of experimentation in pursuit of sustainable rents based on private knowledge. This is fundamentally a neo-Darwinian approach. It has been argued in Nightingale and Laurent (2001) that social and cultural theory is ultimately swallowed by Darwin's "universal acid," as Dennett so tellingly put it (Dennett, 1995). Complexity and self-organization theory is the most recent advance of the neo-Darwinian project (Foster and Metcalfe, 2001).

The second is the New "Old Institutionalism," which is about how agents with minds construct and use complex systems of rules. Current orthodoxy has largely ignored the cognitive dimension of human behavior. This strand of course began with Veblen, finding new life in the development of both evolutionary thought and its application to human institutions. American Institutionalism saw the difficulties of Veblen's imprecision and contradictions, and neglected the biological metaphor introduced by Veblen in favor of a vague developmental notion of institutions as historical determinants of economic outcomes. Current research on Veblen's themes often ignores his contribution, but continuity of ideas remains clear. Organizational ecology, and other resource and systems-based views of the firm, is one such well-defined field on inquiry. Evolutionary psychology is another (Casimides and Tooby, 1994). Both these are converging in the economist's sphere, seeking explanations of selection processes and system regularities in habits, routines and the causes for organizations' and other institutions' persistence as well as entry and exit. The means by which knowledge is conserved as well as transformed and created is at the center of this program.

The third is the complex systems view of economic systems. Methodological Individualism is one of the principles on which modern orthodox economics is based, as an article of faith, and a justification for the reductionism that has bedeviled areas such as macroeconomics. The antithesis of this is an organic approach that can be traced to, among others, the American pragmatist philosopher, Charles Sanders Peirce. In essence, the concept of a system rather than some atom within an aggregation of atoms, as the entity of interest, distinguishes the organic approach from MI. Geoff Hodgson's *Economics and Evolution* (Hodgson, 1993) has an extended exposition of the importance of this branch of theory. Reductionism, one of the fundamentals of MI, insists on "micro-foundations" for any explanation. An organic, systems or hierarchical approach insists that this demand is not only irrelevant but misleading. Such a demand results in attempting to use inappropriate theory, and has long been abandoned in the physical and life sciences (ever heard of a sub-atomic theory of ocean waves?).

This range of heterodox economic theories, all of which are close relatives of very orthodox theories in other fields of science, are united against the neo-walrasian orthodoxy, even with the *ad hoc* auxiliaries added by this year's Nobel prize-winning information economists, by a single critical feature. They are all theories of connections between knowledge carriers, be these individuals (in a theory of intra-household decisions), firms (in a theory of market structure), or sectors or national economies (in a theory of macroeconomic performance). They are all dynamic theories of systems evolving endogenously, subject to external shocks, of course. They are theories in which knowledge rather than information is key. They are not Newtonian field theories, in which every point is connected to every other. They can all be subsumed analytically as elements and the connections between them. These dynamic systems theories of evolutionary organization are all graph theory constructs. In other words, using the language of graph theory, the geometry of elements and connections provides a unifying frame with which to develop these alternative economic theories.

This, then, shows there is a progressive alternative to autistic neoclassical/ neowalrasian economics. The emerging synthesis of evolutionary and self-organizational approaches into a framework of complex systems theory is a solid basis upon which to build. It connects evolutionary biology and evolutionary psychology to evolutionary economics (for a popular science account, see, for example, Stuart Kauffman's *At Home in the Universe* (Kauffman, 1995). It provides analytic methods in discrete mathematics and multi-agent simulation models. It is the study of the emergence of order, rather than continuous equilibria. It is ontologically well founded in a growth of knowledge framework where connections are the prime variables in an economic system. Such a unified heterodox synthesis may underpin a broad front of research advances that do not close off alternatives, but open more to scientific development.

[Jason Potts is the author of *The New Evolutionary Microeconomics: Complexity, Competence, and Adaptive Behaviour* (2000). John Nightingale is the co-editor of *Darwinism and Evolutionary Economics* (Edward Elgar, 2001).]

References

Casimides, L. and Tooby, J. (1994) Better than rational. *AER*, **84**, 327–332.
Dennett, D.C. (1995) *Darwin's Dangerous Idea: Evolution and the Meaning of Life*. Touchstone Books.
Foster, J. and Metcalfe, J.S. (eds) (2001) *Frontiers of Evolutionary Economics: Competition, Self-Organization, and Innovation Policy*. Edward Elgar.
Hodgson, G. (1993) *Economics and Evolution*. Polity Press.
Kauffman, S. (1995) *At Home in the Universe: The Search for Lands of Self-Organization and Complexity*. Oxford University Press.
Loasby, P. (1999) *Knowledge, Institutions and Evolution in Economics*. Routledge.
Nelson, R.R. and Winter, S.G. (1982) *Evolutionary Theory of Economic Change*. Harvard University Press.
Nightingale, J. and Laurent, L. (2001) *Darwinism and Evolutionary Economics*. Edward Elgar.
Potts, J. (2000) *The New Evolutionary Microeconomics*. Edward Elgar.

The Russian defeat of economic orthodoxy

Steve Keen (University of Western Sydney, Australia)

Many armies have followed a triumphant march into Russia with an ignominious withdrawal. Orthodox economics is merely the latest invader to succumb to this dismal tradition. But this theory did more damage to the Russian Bear than most military invaders.

Neoliberals were jubilant at the fall of the Berlin Wall. Not only had capitalism proved superior to communism, but the economic theory of the market economy had, it seemed, proved superior to Marxism. A task of transition did lie at "the end of history" – though not from capitalism to communism as Marx had expected, but from state socialism back to the market economy.

Such a transition was clearly necessary. In addition to the clear political and humanitarian failures of centralized Soviet regimes, economic growth under central planning had failed to maintain its initial promise. Once impressive performances gave way to stagnant economies producing dated goods, whereas the market economies of the West had grown more rapidly (if unevenly), and with far greater product innovation.

As the most prominent intellectual advocates for the free market over central planning, neoclassical economists presented themselves as the authorities for how this transition should occur. Above all else, they endorsed haste. In a typical statement, Murray Wolfson (1992) argued (p. 42) that:

> . . . market systems are much more stable than most people who have been brought up in a command economy can imagine. The flexibility of market systems permits them to absorb a great deal of abuse and error that a rigidly planned system cannot endure.

The terms "abuse" and "error" were unfortunately prophetic – for the rapid transition imposed a great deal of abuse and error on the peoples of Eastern Europe. A decade later, incomes have collapsed, unemployment is at Great Depression levels, poverty is endemic. The transition has in general been not from socialist to capitalist, but from socialist to Third World.

Wolfson is far from being a leading light of neoliberal economics, but his arguments in favor of a rapid transition are indicative of the naivety of those whom Joseph Stiglitz would eventually blame for abetting the theft and destruction of Russia's wealth. Their key failing was a simplistic belief in the ability of market economies – even proto-market economies – rapidly to achieve equilibrium. This led them to recommend haste in the transition, and especially in privatization of state assets – a haste that effectively handed over state assets to those in a position to move quickly, the old Party apparatchiks and organized crime.

Reading these pro-haste papers one decade after the transition debacle, one can take little comfort in realizing how different the outcome of this rapid transition was to the expectations economists held:

> Even though we favor rapid privatization, we doubt that privatization will produce immediate, large increases in productivity. . . . Nonetheless, we believe that in order to enjoy these enormous long-term gains, it is necessary to proceed rapidly and comprehensively on creating a privately-owned, corporate-based economy in Eastern Europe.
>
> Lipton and Sachs (1990)

> The motivation for comprehensiveness and speed in introducing the reforms is clear cut. Such an approach vastly cuts the uncertainties facing the public with regard to the new "rules of the game" in the economy. Rather than creating a lot of turmoil, uncertainty, internal inconsistencies, and political resistance, through a gradual introduction of new measures, the goal is to set in place clear incentives for the new economic system as rapidly as possible. As one wit has put it, if the British were to shift from left-hand-side drive to right-hand-side drive, should they do it gradually . . . say, by just shifting the trucks over to the other side of the road in the first round?
>
> Sachs (1992)

It might be thought that, since speed was such a key aspect of the recommendations economists gave for the transition, they must have modeled the impact of slow versus fast transitions and shown that the latter were, in model terms at least, superior. But in fact the models economists took their guidance from completely ignored time: they were equilibrium models that presumed the system could rapidly move to a new equilibrium once disturbed.

The period of transition coincided with the peak influence of the concept of "rational expectations" in economic theory. This theory argues that a market economy is inhabited by "rational agents" who have, by some presumably evolutionary or iterative learning process, developed complete knowledge of the workings of the market economy and who can therefore confidently predict the future (at the very least, they know what will happen in response to any policy change by the government). The workings of the market economy happen to coincide with the behavior of a conventional neoclassical model, so that the economy is always in full employment equilibrium.

When this theory is put into a mathematical model, it results in a dynamic system known as a "saddle," because the system dynamics are shaped like a horse's saddle.

In conventional dynamic modeling, a saddle is an unstable system: the odds of the system being stable are the same as the odds of dropping a ball on to a real saddle and having it come to rest on the saddle, rather than falling off it. But if you were so lucky as to drop the ball precisely onto the saddle's ridge, and it stayed on that ridge, it would ride up and down it for quite a while until it finally came to rest.

In rational expectations modeling, the saddle system that sensible dynamic models would say is unstable becomes stable but cyclical. The "rational agents" of the models all know the precise shape of the saddle, and jump onto its crest instantly from wherever they may have been displaced by a government policy change. Then the economy cycles up and down the ridge of the saddle, eventually coming to rest in full employment equilibrium once more. This is how devotees of rational expectations explain cycles, given their belief in the inherent equilibrium-seeking nature of a market economy: the system cycles up and down the sole stable path until coming to rest until it is once again disturbed.

These perspectives on individual behavior, the formation of expectations, and the behavior of a market economy, are dubious enough in their own right. Rational expectations "logic" is truly worthy of the moniker autistic, since it is based on a proposition that, if properly handled, negates its own predictions. This is the proposition that, as Muth (1961) put it, "Information is scarce, and the economic system generally does not waste it."

Since in neoclassical economics scarcity is the basis of value, then information should, according to this theory, have a cost. If it has a cost, then agents should economize on its use – they will not use "all available information," but only the subset of information that they can afford, given their preferences for knowledge. Therefore individual agents will not know the full character of the economy, and most will certainly not know its "stable manifold." Rational agents therefore cannot be expected to jump immediately to the equilibrium path of the economy unless they are irrational enough to expend the enormous amount of revenue that would be necessary to buy all the scarce information.

The foundations of "rational expectations" economics are thus internally inconsistent, and the fact that they were taken seriously in the first place is a clear sign of how truly autistic economic theory has become.

But if it was autistic to give this theory credence in the West, how much more so was it to apply this model to the behavior of people in an economic system in transition between central planning and market capitalism? How can the "agents" in a transitional system develop a mental model of a market economy with which they predict the future behavior of the actual economy, if they have not previously lived in a market economy? Are we to presume instead that people can instantly develop the understanding of something as complex as a market economy – and are we to grace this belief with the adjective "rational"?

Lest this seem an overly harsh rhetorical flourish, consider the following discussion of how fast the transition should be from Wolfson's 1992 paper. He begins with a statement that a sensible person might expect would lead towards the conclusion that people must be given time to learn how to react to market signals (p. 37):

> Indeed, when government actions become so large that their effect on prices causes wide divergence from individual choices, one cannot determine what those choices would have been. As a result, no reliable guidelines exist for government choice. Even with the best of intentions, unlimited collective choice destroys the very information base for rational decisions.

He immediately follows up this apparently sensible statement with the following proposition (p. 37):

> Central planners seemingly should at once resign their posts and close their offices. Their departure simply would signal the market to move immediately to equilibrium.

What market? But, oblivious to logical contradictions, he elaborates (p. 39):

> For example, suppose the government were planning a gradual transition from a regime of administered prices to market prices to take place a year from now. What would happen 364 days hence? Obviously, people would refuse to make any but the most urgent transactions at the old prices, or an illegal market would immediately jump to the new prices. Those individuals who would have to sell their goods and services at a lower price on day 365 would find no legal customers on day 364. Similarly, those who would receive higher prices at day 364 would not sell legally on day 363, 362, 361, and so on. The economy would either come to a complete stop or would legally or illegally anticipate the future. In the face of rational and reasonably knowledgeable economic agents, delay invites disaster.

"Rational and reasonably knowledgeable economic agents"? Where did they come from, and how did they acquire so profound a knowledge of the market system they have not as yet lived in that they can predict its behavior (and prices in it a year into the future) before they experience it? Yet, presuming their existence and their intimate knowledge of the behavior of an economic system that does not yet exist, Wolfson advises that (p. 39):

> A rational expectations conclusion is that quitting communism Cold Turkey is the only way to get from A to B. In practice, governments must make the national currency convertible and allow it to float on legal as well as black markets, abolish the system of subsidies and direct plans and quotas, close plants that cannot compete, come quickly to a privatization of industry even if some inequities result, strictly control the money supply, and allow goods and services to find their own price on national and international markets.
>
> *(Wolfson does qualify his arguments with some concessions to reality, but in the end his recommendations are all for speed on the basis of a belief in the self-adjusting properties of the market economy.)*

While there were significant differences in how the program of transition was implemented, in general this rapid and complete exposure of the once relatively closed economies of the East to the West was the rule. Away from the fantasies of rational expectations economics, what this rapid exposure to international competition did was give ex-socialist consumers instant access to Western goods, and expose Eastern European factories to open competition with their Western counterparts.

As Janos Kornai details so well, the soft budget constraints of the Soviet system had resulted in "cashed up" consumers on the one hand, and technologically backward and shortage-afflicted factories on the other. The consumer financial surpluses, accumulated during the long wait between placing orders for consumer durables under the Soviet system and actually receiving the goods, were rapidly dissipated on Western consumer goods. The Eastern businesses, now forced to compete with technologically far superior Western firms, were rapidly destroyed, throwing their workers into unemployment. With accumulated buying power dissipated and freely floating currencies, exchange rates collapsed – for example, Romania's Lei has gone from about 1,000 to the US dollar in 1993 to 32,000 to the dollar today.

A sensible dynamic analysis of the plight of the ex-socialist economies – one that really did take time into account – would have predicted this outcome from a too rapid transition. Even if the technological advantages of the market system over Soviet-style industrialization had amounted to just a 1 percent difference per annum in productivity, the 45-year period of socialism would have given market economy firms a 55 percent cost advantage over their socialist counterparts. And, of course, the product development aspect of technological innovation had made far greater differences than this merely quantitative measure of costs – Western firms would have decimated socialist ones on product quality alone, even without a cost advantage.

A time-based analysis would therefore have supported a gradual transition, with substantial aid as well to assist Eastern factories to introduce modern production technology and process control methods. It should also have been obvious that for a market economy to develop, one needs the minimum distributive systems of a market: systems of wholesale and retail distribution, respect for written contracts, systems for consumer protection, laws of exchange – all things that take a substantial time to put into place.

With the obscene haste with which the actual transition was implemented, the only non-market systems that could rapidly develop were those that were already in place in the preceding socialist system – the systems of organized crime that had always been there to lubricate the wheels of the shortage-afflicted Soviet system, just as market intrusions once permeated the feudal systems out of which capitalism itself evolved in Europe.

It is of course too late now to suggest any alternative path from socialism to the market for these no longer socialist economies. The new transition they must make is from a de-industrialized Third World state back to a developed one, and that transition will clearly take time.

[Steve Keen is the author of *Debunking Economics: The Naked Emperor of the Social Sciences* (Zed Books & Pluto Press).]

References

Lipton, D. and Sachs, J. (1990) Privatization in Eastern Europe: the case of Poland. *Brookings Papers on Economic Activity*, 2, 295.

Muth, J.F. (1961) Rational expectations and the theory of price movements. *Econometrica*, 29(2), 315–335.

Sachs, J. (1992) The economic transformation of Eastern Europe: the case of Poland. *American Economist*, 36(2), 5.

Wolfson, M. (1992) Transition from a command economy: rational expectations and cold turkey. *Contemporary Policy Issues*, 10, 37–42.

The tight links between post-Keynesian and feminist economics

Marc Lavoie (University of Ottawa, Canada)

My aim here is to show that there are tight methodological links between post-Keynesian economics, as I understand it, and feminist economics, as presented by Julie Nelson (1995) (who also argued why PAE needs feminism, in the October 2001 issue of the *PAE Newsletter*). I should point out that others, specifically Lee Levin, have also found substantial points of convergence between feminist economics and post-Keynesian economics.

In her paper, Nelson considers models, methods, topics and pedagogy. The first three issues only will be dealt with here, but, as the French students have shown in the autistic economics debate, pedagogy is also crucial.

Within the issue of models, Nelson questions the use and definition of rationality, as well as the role of methodological individualism; in methods, she discusses the realism of hypotheses; in topics, she challenges the neoclassical obsession with exchange economics. I shall show that these elements that Nelson highlights as key methodological features of feminist economics can also be found in the characterization of post-Keynesian economics.

In my book on post-Keynesian economics (Lavoie, 1992a), and in a previously written article (Lavoie, 1992b), I have argued that there are four essentials, or presuppositions, that distinguish post-Keynesian economics, along with several other heterodox schools such as the Institutionalists and most Marxists, from mainstream neoclassical economics. These four essentials can be set up as four antagonizing doublets, the first term of each doublet applying to neoclassical economics, and the second to post-Keynesian economics and its heterodox brethren. These are: substantive or hyper-rationality versus procedural or reasonable rationality; methodological individualism versus some form of organicism or holism; an instrumentalist/idealist ontology versus realism; exchange versus production.

In neoclassical economics, the assumed capacities of the individual are daunting: it is always possible for agents to optimize, and to behave as if the future could be predicted, with some probabilistic certainty. In post-Keynesian economics and other heterodox schools, agents have bounded capacities to acquire and treat information; in addition, their environment can be highly uncertain, as decisions to be taken themselves may change the future economic environment. Procedural rationality, or reasonable rationality, goes beyond maximization subject to constrained computational abilities. The solution sought can only be a satisfying one, for in general no one knows what the optimal solution is, nor whether there ever existed such an optimal solution. Within this world, one is compelled to function on the basis of procedural rationality, often relying on rules, habits, and the judgment of others, who we assume to be better informed.

The use of rules, customs, and conventions brings in organicism, holism and intersubjectivity. In post-Keynesian economics, individual behavior is interdependent. Individuals are influenced by their social environment, social classes, or gender. There is organic interdependence. For this reason, social classes and their institutions play a crucial role in the analysis. By contrast, the mainstream neoclassical agent is generally seen as an atomistic being, devoid of any class link or social attachment.

The third essential of post-Keynesian economics, related to epistemology, is realism. Realism is rather vague, as it can be defined in many different ways – specially with the advent of critical and transcendental realism – but I shall define it as a school driving at putting forth realist hypotheses based on stylized facts, and determined to offer explanations and tell a story. In neoclassical economics, a form of idealistic instrumentalism reigns. High-brow theory – general equilibrium theory – defines the hypotheses that are required to describe the world as they wish it would be; vulgar theory starts from these unrealistic premises to build partial equilibrium models and to test their models.

Finally, there is the issue of the definition of economics. Mainstream economics is the science of scarcity, the study of the optimal allocation of scarce means. All models are variants or extensions of the exchange economy. Producers are arbitrageurs acting in a form of indirect exchange. By contrast, post-Keynesian economics is concerned, as the classical authors were, with production and distribution. The major issue is not how to allocate resources, but rather how to get rid of unemployed resources and how to increase production and living standards.

These four essentials of post-Keynesian economics can be found in Nelson's (1995) depiction of feminist economics. She criticizes the mainstream "rational, autonomous, self-interested agent, successfully making optimizing choices subject to exogenously imposed constraints" (p. 135). In place of this atomistic agent with hyper-rationality, Nelson wishes an agent "socialized into family and community groups," a "dependent, emotional, connected" human being – in other words the organic economic actor that I described above.

For example, Nelson (1995: 136) points to models, such as wage efficiency models *à la* Akerlof, that emphasize the notions of fairness and equity. We know that these kinds of models have long been advocated by Marxist economists; and post-Keynesian economists have also tied fairness to economic behavior for instance, Adrian Wood in his theory of pay (Wood, 1978). Nelson also points toward Keynes's notion of animal spirits and conventions, which are recurrent themes along with fundamental uncertainty and liquidity preference in post-Keynesian economics. Decisions in an environment of fundamental uncertainty, as pointed out above, cannot be guided by mainstream hyper-rationality; it requires procedural rationality.

In some ways, Nelson (1995: 139) favors realism, as the post-Keynesians do. She denounces the neoclassical emphasis on "logic, without sufficient attention to grasping the big picture," which leads to "empty, out-of-touch exercises in pointless deduction . . . for the sake of precision" – the idealism of a segment of neoclassical economics. Nelson recommends the use of metaphors and story-telling. As post-Keynesian Paul Davidson has written on a number of occasions, it is better to be vaguely right than precisely wrong.

The fourth essential doublet, that of exchange versus production, is directly tackled by Nelson (1995: 142–143). She points out that classical economists used to be concerned with production and the distribution of all the necessaries and conveniences of life. This is contrasted to the neoclassical definition of our field, "the processes by which things – goods, services, financial assets – are exchanged." For her, the definition of economics should be based on "provisioning" rather than "marketization" or the use of a narrow model of individual choice.

There are other passages in Nelson's account of feminist economics that are reminiscent of ideas that have been long advocated by some post-Keynesian economists. For instance, when Nelson' (p. 137) says that "the feminist analysis suggests that there should not be just one economic model, but rather many economic models, depending on the usefulness of various modeling techniques in the various applications," one is struck with the similarity of such a statement to the Babylonian approach, the main proponent of which has been post-Keynesian (Dow, 1990). Dow's Babylonian approach sees research as examining an issue from "a variety of starting points" (p. 146), by using a range of different methods and techniques (as also argued by Nelson), and by using a pluralism of models.

Finally, Nelson (1995: 141) points out that the objectivity of the researcher, which is the hallmark of positive economics as conceived by mainstream colleagues, is an illusion. This was also pointed out by post-Keynesian Joan Robinson, who argued that, since ideology and economics were intimately tied up, economics was little different from a branch of theology. Robinson loathed those who claimed objectivity in the social sciences, saying that they either deceived themselves or tried to deceive others. For Robinson (1964: 27), "the objectivity of science arises, not because the individual is impartial, but because individuals are continually testing each other's theories."

The post-autistic movement, which got started by the French students asking for more pluralism in the classroom, ironically contributes to more objectivity in economics.

References

Dow, S.C. (1990) "Beyond dualism," *Cambridge Journal of Economics,* 14(2).

Lavoie, M. (1992a) *Foundations of Post-Keynesian Economic Analysis.* Aldershot: Edward Elgar.

Lavoie, M. (1992b) "Towards a new research programme for post-Keynesianism and neo-Ricardianism." *Review of Political Economy*, 4(1).

Nelson, J.A. (1995) "Feminism and economics," *Journal of Economic Perspectives*, 9(2).

Robinson, J. (1964) *Economic Philosophy.* London: Penguin Books.

Wood, A. (1978) *A Theory of Pay*. Cambridge: Cambridge University Press.

Is the concept of economic growth autistic?

Jean Gadrey (University of Lille, France)

Since Malthus, economists have been debating the "limits to growth" in an attempt to identify those factors that might lead to an inexorable slow-down in growth, or even to a "steady state." At the beginning of the 1970s, the studies carried out by the "Club of Rome" brought the terms of the debate up to date again, drawing on analyses of the increasing scarcity of natural resources. We will not engage with this debate, which is undoubtedly worthy of interest, for two reasons. First, history can be said to have decided the matter, at least up to now: capitalism has repeatedly pushed back the limits in question and given the lie to prophesies inspired by the Malthusian approach. Second, and more importantly, it seems to us that the main question raised by the virtually unanimous assertion that growth needs to be as strong as possible concerns not the rate of growth, but rather the concept itself and the tools used to measure increasing wealth. The issues addressed in debates on the limits to growth seldom include the limits of the concept itself.

The invention of growth

The concept of economic growth, in the sense attributed to it today,[1] is a relatively recent invention, a by-product, as it were, of industrialization. It came into its own with Fordism, the three decades or so of growth and prosperity following the Second World War, and the national accounting systems of the twentieth century, which were themselves developed in a particular economic context — one that saw the expansion of heavy industry and the mass consumption of standardized goods. What is economic growth? It is the rate of increase, from one period to another, in the flows of goods produced and/or consumed within a given institutional space, which may be a firm, an industry, a national or regional territory, etc. However, if this statistical operation is to be carried out successfully from period to period, there has to be agreement on the nature of the goods whose "volumes" are being measured, and these goods should not be continually changing in nature or in quality. The ideal situation is one in which, first, the transformations carried out during the production process affect mainly the quantities of the goods produced rather than the nature and qualities of those goods. In this way, product standards remain unchanged from period to period. Secondly, there should be stable conventions governing the types of products to be included in the accounts.

Broadly speaking, these conditions were met during the "Fordist" period, which saw the expansion of the mass production and consumption of highly standardized goods and services that benefited from economies of scale, the mechanization of agriculture, the heavy and inflexible automation of the manufacturing industry (before the advent of the computer), the establishment of large retail outlets and other "retail factories," the increased take-up of banking services by households and their increasing connection to water, gas and electricity suppliers and to telephone networks, and even the development of "Fordist" tourism in the 1960s – the ideal type of which is of course the Spanish model. While it is true that the quality of these goods and services improved over time, it was the increase in their volume that was the major component of this mode of development, whose progress could be followed as the annual product flows and year-on-year increases were entered into the national accounts, providing a picture of economic growth. As far as households were concerned, the corresponding indicator of progress was the "standard of living," which was measured in the same way – on the basis of the annual flows consumed. Thus the criterion used to assess economic "well-being" was the level of consumption: the more goods and services were consumed, the higher economic well-being was judged to be. At the heart of this economy based on growth in the flows of standardized goods and services lay gains in labor productivity.

Contemporary economies, growth and productivity

Can the analysis of contemporary economies rely exclusively on the use of similar tools (growth, productivity, standard of living) to measure and evaluate their own progress? There must be considerable doubt about this.

As far as the manufacturing industry is concerned, demassification (a term coined by Alvin Toffler as early as 1970[2]), increasing variety, product innovations that reduce product life cycles and, in some cases, the introduction of individualized or "customized" products, together with the sale of integrated packages (products/services/after sales), have all served to weaken measurement conventions based on quality standards that were comparable over time.

The difficulties and uncertainties of these measurements are further compounded in the service sector. While some service industries are still at the "industrial" stage of providing standardized services, many others do not readily lend themselves to the application of the traditional industrial concepts. What do terms such as "growth" and "productivity gains" mean when applied to services such as consultancy, education, health, social welfare, research or insurance? Where are the standard product units that would make it possible to compare the quantities produced over time? If the production and diffusion of knowledge is playing an increasingly important role in the developed economies, what are these units of knowledge whose increased volume is being followed?

One of the greatest ambiguities in the desperate and generally fruitless search for new "conventions" that would make such activities amenable to the application of the industrial concepts of growth and productivity can be illustrated by considering the case of health services. In such activities, is the product whose growth we are seeking to measure (and whose definition subsequently determines the measurement of productivity gains and standard of living) synonymous with the flows of actions, of medical and surgical treatments and of patients treated? Or should we look beyond these flows and recognize that what counts (the real "product") is the improvement in the health of the individuals and population concerned? If the flows approach is adopted, successful preventive policies, for example, will lead to reductions in the measurement of growth and standards of living! However, if priority is given in evaluations to improvements of state, those same preventive policies could be judged to be positive contributions to the individual and collective quality of life. This would constitute a shift away from (economic) growth towards (social and human) development. We would not, for all that, be abandoning the use of statistical indicators of that development (the name of Amartya Sen, a Nobel prize-winner in economics, is associated with important advances in this area linked to studies carried out under the auspices of the United Nations Development Program), and there would still be a need for proper economic analyses of the effectiveness of the actions and services through which these improvements in state are to be achieved. What is different is the favored indicator of progress (the others are not entirely dispensed with, however), and the conventions on which evaluation is based.

This example of the healthcare sector and its output indicators is in no sense specific. Similar dilemmas can be found in most activities based on the production and exchange of knowledge (education, research, consultancy of all kinds), in "relational" neighborhood services (help for the elderly, childcare, etc.), social work, insurance, etc. – that is, in the vast majority of activities that have seen the strongest growth in employment over the past 25 years. Notions such as the growth in processing flows and productivity gains are of much less relevance in assessing progress in these sectors, which play a major role in developed economies. The increase in wealth, in value created or value added or in productive efficiency, certainly seems to require mechanisms for assessing the effects or impacts of those activities on the proper functioning or development of the realities they operate on, whether they be individuals, organizations, or technical or social systems. Does the wealth or value produced by a service that helps to maintain technical, economic or social systems, or even human beings, increase with the number of "trouble-shooting" interventions or repairs (which is the solution usually adopted by growth indicators) or, conversely, with the ability of that service to reduce the number and gravity of the dysfunctions? Is the wealth-generating capacity of an educational system measured by the number of hours teaching delivered or the number of training sessions organized, or should we adopt different conventions for assessing the contribution of the education system to the development of its users' knowledge, personalities and socialization?

The new growth of the "new economy," we are told, is based on the new information and communication technologies that constitute a new, universal technological paradigm. This assessment is somewhat exaggerated, but let us accept for the moment that it is true. Can such an economy, based on information, communication and knowledge, be conceptualized and managed in terms of growth? The answer is obviously no: the relative "dematerialization" of wealth has gone hand-in-hand with the gradual disappearance of those stable reference units used to measure agricultural and industrial output. True, it is possible to count software programs (or the lines of programming in each package), computers, Internet connections or bank transactions, but it is well known that "what counts" is processing and problem-solving capacity, reliability, or the useful information that can be easily obtained by means of "intelligent" and "user-friendly" procedures. Once again, the progress of this information economy lies less in the growth of units produced than in the impact of these ICTs on the functioning of other technical and human systems. This requires the services thus obtained to be evaluated from a development perspective that might include certain growth indicators but would not be reduced solely to such measures.

Financial criteria and the discourse on progress

Thus if the main pillars of contemporary developed economies are services, permanent innovation, knowledge and the new information and communication technologies, we can reasonably suppose that it requires us to move away from the economic growth paradigm towards a new paradigm based on the evaluation of economic and social development. In other words, we need to shift away from the economics of measuring flows and costs towards the socio-economics of judging improvements in state, quality, and individual and collective well-being.

Now the advocates of the "new economy," namely some in the world of politics and the media and a handful of economists, have not reached this point. They extol the merits of their new model in the language of the old model, using the concepts that enabled economics to portray itself as a "hard" science, laying down technical laws comparable to the law of gravitation.

One objection can be raised here. Observation of the management practices adopted by firms in high-tech sectors and the financial institutions that support them clearly shows that these major players in the new economy have long understood that the realities they are managing can no longer be conceptualized with the old concepts. They have successfully put the growth paradigm into context . . . . Neither Bill Gates and his kind nor the pension funds that influence the management of an increasing number of companies need the old micro- and macro-economic concepts to manage the performance of the firms in their possession. Their tools are indicators of financial return, or, to use the language of the day, of the "creation of shareholder value." However, beyond the boundaries of their companies and financial networks, what they need is a discourse that publicly legitimizes their outstanding contribution to the public good. This is where the majority of economists, the economic media, Alan Greenspan and others play their part, making their statements in the name of prosperity, growth and productivity.

There are other ways of putting the growth paradigm into context than by imputing a monetary value to all the activities and all the products in competitive markets or the financial markets. In policy terms, the first point at issue in the observable present economy is not the choice of strong growth rather than slow growth. Rather, it is the choice of a mode of thinking distinct from both the industrialist mode of judging progress inherited from the Fordist era (based on the notions of growth, productivity and standard of living) and the financial mode of calculating the shareholder value of all activities. This new mode would be one based on a pluralistic evaluation of social development, of quality of life, and of the improvement in various individual and collective states. Putting both the growth and productivity paradigm and the financial magnitude paradigm into context simultaneously obviously does not mean we are depriving ourselves of economic and financial indicators, when relevant, as a means of quantifying increases in product flows and the efficiency with which those flows are produced, particularly in activities that produce relatively standardized goods and services. These indicators should be part – with others – of the development evaluation paradigm, but their role should be a subordinate one. What does the phrase "controlling health expenditure" mean, for example, if not a policy based, over and above statistical observation of the volume of medical and paramedical actions and their costs ("accounting control"), on assessments of the relevance of these practices to individual and collective health objectives under debate? Should home help services for the elderly be evaluated in terms of their ability to reduce old people's dependency, to give them as much autonomy as possible by cooperating with their relatives and with voluntary workers to that end, thereby reducing the outside assistance required to the minimum? Or should they be measured on the basis of the volume of visits, actions or hours of intervention, in accordance with the argument that an increase in dependency encourages growth?

To conclude on a similar note, we will mention a modest but interesting attempt to suggest a possible path out of this dilemma. American researchers[3] have developed a synthetic national indicator of "social health" in the USA by aggregating nine existing social indicators that it has been possible to monitor statistically since 1959: the index of inequality between rich and poor, average weekly earnings, infant mortality, child poverty, the adolescent suicide rate, the murder rate, unemployment, old age poverty and the cost of care for the elderly that is not reimbursed. They then plotted the index of the growth of GDP and this national index of "social health" on the same graph. From 1959 until the early 1970s, the two indexes evolved in parallel with each other. In the mid-1970s, however, they became uncoupled from each other in spectacular fashion: GDP continued its remarkable growth, while the social health indicator fell sharply, particularly during the lengthy period between 1978 and 1993. Moreover, this finding is relatively insensitive to the weighting coefficients used to construct the synthetic social indicator. The main value of this type of research is not that it provides a definitive new objective measure of social progress, even less of Gross National Happiness, but that it feeds into debates on the development of more precise pluralistic evaluations based on a limited number of indicators whose significance lies in the fact they are the product of careful thought and discussion, rather than being chosen unilaterally by researchers or experts. This, among other things, is what makes the work of the UNDP (United Nations Development Program) on indicators of human development so interesting.

[This essay's ideas are developed further in Jean Gadrey's book *Nouvelle économie nouveau mythe?* (2001). An English translation, *New Economy, New Myth?* will be published later this year by Routledge.]

Notes

1   Our contemporary concepts have more distant origins, since they date from the early days of the Industrial Revolution, and in particular from the work of Malthus. However, it was not until the State took control of "industrial policy" and planning (in Europe, just after the Second World War) that these ideas led to the development of measuring tools, institutions and figures that could be fed into the public debate as indicators of progress.
2   Toffler, A. (1970) *Future Shock*, Bantam Books.
3   See Miringoff, M.L. and Miringoff, M. (1996) *The Growing Gap Between Standard Economic Indicators and the Nation's Social Health*, Challenge, July 1996.

Ontology, epistemology, language and the practice of economics

Warren J. Samuels (Michigan State University, USA)

The post-autistic movement in economics is the latest, certainly a welcome, effort to restructure and refocus the teaching and practice of economics. Limitations of space prevent the articulation of everything that needs to be said about the movement, but a few key points can be made, especially regarding some ontological, epistemological, and linguistic concerns.

Some preliminary points:

1   The practice of economics has always been more diverse than Whig historians have made it out to be. This was true of both the interwar period and the period, following the Second World War, of manifest neoclassical hegemony. Heterogeneity has characterized economics as a whole, heterodox economics, and orthodox economics.

2   A driving force within economics is status emulation. Decisions as to department type, membership, publication outlets chosen and rewarded, curricular content, attitudes toward mathematics and econometrics, the sociology of training graduate students, the finessing of criticism, and so on, are driven by considerations of rank and power. Some heterodox economists have undertaken work to impress – be read by – leading orthodox economists rather than to promote their heterodox paradigm. Some economists within orthodoxy have downplayed the radical aspects of their ideas so as to avoid endangering their status. The combination of heterogeneity and status emulation has resulted in increased hierarchy, including the gradual weakening of heterodoxy and general heterogeneity.

3   Every discipline, every school of thought and every reform movement must confront the tension between being so diffuse that it stands for very little and being so definitive that it appeals only to a narrow and perhaps fanatical group.

4   Economists have, for almost two centuries, been concerned that the discipline does not speak with one voice. One concern is that a multi-vocal economics would not be perceived to be a science – and during that period of

time status emulation has increasingly taken the form of emulating one or another version of what is perceived to be "science."

I now turn to my principal topics: ontology, epistemology, and language.

Ontology has to do with the ultimate nature of reality and of those objects that putatively comprise reality. With regard to economics, the key questions are, first, is there a fundamental, ultimate economic reality? Second, if so, what is it?

The realist position is that such an ultimate reality exists. The burden of the realist position is that realists do not agree as to what it is. One must choose between alternative specifications of reality. The idealist position, in partial contrast, is that no such given ultimate reality exists and that it is thereby open to human social construction. The burden of the idealist position is that idealists do not agree as to what it should be. One must choose between alternative specifications of the ideal, socially constructed economy. In the light of such ubiquity of choice, the use and role of ideology in channeling social construction is understandable.

In economics, a further dichotomy exists. The principal approach to the economy within mainstream neoclassicism is that of positing a pure a-institutional conceptual model of "the market" and examining it under the aegis of the neoclassical research protocol; that of seeking unique determinate optimal equilibrium results. The main alternative approach is to study actual markets and the institutions that form and operate through them. Those who follow the former approach feel that they are reaching conclusions applicable to all economies, even if not to any economy in particular. Those who follow the latter approach both wonder about conclusions that apply to no particular economy and emphasize that – in the allocation of resources, etc. – institutions matter.

The conflict between these two approaches involves both ontology and epistemology: ontology, in regard to the nature of reality: purely conceptual market or actual institutionalized markets; epistemology, as to the object, domain or level of inquiry with respect to which principles of "true" knowledge apply.

This should not be an either-or matter. Abstraction is inevitable. There can be different pure a-institutional conceptual models of the market; some can be orthodox and others heterodox. There can be different modes of putatively actual markets and the institutions that form and operate through them; some can be orthodox and others heterodox. Individual economists can have different notions of what constitutes interesting and useful objects of study. Kevin Hoover, in his message on the HES list of 9 September 2000 pertaining to autism in economics, correctly combines the possibility, if not inevitability, of narrow, hyper-focused research that is also, on its own terms, quite accomplished activity.

It seems to me that to some extent economics already is ontologically pluralistic, but that it is not enough so.

Epistemology has to do with the rules or criteria by which a statement is to be deemed true. Two approaches, or classes of approaches, to epistemology have been followed. By prescriptivism, the quest is for specific conclusively prescriptive rules; by these rules and by these rules alone may truth be determined. By conditionism, no such singular conclusive quest is contemplated; a variety of rules is formulated, and thinkers make their choice(s) from among them.

Transcending even those rival approaches is a fundamental dichotomy as to the nature of truth (rationalism versus empiricism) and a parallel one as to procedure (deduction versus induction). Without examining these dichotomies closely here, it can be said first that both rationalism and empiricism and both deduction and induction are also complements, each mutually influencing the conduct of the other; and second, that deduction yields not truth – defined as correct description or explanation – but validity – understood as a conclusion properly derived from premises, given the system of logic.

It seems to me that to some extent economics already is epistemologically pluralistic, but that it is not enough so.

I would make the same points with regard to theoretical pluralism, including pluralism of models.

I come next to *language*. Here I begin with two dichotomies. The first juxtaposes language as (an effort at) truth with language as (an effort at) power. The former has to do with description and/or explanation, as at least an end in itself; the latter has to do with the motivation of belief and/or behavior. The former informs; the latter moves.

The second dichotomy juxtaposes (through the early Ludwig Wittgenstein) language as corresponding (in substance or logical structure) to reality with language as a tool. The former ties and subordinates us to reality; the latter ties and subordinates reality to us.

One's position with regard to these dichotomies will be reflected in how one treats theories of profit, the existence of the Federal Reserve System, and/or cross-elasticity of supply.

Other problems of language in economics include the following.

Definitions often assume, embody, and give effect to theories: theories as hypotheses. Definitions not only define words: when the words are used they define the world for us, and that definition may misleadingly or incompletely define the world.

Very often terms are used in a primitive or generic sense. Terms like "private," "public," "voluntary," "freedom," "coercion," "property," "morality," "liberty," and so on are used with unspecified meaning. They are kaleidoscopic, subject to selective perception, and almost invariably given variable specification. Their use facilitates the entry into analysis or argument of selective implicit antecedent normative premises. This allows an author to escape questions of both substantive content and the mode of its determination, thereby usually begging an (if not the) important substantive question, leaving it to each reader to provide substantive content. Such terms are often identified with the status quo somehow selectively perceived – often the point at issue.

Economists generally work with some notion of a pure abstract a-institutional conceptual model of the economy. Economists also tend to identify the status quo with that conceptual model. This can only be done by assuming that the primitive terms of the model are to be understood only in terms of the status quo. One problem is that the so-called status quo is a matter of interpretation – selectively perceived and identified. Second, the status quo itself is the ultimate object of inquiry. By identifying it in particular, selective terms, and identifying it with the pure conceptual model, economists selectively reify the existing system, rendering it more concrete than it really is. A further problem is that the primitive terms of the model itself – such as "competition" – can be given variable specification.

Specific, definitive texts do not necessarily have definitive meanings. Selective interpretation engenders different reifications. As conditions and therefore interests change, different readings of texts are advanced and adopted. All this is part of the role of language in the continuing social construction of reality, a putative reality that is given selective reification.

It seems to me that to some extent economists already are sensitive to problems of language, but that they are not enough so.

Such views as I have promoted here can advance post-autistic economics; and a strong post-autistic economics can advance both such views and economics.

[Warren J. Samuels is Professor Emeritus of Economics at Michigan State University. The foregoing is based in part on: Deduction and the practice of economics: the necessity of a sense of limits. *Journal of Economic Methodology*, **8**, 99–104; Some problems in the use of language in economics. *Review of Political Economy*, **13(1)**, 91–100; Methodological pluralism. In: *The Handbook of Economic Methodology*, B. Davis, D. Wade Hands and U. Maki, (eds.) Edward Elgar, 1998, pp. 300–303; The case for methodological pluralism. In: A. Salanti and E. Screpanti, (eds.), *Pluralism in Economics*. Edward Elgar, 1997, pp. 67–79, and Methodological pluralism: the discussion in retrospect. In: A. Salanti and E. Screpanti, (eds.), *Pluralism in Economics*. Edward Elgar, 1997, pp. 308–309; Postmodernism and knowledge: a middlebrow view. *Journal of Economic Methodology* 3, 13–120.]

Is the utility maximization principle necessary?

Katalin Martinás (Department of Atomic Physics, Roland Eotvos University, Hungary)

Microeconomics and thermodynamics are both based on the idea of exchange. In thermodynamics the irreversibility of exchanges is a key idea and one that my physics students sometimes have difficulty understanding, so about twenty years ago I went looking for examples of irreversibility in economic theory that I could use in my teaching of thermodynamics. What I found, however, was no irreversibility in the neoclassical paradigm. As a physicist this struck me as preposterous and incredible. Without irreversibility, microeconomics might be a wonderful mathematical theory, but it could not offer a theory of economic activity. This encounter marked the beginning of my long-term interest in economic research.

Most economists living today grew up with the idea, even if not always agreeing with it, that there is and should be a master theory, neoclassicalism (Fullbrook, 2001). Central to this theory are the principles of utility and profit maximization. I am going to argue that in spite of their ever-growing dominance in journals and textbooks (in Hungary they are now taught in secondary schools), these maximization principles are neither sufficient nor necessary conditions for building a mathematical economic theory.

"Childish pleasure"

The founding fathers of modern theoretical economics chose profit and utility maximization as foundational principles for the description of economic decisions, a choice that resulted in a timeless mathematical economics. From its earliest days, however, neoclassicalism has been subject to empirical and theoretical critiques that have called the legitimacy of its maximization principles fundamentally into question. Already in 1918, Gustav Cassel wrote (Cassel, 1918):

> This purely formal [utility] theory, which in no way extends our knowledge of actual processes, is in any case superfluous for the theory of price. It should further be noted that this deduction of the nature of demand from a single

principle, in which so much childish pleasure has been taken, was only made possible by artificial constructions and a considerable distortion of reality.

Cassel's charge of childish pleasure is justified because the existence of the utility and maximizing principles have been refuted from various points of view. Briefly, I will review some of the arguments.

It does not exist

Hall and Hintch in 1939 investigated whether entrepreneurs did in fact conduct the price and output policy that was ascribed to them in neoclassical theory. These Oxford economists chose to use the "method of direct question" to find this out. The results were clearly negative. Almost all businessmen followed a "full cost" pricing rule; that is they took prime (or "direct") cost per unit as the base, added a percentage to cover overheads (or "indirect" cost), and made a further addition for profit (Vromen, 1995).

It may not exist

Profit and utility maximization demand perfect information. Moreover they need the perfect knowledge of the future too. Furthermore, as the decisions (and actions) take finite time, in real life the action and the result appear in different environments. Maximization at the moment of decision does not necessarily mean maximization for the result. The world changes. That problem is "solved" via the assumption of equilibrium (not changing environment). This results in a timeless theory. The (in)famous proof of the existence of a general equilibrium state is in some sense a tautology, as it is a built-in conclusion.

It cannot exist

It is an oxymoron for a human being to be an economic agent in the neoclassical sense, because an economic actor cannot behave simultaneously as a profit and a utility maximizer (Jensen and Meckling, 1994). In standard economics, production and consumption are two different activities done by different actors. However, in reality the same human being is often both a producer and a consumer. True, not every consumer is a producer, but all producers are consumers. Both production and consumption require human time, so that in reality any profit and utility maximizing by a producer/consumer would have to be done against the same limited fund of time. Consequently a description of the real behavior of such agents would have to incorporate both dimensions simultaneously. Neoclassical theory does not do this.

It must not exist

It violates the traditional ethical principles of humanity (Scitovsky, 1965).

It does not need to exist (it is not necessary)

There is a general belief that utility maximization principle is needed to ensure an ordering of the commodity space, and that it is the only possible approach. This is not the case. A weaker postulate – the no-loss rule – is sufficient to construct an economic theory (Bródy *et al.*, 1985; Ayres and Martinás, 1996; Martinás, 1996; Zsolt and Martinás, 2000).

The no-loss rule

The no-loss rule first appeared in the Austrian School when Menger stated the necessary conditions for an exchange (Menger, 1871). For a free exchange of goods among economizing individuals the following triad of conditions must be fulfilled:

1   One economizing individual must have command of goods that have a smaller value to him/her than other quantities of goods at the disposal of another economizing individual who evaluates the goods in reverse fashion,
2   The two economizing individuals must have recognized this relationship, and
3   They must have the power actually to perform the exchange of goods.

The absence of any one of the above three conditions means that an essential pre-requisite for an exchange is missing. The first condition, essential in free economic exchange, is the no-loss rule: an economic individual never acts if that action would result in an immediate loss. The no-loss rule is postulated as a decision rule for economic agents instead of utility/profit maximization. It is extremely important to note that the no-loss rule holds only for the moment of action. The natural and economic environments, as well as the economic agents themselves, are in continuous transition, so that today yesterday's decision may seem to have been a bad decision. The no-loss criteria is weaker than the utility maximum principle; it presupposes only that every economic unit has common sense, and hence does not do anything that impairs its economic state. It does not presume perfect "rationality," that is, it does not suppose perfect foresight, and nor does it necessarily follow that the actions taken are optimal.

Some basic features of the no-loss approach

Under this approach an economic system (state, market, etc.) consists of economic agents interacting through exchanges of materials (goods), money and information. An economic agent (EA) is the smallest entity with an implicit or explicit decision-making rule. In most cases the EA is either a firm or an individual. EAs are characterized by the scope of their activities, by their knowledge, their experiences and their stocks. Their list of stocks (N) may contain money (M), but money is not conceptually necessary.

Every economic activity of an agent is represented as a decision. There are "free" decisions (concerning production and trade – based on the economic interest of the EA) – and "forced" decisions. The latter result from physical/biological constraints (e.g. degradation, depreciation) and political constraints (e.g. regulations of the state, taxes, or robbery).

A necessary criterion for every voluntary action (free decisions) is that the agent's economic welfare will not be worse than in the initial state. This no-loss rule only forbids those decisions that would result in a worse economic state than the initial one. That is a fundamental difference from the utility and profit maximization principles: the latter define the actual decision, while the no-loss rule specifies only that an action is allowed or forbidden.

The no-loss rule demands that every economic agent is characterized by a function, called the wealth function, $Z(X,\ldots,M)$, where X represents stocks, and M money. The wealth function is a measure, in non-monetary units, of the wealth or welfare of the economic actors. The wealth function reflects the "wealth" state of the economic agent (individual or firm) as self-evaluated. It represents the potential use (including, but not limited to, possible current or future consumption), as opposed to the utility function, which shows the level of satisfaction from that consumption. In some senses the notion of utility is retrospective (and applies only to individuals), whereas the notion of wealth is prospective and applies equally to firms. The characterization of all agents by a non-decreasing function parallels the traditional treatment of individuals in economics. However, previously firms have never been treated in this manner. The wealth function of a firm means that the firm also evaluates commodities (in terms of its business and technological possibilities), as do individual consumers. The evaluation of stocks of commodities means that the firm is capable of anticipating the possible changes in future wealth that a set of existing stocks affords.

The most important properties of the wealth function are (Ayres *et al.*, 1996):

1   Since wealth is a positive attribute (in the absence of the possibility of net debt), a function that measures wealth must be non-negative. Normally $Z > 0$.

2   Wealth comprises all goods and money, or money-equivalents (like receivables) that are owned outright (net of mortgages, debts or other encumbrances). The terms "own," "owned," "ownership" etc. are shorthand for a more cumbersome phrase, such as "to which the economic agent has enforceable exclusive access."

3   An increase in the agent's ownership of stocks of beneficial goods or money results, *ceteris paribus*, in an increase in the agent's wealth. In case of an incremental increase in the stock of a beneficial good (as opposed to a waste), we can assert $dX > 0$, and $dZ > 0$. Similarly, if $dM > 0$, $dZ > 0$.

4   An economic agent's wealth can only increase or stay constant (but never

decrease) as a consequence of voluntary actions consistent with the no-loss rule. The payment of taxes (for example) is considered to be involuntary and unavoidable.

5 The wealth function may have the property of homogeneity in the first degree (doubling all stocks will double wealth) This is a useful property when the time comes to select representative mathematical forms.

The no-loss rule defines the direction of economic processes. An agent agrees to a process only if it leads to $dZ > 0$. A force law of economic processes is introduced. The magnitude of actions is proportional to the anticipated wealth increase. The result is a non-linear, non-equilibrium dynamic equation system. Computer simulations of a market economy through the history of the individual economic actors can be performed. These simulations provide tools to investigate the effect of different economic policies, institutions, environmental impacts on the economic system. We have shown how to integrate firms in this model (Zsolt and Martinás, 2000). We have found that the usual general equilibrium solution is only a special case.

Description of economic phenomena with help from the no-loss rule is promising for at least three reasons. First, the no-loss rule has long been a premise for economists. Second, the no-loss rule can handle straightforwardly the main elements of economic models – consumers, producers, commodities, trade and production. Finally, it is a non-equilibrium approach.

I gratefully acknowledge the kind help of Edward Fullbrook in improving the present paper.

References

Ayres, R.U. and Martinás, K. (1996) "Wealth accumulation and economic progress". *Journal of Evolutionary Economics*, 6(4), 347–359.

Bródy, A., Martinás, K. and Sajó, K. (1985) Essay on Macroeconomics. *Acta Oec* 36, 305. (Reprinted in *Thermodynamics and Economics*, Kluwer, 1994).

Cassel, G. (1918) *Theory of Social Economy*, p. 81.

Fullbrook, E. (2001) "Real science is pluralist." *post-autistic economics newsletter*, issue no. 5, article 5. http://www.btinternet.com/~pae_news/review/issue5

Jensen, M.C. and Meckling, W.H. (1994) "The nature of man." *Journal of Applied Corporate Finance* 7(2), 4–19.

Martinás, K. (1996) "Irreversible microeconomics," In: K. Martinás and M. Moreau (eds), *Complex Systems in Natural and Economic Sciences*, ELFT, p. 114.

Menger, C., (1871) *Principles of Economics*, (trans. J. Dingwall and B.H. Hoselitz, The Free Press, 1950.

Scitovsky, T. (1965) *The Joyless Economy*. Oxford University Press.

Vromen, J.J. (1995) *Economic Evolution*, Routledge.

Zsolt, G. and Martinás, K. (2000) "An irreversible economic approach to the theory of production." *Open Systems and Information Dynamics*, 7, 1–15.

Quo vadis behavioral finance?

George M. Frankfurter (Louisiana State University, USA)
Elton G. McGoun (Bucknell University, USA)

In the science fiction television and film series *Star Trek: The Next Generation*, there is a species called the Borg, a collective of techno-organic drones acting in concert as a single organism. In their pursuit of perfection, they roam the galaxy in search of other species, whose capabilities they acquire through a process of assimilation – turning their captives into Borg and effectively absorbing their knowledge into the hive's mind. The first line of every encounter with the Borg is familiar to *Star Trek* aficionados: "Resistance is futile. Prepare to be assimilated."

It seems that this sci-fi dream world is worryingly more than *apropos* to describe the state of affairs of the field of finance, both as a scientific endeavor and a subdiscipline of economics. Academic finance has been an outgrowth of neo-classical economics, Friedmanian instrumentalism (Friedman, 1953) and Fama's efficient markets hypothesis (EMH) (Fama, 1965, 1970). It is an autistic world, in which there exists this mythical economic individual, the *homo economicus* (or, as our European colleagues correctly spell it, *oeconomicus*). This world is called financial economics, or modern finance. Financial economics is an orthodox world where the leaders of the church are vigilant to nip in the bud any criticism, or questioning of this world's methodology.

The only serious challenge to the modern finance dogma over its 50-year existence has been the appearance of behavioral finance. Behavioral finance got its start with the importation of prospect theory (Tversky and Kahneman, 1974; Kahneman and Tversky, 1979), a challenge to the axioms of Von Neuman and Morgenstern (1967) on which the psychological makeup of the *homo economicus* is built. At first, De Bondt and Thaler (1985, 1987) showed that, contrary to the predictions of the EMH, markets over-react. Many followers also showed under reaction. Both these "reactions" were translated to a real-world strategy referred to as contrarian[1] (Dreman, 1998).

Concurrently, others too numerous to mention questioned the empirical proxy of the EMH, the capital asset pricing model (CAPM). These works showed the presence of statistically significant "effects" that the CAPM could not account for. Discoveries of these effects were lumped under the rubric of anomalies.

In an interview with Fama, appearing on the CAPITALIDEASONLINE.COM website,[2] Fama expands his views on behavioral finance:

> Well, my good friend, Dick Thaylor [sic., the reference is to Richard Thaler who moved a few years ago from Cornell to Chicago in the latter university's attempt to cover all the bases] is kind of the guru of behavioral finance and every time he walks down the corridor, I ask him a question. The question isn't a complete question, but a person on the street wouldn't know what was going on. My question is always the same: *Now what is it?* He knows what *it* refers to. It's behavioral finance, and the reality is they haven't defined the top. They haven't defined the area. What it is at this point is unkindly speakings, just dredging for anomalous looking things in the data. But the fact is that even in a perfectly efficient market, every data set would be on the foremost phenomenon just on a strictly random basis. So that's not evidence for or against anything. If you don't have a specific view of what behavioral finance is in the way it manifests itself in the behavior of prices and returns, you don't really have anything to work with because everything you observe really can be rationalized in the context of an efficient market. For example, all of these studies on behavioral finance basically look at how prices react to different kinds of announcements. So sometimes, it seems to be the case that prices underreact, sometimes it seems to be the case that prices overreact, but that's exactly what you predict in an efficient market. You're going to see drift one way or the other, but it will be random. So if you don't have a theory that predicts when it's going to underreact and when it's going to overreact, you don't have anything. It looks to me like an efficient market, just a random price behavior.

Professor Fama has a paper coming out soon on the subject, "Market Efficiency Long Term Returns on Behavioral Finance."

For Fama, the number one count on the list of indictments of behavioral finance is its less than perfect prediction power. Now, let that paradigm cast the first stone that either established a perfect record of predictions or didn't suffer from the discovery of anomalies. In fact, as far as predictions go, Fama's own research concluded that the CAPM has no predictive power (Fama and French, 1992). Then what makes the EMH something above doubt and behavioral finance "just dredging for anomalous looking things?"

In the same swoop, Fama also promotes a colleague to the dubious rank of "the guru of behavioral finance." This is not only an ill-concealed insult, but also an insinuation that Professor Thaler somehow stumbled into a major university straight from the ashram of behavioral finance (perhaps a Hindu cult?). We are also doubtful that Dick Thaler cannot answer Fama's question, because this is the same Thaler who in a recent article in the *Financial Analysts Journal* (Thaler, 1999) had this to say: "I predict that in the not-too-distant future, the term "behavioral finance" will be correctly viewed as a redundant phrase. What other kind of finance is there?"

In the paper the interview refers to, Fama (1998) artfully reduces behavioral finance to the "anomalies literature." What Fama conveniently forgets is that behavioral finance is not just the anomalies literature, or even over- or under-reaction, but the realization that the axioms and assumptions of modern finance/financial economics on which his EMH is built is an autistic world.

Or does he forget? Being conspiracy theorists, it is our belief that the label "the anomalies literature" is a carefully chosen signifier that necessarily puts behavioral finance at a level below the EMH. This is so because one may deal with anomalies as puzzles that eventually must be solved. One may make a note of anomalies for further reference, or one may just forget about them. The last choice is the one researchers in financial economics seem to select. We conjecture that this choice is influenced by the sociology of the field; that is, the totalitarian control of the orthodoxy over the nobility press on which promotion and tenure depend.

In an almost unique move in the financial economics literature,[3] Fama (1998) also cleverly uses the argument of both Kuhn (1970) and Lakatos (1970) that once a paradigm has been established only a new and more powerful paradigm can replace the old one. What Fama doesn't mention is that the EMH/CAPM is an arriviste paradigm. It is one that, we suspect, is promoted for ideological reasons (the market knows best, keep government out, etc.), and in fact has been often found to be invalid. Because it cannot be falsified, Fama ought to have argued that it should never have been put on the pedestal of a paradigm.

Unfortunately for behavioral finance, its practitioners are drawn like a doomed species into the tractor beam of financial economics, and their work is concentrating on proofs of market efficiency, or lack thereof, using the same statistical methods (and methodology) the proponents of the EMH have been using from time immemorial. An alternative and more promising avenue would be to define behavioral finance's methodology without paying any attention to the vapid issue of whether markets are efficient or not. This is no small task, because the methodology of a science is a complex and multileveled ziggurat (Frankfurter, 2001). However, this is the only way behavioral finance can survive before it is totally assimilated by the Borg. Behavioral finance, therefore, is on the road to Damascus. This is why we are asking the question: *Quo vadis* behavioral finance?

[George M. Frankfurter and Elton G. McGoun are the authors of *From Individualism to the Individual: Ideology and Inquiry in Financial Economics* (May 2000).]

Notes

1 The word contrarian was coined to signify a strategy contrary to the teachings of the EMH.
2 Or go straight to link: http://www.ifa.tv/Library/Support/Articles/Scholarly/TextInterviewEugeneFama.htm
3 Unique in the sense that it invokes the philosophy of science to bolster an argument.

References

DeBondt, W. and Thaler, R. (1985) Does the stock market overreact? *Journal of Finance*, 40, 793–805.

DeBondt, W. and Thaler, R. (1987) Further evidence on investors' overreaction and stock market seasonality. *Journal of Finance*, 42, 557–581.

Dreman, D. (1998) *Contrarian Investment Strategies: The Next Generation*. New York: Simon and Schuster.

Fama, E.F. (1965) The behavior of stock market prices. *Journal of Business*, 38, 34–105.

Fama, E.F. (1970) Efficient capital markets: a review of theory and empirical work. *Journal of Finance*, 25, 383–417.

Fama, E.F. (1998). Market efficiency, long-term returns, and behavioral finance. *Journal of Financial Economics*, 49, 283–306.

Fama, E.F. and French, K.R. (1992) The cross-section of expected stock returns. *Journal of Finance*, 47, 427–465.

Frankfurter, G.M. (2001) Method and Methodology. *Homo Oeconomicus*, 18, 465–491.

Friedman, M.M. (1953) The methodology of positive economics. In: Friedman, Milton M. (ed), *Essays in Positive Economics*. Chicago: University of Chicago Press.

Kahneman, D. and Tversky, A. (1979) Prospect theory: an analysis of decisions under risk. *Econometrica* 47, 263–291.

Kuhn, T.S. (1970) *The Structure of Scientific Revolutions*. Chicago: The University of Chicago Press.

Lakatos, I. (1970) Falsification and the methodology of scientific research programmes. In: Lakatos, I. and Musgrave, G. (eds), *Criticism and the Growth of Knowledge*. Cambridge, UK: Cambridge University Press.

Thaler, R.H. (1999) The end of behavioral finance. *Financial Analysts Journal* 16.

Tversky, A. and Kahneman. D. (1974) Judgment under uncertainty: heuristics and biases. *Science*, 185, 1124–1131.

Von Neuman, J. and Morgenstern, O. (1967) *Theory of Games and Economic Behavior*. Princeton, NJ: Princeton University Press.

Psychological autism, institutional autism and economics

James G. Devine (Loyola Marymount University, USA)

As an economist with a son having heavy autistic leanings, the discussion of the "Autistic Economics" quickly caught my attention. I had never thought of the economics profession or its neoclassical orthodoxy as "autistic." I think that this way of thinking can be useful, at least as a preliminary step, allowing the economics profession eventually to transcend autism. But as with all analogies, we must examine not only the similarities between autism and orthodox economics, but also the differences.

The autism spectrum

As a layperson interested in psychology, I have reached a preliminary understanding of autism, based on others' research and on discussions with other parents of autistic or semi-autistic children. "Autistic disorder" is a social communication disorder and a developmental delay, involving "restricted, repetitive, and stereotyped patterns of behavior, interests, and activities."[1] I interpret this constellation of symptoms as being the result of an organically-based (neurobiological) sensory-processing problem, which is much like the opposite of being deaf. Instead of hearing too little, a person with autism may hear *too much*, and be unable to filter out the noise or prioritize the information received to make it intelligible. The external stimuli that most treat as normal seem to be a constant barrage of blackboard chalk scraping the wrong way. Not surprisingly, autistic people slam their hands over their ears, trying to shut out the meaningless cacophony. Alas, for such people information overload occurs not simply with sound, but with the other commonly-known senses (sight, taste, smell, touch), along with proprioception (the sense of movement through space) and the vestibular sense (understanding one's own body's internal signals). So folks with autism tend not only to shut out external stimuli, but also to be extremely anxious, to communicate poorly with others, and to be physically uncoordinated.

Just as with "neurotypical" individuals (i.e. many or most of those reading this essay),[2] each person with autism or autistic tendencies is unique. Different individuals with autistic problems have different combinations of these sensory-processing difficulties, so that one may be better at screening sounds than at prioritizing and understanding visual information – and so forth. Some, but far from all, compensate for processing problems in one sphere with genius in another, as in the film "*Rainman.*" There are also degrees to which the whole neurobiological package hits an individual – and the amount of emotional or intellectual resources she or he has to resist impairment. Thus, professionals write of the "autistic spectrum," the continuum from hard-core autism to high-functioning autism, to Asperger's syndrome or borderline autism (*AS*), to the loner mentality so common among professors, accountants, and computer specialists.[3]

In terms of behavior, folks on the autism spectrum tend to be isolated from the world; have troubles with communication with others; engage in repetitive body movements; insist on sameness, repetition, and routine; and seem to treat others as objects.[4] Those with *AS* have been described as follows:[5]

> Persons with *AS* show marked deficiencies in social skills, have difficulties with transitions or changes and prefer sameness. They often have obsessive routines and may be preoccupied with a particular subject of interest. They have a great deal of difficulty reading nonverbal cues (body language) and very often the individual with *AS* has difficulty determining proper body space. Often overly sensitive to sounds, tastes, smells, and sights, the person with *AS* may prefer soft clothing, certain foods, and be bothered by sounds or lights no one else seems to hear or see.[5]

This is just a partial list of symptoms, but the general idea is clear: people with autism have a hard time doing anything but living inside their heads, no matter how friendly the social environment is.

It is not surprising, therefore, that one autistic mother that I know had to explain to her two autistic children that there was something "out there" called "society" that had norms and mores they had to learn and obey. Those on the spectrum instinctively see Baroness Thatcher's dictum that there is no society, only individuals,[6] as self-evident.

Autism and economics

The orthodox economist's a priori agreement with Thatcher's assertion – i.e. its commitment to methodological individualism – suggests that the textbook *homo economicus* (*HE*) might be autistic. For example, as with *HE*, autistic individuals often have preferences that are little shaped by their social environments (or at least seem that way to frustrated parents or partners).[7] But there are major differences. First, unlike for neurotypicals or *HE*, information-processing problems are extremely important to autism, as with Herbert Simon's "bounded rationality."

Second, just as with neurotypicals but unlike *HE*, people with autism have con-
sciences, are torn by inner mental and emotional conflicts, and often want to
connect socially with other human beings, if they can.[8]

Instead of being autistic, *HE* is more robotic or cybernetic in nature. The use
of this kind of one-dimensional "man" in theoretical work is appropriate to a profession suffering from "institutional autism" (see below). Someone with autism is
likely to treat other human beings as if they were furniture or automatons. Put
another way, like those with autism, the economics profession's dominant vision
lacks a "theory of mind." This means that, like autistic individuals, those who
employ *HE* as a theoretical concept "do not understand that other people have
their own plans, thoughts, and points of view. . . [and] have difficulty understanding other people's beliefs, attitudes, and emotions."[9]

Turn now, before any analysis of their etiology, to other specific "autistic"
symptoms of the profession. The original statements by the rebellious French
economics students[10] define autistic economics in terms of its one-sided and
exclusionary interest in "imaginary worlds" (as opposed to empirical study),
"uncontrolled use of mathematics" (as an end in itself rather than merely as a
tool), and the absence of pluralism of approaches in economics (the monopoly of
the neoclassical approach).

The first two of these characteristics seem at first to fit with the idea of autism.
Indeed, they merge into one symptom in many cases, since mathematics almost
always portrays an idealized and thus imaginary world.[11] However, there is a
major difference from autism here: many folks with autism have difficulty with
abstract thought, since they are overwhelmed by the concrete details of life.
While the focus on an imaginary internal world is an obvious result of autism, the
use of abstraction should be seen instead as a *defense mechanism* against the confusion arising from the blooming, buzzing, confusing concreteness of the empirical
world.

The third characteristic – a tendency for a single paradigm to dominate –
seems to fit well with an autistic person's rigidity and desire for sameness,
expressed as a preference for clear simple answers rather than intellectual debate
or critical thinking. However, it does not explain why neoclassical economics –
which includes methodological individualism and the focus on *HE* – is the preval-
ent orthodoxy. Nor does this list of "symptoms" say anything about treatment. So
the profession must be described.

An autistic profession?

It would be a mistake to apply the psychological description of autism to economics in an unvarnished way. Even though high-functioning autistic people are
often attracted to academia, where they can lecture others without listening,
engage in research alone, and develop beautiful mind pictures, it is hard to say

that a majority – or even a large minority – of economists have autistic tendencies. Individuals on the autistic spectrum do not have to specialize in economics
to succeed in academia since there are other outlets for expression of their pro-
clivities besides economic theory.[12] Being able to "work well with others" helps
one achieve success in academia, as in most spheres, so that those with autistic
tendencies would need to be very smart or to work very hard to compensate for
social skills deficits. In sum, self-selection can only be one part of the basis for
autistic economics.

More profoundly, it would be a mistake to apply an autistic person's own
highly individualistic perspective, i.e. seeing "economics" as a simple aggregation
of isolated economists. Instead, the economics profession is an institution,
spawning a collective product and should thus be analyzed in a sociological or
social–psychological (institutionalist) way. The profession trains people to accept
autistic assumptions (and attracts those who do so already), and rewards them for
doing so. Thus, the autistic aspect of the field involves more than the sum of its
parts.

Again delaying a full discussion of the basis for this institutional autism, it must
be stressed that the French students' summary does not apply exactly to the
empirical world. As with psychological autism, there is a spectrum. The hard-
core autistic walling-off from the societal environment can be seen most strongly
in the specific, highly abstract, axiomatic, or "Bourbakist," school that the students protested against.[13] Further down the spectrum toward "normal," the
approach of only dealing with the world by lecturing or dictating to it (as with
Asperger's syndrome) can be seen with the International Monetary Fund, which
applies the same preconceived vision of the ideal market system (and the same
neo-liberal set of policy imperatives) to every country it encounters. At the other
end of the spectrum, there are all sorts of economists who work for government,
business, foundations, and even labor unions; the fact that these real-world institutions are willing to pay for their contributions indicates that these economists'
degree of social connectedness is adequate to the task. They may use abstract
mathematics or econometrics, but it would be libelous to apply the autistic tag to
these economists.

The existence of a spectrum does not mean that the profession itself lacks
institutional autism. The autistic economics of the Bourbakists and their Anglo-
phone counterparts, or the IMF and similar organizations, define the most prestigious segment of the economics profession, the one that "smart young economists
on the rise" wish to emulate. Thus, autistic economics tends to dominate the "Big
Name" departments, along with most professional journals, departments, professional associations and textbooks.

Since much of the socio-institutional basis for the prevalence of autistic economics is shared with other academic fields, the nature of the subject matter must
be considered. As a "soft science" dealing with the complexity of human social

interaction as participant–observers, economists cannot approach the objectivity – and the ability to attain consensus – of the physical sciences. However, we deal with a much simpler subject matter than does, say, the sociology profession, so that some hope of consensus arising exists, at least on key issues. That is, economics is in the middle of a spectrum between obvious consensus on many issues and the extreme inability to form one. In this context, economists seem to have an autistic drive for sameness – a "physics envy" wish to imitate the natural sciences' ability to attain consensus. Unlike sociology, for example, they can do so partly by restricting the subject matter to easy topics such as markets and market-like processes, and thus by restricting the acceptable ways of thinking.

To explain physics envy and other autistic symptoms, the profession must be understood as an artificial societal institution, created by people, that has taken on a life of its own partly independent of individual preferences while feeding back to shape those preferences and perspectives. Having roots in medieval guilds, academic institutions such as the economics profession center on a hierarchy topped by Big Name professors, universities, professional associations and journals. Lacking a basis for true scientific objectivity, the identity of these Big Names cannot be decided as in physics. Thus, which professors, universities, professional associations and journals are most influential are selected by the already-existing Big-Names – i.e. by "the insiders" or the "superstars."[14] Thus, the dominant ideology of the past is perpetuated over time.

Despite the top-down organization of the profession, it would be a mistake to assume that either a monopoly or a conspiracy exists. Competition also plays a role, in which "success" is defined by rising in that hierarchy. By the pyramidal nature of such hierarchies, the rise of one individual toward the top excludes others from such success, so that competition encourages individuals to over-invest time and effort in order to succeed.[15] Departments, associations, journals and textbooks also compete to attain the pinnacle of prestige and power defined by the current in-group.

This system implies a dynamic that perpetuates autistic pathology over time: people at the bottom of the hierarchy are not only trained to think and practice the dominant ideology, but find it in their professional interest to do so wholeheartedly and sincerely. Otherwise, they do not get the desired publications, jobs, promotion, tenure, attention and fame. Those who accept the dominant world-view most profoundly are most able to be creative in developing new applications, and are seen as *Wunderkinder* who can rise to the top. This result is reinforced by self-selection, as the deviants leave the profession or sink into professional backwaters. Of course, those who rise feel they must teach it to those further down the hierarchy (students), since they believe in it and want the students to succeed at the higher levels of a profession they value. Those textbooks produced by Big-Name economists (or their conceptions) tend to dominate, while the "winner-take-all" nature of the textbook market limits the number of textbooks available.[15] Finally, the neoclassical approach of excluding critical thinking and intellectual debate makes the task of teaching easier.

The self-referential nature of this system encourages the focus on imaginary worlds, including that of mathematics. The latter also plays a major role because of its use in grading subordinates' success, a crucial part of any hierarchy. It has always been very difficult to judge how hard or well an academic actually works, while such decisions often threaten to become unpleasant political processes. Student course evaluations are almost always inadequate, as is the number or size of a professor's publications (along with the number of times they are cited). But most feel that the quality of her or his mathematical technique can readily be judged. Simultaneously, the ambitious scholar can bemuse the older professors whose mathematical techniques are rusty or out-dated by applying the newest and fanciest methods. Just as we see the prevalence of jargon or obscurantism in other fields, in economics the one-upmanship of academic competition encourages the over-use of mathematics and the embracing of physics envy.

However, the institutional autism of the profession exists in a societal context. The economics profession cannot be understood without stressing its separation from the other social sciences. During the last century or so, the economics profession has defined itself in comparison to other fields. This, along with their self-satisfied sense of mathematical virtue, has encouraged economists to sneer at other specializations (especially sociology), the way the hatters' guild mocked the laborers – or to try to conquer them, as Gary Becker and his school does. Either way, the main flow of information is from economics to other fields, rather than vice versa. This Asperger-style elitism means that the profession eliminates whole sets of questions and parts of society from analysis, restricting the empirical and theoretical information that economists have to process, adding order to a complex and confusing reality. It allows the economists to maintain their beloved assumptions, however unrealistic.

Of course, the economists' guild exists in a modern capitalist environment, not a medieval one. It must sometimes prove its usefulness to business, government, and other societal institutions, which can threaten to de-fund academic programs that are totally "irrelevant."[16] This, of course, explains why the dominant form of economics is *neoclassical* (studying idealized markets), just as a different style of economics (one emphasizing planning) prevailed in the old Soviet Union. This role for the societal environment implies that the profession cannot be entirely autistic, just as no individual can be so.

This point is reinforced if we define neoclassical economics. This approach can be seen as involving adherence to (1) mathematical method, with an emphasis on (2) utilitarianism and methodological individualism, (3) equilibrium, (4) naturalism, and (5) positivism.[17] Last, but hardly least, in the neoclassical ideal, (6) all human activity is seen as exchange or as organized by markets, in reality or as an ideal.

In terms of the discussion above, all but one of these may be seen as reflecting the profession's autistic attitudes, at least in part. I have discussed the first two of these above. Moving down the list, the centrality of equilibrium seems a symptom of totally autistic thinking in a society such as capitalism in which endogenously-driven change – sometimes drastic, as with financial crises – is the norm.[18] Related is item (4), i.e. the view that human-made institutions such as markets can be reduced to "natural" forces such as individual preferences and technology, in which the complexity and artificiality of human institutions is abstracted from or forgotten. The profession's positivism – i.e. its view that value-free research is an achievable ideal, that the observer is unaffected by being a participant in the system, and that serious philosophical reflection is unnecessary – also fits with a generally autistic attitudes.

However, the emphasis on markets and exchange – as opposed to other kinds of human institutions such as tradition, democratic cooperation and hierarchy – clearly reflects the society in which economists live and learn. Though the neoclassical's vision of exchange and markets may be unduly restricted, idealized, formalized, static and individualized – symptoms of autistic attitudes – the fact that he or she is actually engaged with a real-world problem gives us a glimmer of hope.

Cures?

Returning to the case of neurobiological autism, there is no cure at this point. That is, there is no known method (such as a pill) to definitively prevent or end this disorder. But autism represents a developmental delay – which opens the door for a long-term struggle to speed up that development, to improve an individual's functioning in society. Various methods (from behavior modification to active effort to engage a person socially in his activities[19] to occupational therapy) can speed up an individual's ability to learn to cope with the shower of stimuli. Pills can help handle symptoms (such as anxiety), making it easier for therapists to apply other methods. All of these involve trying to break down the walls between the autistic individual and the empirical world.

What about "curing" the economics profession of its institutional autism? It should not surprise anyone that there is no quick fix. The persistence of autistic symptoms (as described by the French students) is based in the hierarchy and the competition to rise in those ranks. This autism encourages, and is in turn shored up by, a refusal to engage with other social scientists in a serious way, as peers. In addition to efforts to get rid of unnecessary hierarchy and competition, outsiders and deviants may be able to push the profession up the developmental ladder to minimize solipsism. These efforts might be helped by the course of events, as when the shock treatment of the Great Depression pushed the profession away from classical economics and toward Keynes. In any event, the effort to force the profession actively to engage with reality must be central.

However, such empirio-criticism is never enough. Just as autistic individuals need help in making sense of reality, it takes a theory to trump a theory. In many cases that means that we need to do better than the neoclassicists, presenting improved theories to understand empirical reality. These would be conscious of the limits of mathematical method, embrace the heterogeneity of empirical reality, take a deeper understanding of individual social psychology into account, treat economies as undergoing hard-to-reverse processes, involve institutionalist insights, eschew excessive pretensions of unjustified scientific objectivity, and avoid reducing all activity to exchange, partly by learning from the other social sciences.[20] If enough people are willing to make the effort, perhaps the profession will move toward pluralism.

In terms of research, it would be a major mistake to reject the profession or even neoclassical economics totally. In my experience, many interesting insights can be drawn from the more sophisticated work of neoclassicals, especially if treated skeptically with an eye to finding the valid aspects of their work rather than simply rejecting them. Despite their problems, it is better to know the state of the orthodoxy's knowledge than to be ignorant of it. Finally, there are reasons for hope. Magazines such as *The Journal of Economic Perspectives*, which center on presenting ideas without unnecessary formalism, along with such fields as experimental economics (which are by necessity empirical) show the possibility for improvement.

Thanks to Edward Fullbrook, Barkley Rosser, and Lynn Kilroy for their input. Of course, the full weight of any blame for misleading, inaccurate, or ambiguous content is on my shoulders.

Notes

1 *Diagnostic and Statistical Manual* (DSM-IV), (1994) 4th edn. American Psychiatric Association. Category 299.00.
2 See http://isnt.autistics.org/ for an analysis of "neurotypical disorder," which affects 9625 out of 10000 individuals.
3 See, for example, Attwood, T. (1998) *Asperger's Syndrome: A Guide for Parents and Professionals*. London; Jessica Kingsley Publishers.
4 A more complete list can be found in many places. Mine is based on a web-page of the Los Angeles-based United Autism Alliance (http://www.unitedautismalliance.org/knowledge/).
5 See "What is *AS*?" at http://www.udel.edu/bkirby/asperger/.
6 In reality, she said that "there is no such thing as society. There are individual men and women, and there are families." (See http://www.cooperativeindividualism.org/thatcher_society_and_responsibility.html)
7 Contrary to this assertion, autistic children, like neurotypical children, can be very suggestible, absorbing all sorts of attitudes and preferences from the popular culture.
8 Despite its lack of conscience, *HE* is also not sociopathic or psychopathic since a

person with antisocial personality disorder (to use the up-to-date term) often exploits society's mores for his or her selfish aims. This shows a clear understanding of society that both *HE* and the autistic individual lack.

9 From Stephen M. Edelson of the Center for the Study of Autism, "Theory of Mind," at http://www.autism.org/mind.html. The concept – also used in animal ethology – was first applied to autism by Uta Frith.

10 See the "Open Letter From Economic Students to Professors and Others Responsible for the Teaching of this Discipline" and "Petition for a Debate on the Teaching of Economics" (from June and July of 2000, both found at http://www.paecon.net/).

11 Of course, it is quite possible to describe an ideal world without mathematics, as in Utopian novels.

12 However, I doubt that very many autistic individuals study sociology or social psychology, which (as their names suggest) are inherently societal in their nature.

13 See, for example, Mirowski, P. and Weintraub, R. (1994) "The pure and the applied: Boubakism comes to mathematical economics," *Science in Context*, 7, 245–272. A classic case of Boubakism is Gerard Debreu's *Theory of Value* (New York, Wiley, 1959).

14 On the former, see for example, Blanchard O.J. and Summers, L.H. (1986) "Hysteresis and the European unemployment problem." *NBER Macroeconomics Annual*, 1986, pp. 15–78. On the latter, see Rosen, S. (1981) "The economics of superstars," *American Economic Review*, 71, 845–858.

15 For this vision of competition, see Frank, R.H. and Cook, P.J. (1995) *The Winner-Take-All Society: Why So Few at the Top Get So Much More Than the Rest Of Us*. Penguin.

16 Critics of autistic economics should recognize the possibility of the rise of an economics which is totally subservient to these interest groups.

17 See, for example, Mirowski, P. (1988) *Against Mechanism: Protecting Economics from Science*. Towota, NJ: Rowman & Littlefield, pp. 24–25.

18 This point should remembered by those who confuse the opposition to autistic economics with left-wing economics, since the generally conservative Austrian and Schumpeterian schools reject the static conceptions of the orthodox school.

19 By coincidence, Dr Stanley I. Greenspan, the advocate of active social intervention ("floor time") is the brother of economist Alan Greenspan.

20 For one of my efforts on this front, see "The positive political economy of individualism and collectivism: Hobbes, Locke, and Rousseau," *Politics & Society*, 28(2), 265–304. A draft is available at http://bellarmine.lmu.edu/~jdevine/HLR.html.

Name index

Subject index

"The post-autistic economics movement represents an extremely important and widespread uprising against the dominance and hegemony of neoclassical economics at the beginning of the twenty-first century. This book, *The Crisis in Economics*, provides an excellent introduction to the PAE movement. It contains significant documents and essays that define and drive the movement, all drawn from the *post-autistic economics review*. This is a MUST book for all economists, their students and their university libraries."
Fred Lee, *University of Missouri-Kansas City*

"*The Crisis in Economics* offers a superb introduction to the French post-autistic economics movement. It also contains interesting comments on reform of economics teaching by an international group of distinguished economists. A very readable and informative collection on a current topic of great importance to all economics teachers and students."
Peter Groenewegen, Professor Emeritus, *University of Sydney, Australia*

Edward Fullbrook is Visiting Research Fellow at the University of the West of England, UK. *Intersubjectivity in Economics* is another of his books, which is also published by Routledge.

ECONOMICS/ECONOMIC METHODOLOGY

Routledge
Taylor & Francis Group

11 New Fetter Lane,
London EC4P 4EE
29 West 35th Street,
New York NY 10001
www.routledge.com
Printed in Great Britain

ISBN 0-415-30898-4

9 780415 308984